Land, Settlement, and Politics on Eighteenth-Century Prince Edward Island

Land, Settlement, and Politics on Eighteenth-Century Prince Edward Island

J.M. BUMSTED

McGill-Queen's University Press
Kingston and Montreal

© McGill-Queen's University Press 1987
ISBN 0-7735-0566-0

Printed on acid-free paper

Legal deposit 1st quarter 1987
Bibliothèque nationale du Québec

Printed in Canada

This book has been published with the help of a grant from the Social Science
Federation of Canada, using funds provided by the Social Sciences and Humanities
Research Council of Canada.

Canadian Cataloguing in Publication Data

Bumsted, J. M., 1938–
    Land, settlement, and politics on eighteenth-
century Prince Edward Island

    Includes bibliographical references and index.
    ISBN 0-7735-0566-0
    1. Prince Edward Island – History – To 1873.*
    2. Prince Edward Island – Politics and government –
    To 1873.* 3. Land tenure – Prince Edward Island –
    History – 18th century. I. Title.
    FC2621.3.B85 1987   971.7'02   c86-094889-7
    F1048.B85 1987

To Wendy

Contents

FIGURES

Preface

In 1763 at the Treaty of Paris, an island of over 5,600 square kilometres in the Gulf of St Lawrence was transferred from French to British suzerainty, to be subsequently settled as an autonomous colony within the British Empire. Government policy toward what the British initially called the Island of St John – it was later renamed Prince Edward Island to avoid confusion with other places of similar names in the Atlantic region – was experimental and to a substantial extent different from that employed elsewhere within North America after the fall of the Stuart monarchy. Virtually the entire land surface of the Island was turned over to private proprietors in 1767, on the understanding that they would finance both settlement and the administration of the territory. The proprietors did not fulfil their obligations, but did cling tenaciously to their privileges, ultimately becoming an anachronistic group of landlords – partly absentee – on a North American continent where freehold tenure was regarded as the norm. The colony the British government created at the behest of the proprietors did not flourish and merely existed on the fringes of British North America, but it did survive as an autonomous government to become the smallest (in both land area and population) of the provinces of Canada. Its early history, though often tangential to the larger dynamic of Canadian development, was a tumultuous and complicated one.

Historical study of the formative years of Prince Edward Island as a British colony has long suffered from two problems: one the implicit and occasionally explicit whiggism of historians, and the other the tendency of most of the hardy few who have studied the Island's early years to accept too uncritically an interpretation of its development as carved out of the bitter struggles with the proprietors and the British government. In the Island's formative period from the 1760s to the close of the Napoleonic Wars in 1815, no intrinsic or extrinsic reasons existed to assume that – if properly developed – the Island would be any less populous or prosperous than any other part of the British Empire. Indeed, comparisons with heavily populated West Indian islands were common among those who saw a great future for the Island of St John. Much of the criticism of the proprietors and the government came from those who insisted that the retardation of development had to be somebody's fault. The Island was young and a wilderness, but for its residents it was not inconsequential or likely to become so.

Unfortunately for its historical reputation, the Island was too immature to play a crucial role in the events of the American Revolution, and it remained British. Thus, although American historians who study the pre-revolutionary British colonies ought to be interested in the Island of St John, they are not because it does not become a part of the United States. At the same time, Canadian historians display little more interest in the Island because they know that its historical progress leads it merely to admission into Canadian Confederation as a technically equal but practically marginal jurisdiction. In short, because the early history of Prince Edward Island does not fit neatly into the national historical sensibilities of either the United States or Canada, it has not drawn much attention from historians of North American colonization.

For the most part, those who have investigated the early development of Prince Edward Island have been individuals with a close personal connection to it, either through birth or residence. Regrettably, many have tended to become trapped by another and quite different perceptual limitation, the Island's own mythological sense of its past. In recent years, however, much useful work has been done and we can see the beginnings of a renaissance of Island historical writing less wedded to the past. The key point in this past, almost an obsession among Island historians, was the peculiar system imposed on the Island by the British government in the 1760s that led to absentee landlordism and tenant discontent while retarding economic progress. One can see the origins of this point of view from the first efforts of the leading residents unilaterally to alter the landholding system, although it did not become enshrined in print until the nineteenth century. Both Islanders and their historians came to see themselves as innocent victims of an imperial conspiracy which held that the principles of private property were more important than popular opinion or the Island's natural destiny as a prosperous agricultural community. Little attempt was made to distinguish among the various categories of residents, or to appreciate that the ambitions of those on the scene were not necessarily different or less exploitative than the notorious absentee landlords. In order to understand the state of affairs properly, it becomes necessary to produce a considerably more sophisticated view of Island political and social structure than the traditional one of resident tenants and exploiting absentee landlords.

I first came to an examination of the early history of Prince Edward Island through my study into the career of Thomas Douglas, fifth earl of Selkirk, who transplanted over 800 Scots Highlanders to the Island in 1803. As I struggled to understand how Selkirk had become a large landholder, and why his visionary plans met with so little success, I began to realize that the existing secondary literature was not only sparse, but often limited by formulistic assumptions about the Island's early development. Investigation of the available manuscript sources led me to some questions quite different from those that had preoccupied most of my predecessors, and a lengthy sojourn in Scotland fortunately made it possible for me to uncover considerable new evidence, particularly on the settlement activities of other active proprietors – such as James Montgomery and John MacDonald –most of whom were Scots. Some of my findings made their way into my book on early Scottish emigration to Canada, entitled *The People's Clearance*, which focused on emigration from Scotland, rather than on immigration to and settlement in Canada. In that book I promised studies of the early settlements in the New World that involved Scots, and the present volume is part of the fulfilment of that promise. Sections of this book have appeared in different form as articles in *Acadiensis*, the *Dalhousie Review*, *The Island Magazine*, and *The Dictionary of Canadian Biography*.

Like all scholars, I have had considerable assistance in the enterprise. Staffs at a number of British and Canadian libraries and archives deserve special thanks, particularly those at the Scottish Record Office, the National Library of Scotland, the Scottish Catholic Archives, the University of Edinburgh Library, the Public Record Office (Kew), the British Library, the Public Archives of Canada, the National Library of Canada, the Public Archives of Nova Scotia, the Toronto Public Library, the University of Manitoba Library, the Centennial Library in Charlottetown, and the University of Prince Edward Island Library. I am especially indebted to the Public Archives of Prince Edward Island, and to Nicholas DeJong and Harry Holman there. Harry Baglole and Phil Buckner offered much sound advice and assistance, particularly in the early stages of the research. Ian Robertson has been a friend throughout the gestation of this book, and commented usefully on several draft chapters. I am grateful to St John's College and June Renton for typing the first draft of the manuscript, and to the Marjorie Young Bell Faculty Fund at Mount Allison University for funds to type the final version. Maps were redrafted (by permission of the publisher, from A.H. Clark, *Three Centuries and the Island* [Toronto: University of Toronto Press 1959], pp. 53 and 59) with the assistance of a small grant from the University of Manitoba/SSHRC Research Grants Committee. My family put up with someone whose mind was often elsewhere while this work was in progress, at the same time that it provided the support necessary to keep going. None of the above, of course, are responsible for any errors that may have crept into this work; for those I alone am to blame.

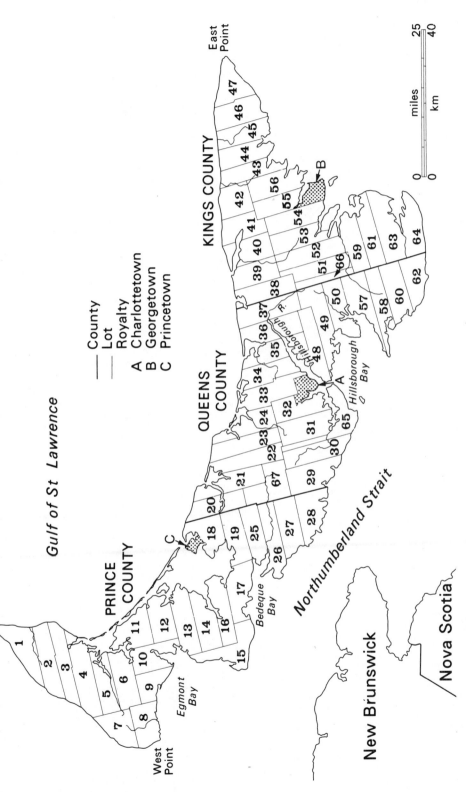

Figure 1   Island of St John as surveyed by Samuel Holland in 1765 (from an original survey by Holland, in the Public Archives of Prince Edward Island)

Land, Settlement, and Politics on Eighteenth-Century Prince Edward Island

Prologue: The French Regime

In late June 1534, Jacques Cartier sighted and briefly visited what is today known as Prince Edward Island; however, its settled development did not begin in earnest until well into the eighteenth century. Cartier probably was not the first European to view and be favourably impressed by the crescent-shaped wedge of land off the coast of mainland Nova Scotia. Basque and other fishermen had doubtless reached the Island years earlier – perhaps even before John Cabot's celebrated landfall in Newfoundland in 1497 – and the Micmac Indians, of course, had at least summered there for centuries. Notwithstanding the enthusiastic comments by Cartier ("The finest land one can see, and full of beautiful trees and meadows") and a century later by Nicholas Denys in his *Description and Natural History of Acadia*, the Island was generally regarded as difficult of access and lacking in first-rate harbours.[1] It was true that the north coast, despite its proximity to the St Lawrence fishery, was characterized by shifting sand dunes standing between its many coves and the open sea. Moreover, neither fisherfolk nor Indians had any great incentive to publicize the many advantages of Abegweit (as the native peoples called it) or Île Saint-Jean (as the French labelled it) for permanent settlement, since such development clearly ran counter to their own best interests.

Some scholars go so far as to suggest that Denys, who was granted the Island among other territories in 1654, "may have deliberately suppressed some of his knowledge," but it seems more likely that lack of precise information, rather than deliberate misinformation, was the basic problem.[2] In any event, summering fishermen and summering Indians constituted the bulk of the resident population of the Island throughout the seventeenth century. After Denys, a succession of French adventurers were granted fishing concessions that included the Island, usually specifying permanent settlement as a condition of tenure. Without exception these operations failed, both in financial and in practical terms. A sedentary fishery based on the Island did not spring instantly to life, and permanent habitation was more a product of the pressure of international rivalry in the Gulf of St Lawrence than of the attractions of the Island.

In 1710 the British captured Port Royal, the major French settlement in Acadia, and in 1713 the Treaty of Utrecht transferred Acadia and its people (minus Cape Breton and the islands of the Gulf of St Lawrence, including Île Saint-Jean) into British hands. Soon after the capture of Port Royal, Acadians had begun moving to the Island as an alternative residence, and French officials in America began insisting on its value as a potential colony. Following the losses at Utrecht, French official policy was to move the Acadian population onto French territory, although the bulk of the people were extremely reluctant to leave their traditional homes. As part of the new policy, le comte de Saint-Pierre – under confused circumstances – was in 1719 granted in *franc-alleu noble* Île Saint-Jean and adjacent islands by the French Crown, which reserved to itself the administration of justice, mining production, and some timber rights. Saint-Pierre, while technically responsible to Louisbourg, was in effect an autonomous landlord. In return for his grant, he was obliged to settle 100 *habitants* the first year and 50 annually thereafter, assisting them with livestock and building roads as required.[3]

Although this first serious attempt at settlement was not based upon identical assumptions and conditions as those – both French and British – that followed it, there are sufficient similarities and parallels with later efforts to require some general comment. As would be the case subsequently with both French and British policy for the Island, the French Crown was in 1719 unwilling to finance the cost of settlement itself, and was prepared instead to create a semi-feudal landlord with responsibility for colonization. If such an attitude would persist long into the future, it also had deep roots in the past. All European governments had employed some variation of the strategy virtually since the first sightings of the New World, and it had its origins in medieval expansion within Europe itself. No state or head of state wanted settlement of new territory to be a financial drain, and the standard way to encourage private capital to take over responsibility was by offering either commercial concessions or semi-feudal power, or both. Whether such policies were effective is a nice question, but European experience with privately financed settlement was not entirely negative; indeed, most overseas colonization was executed privately. Failures – and there were many – did not really matter. From any government's perspective, privately financed disasters simply cancelled grants, with yet another promoter given the chance. Eventually something might work, and there were sufficient illustrations of success to encourage continuation of the policy.[4]

Why, given the record of failure, was the private sector prepared to be exploited in this way? In the lengthy history of North American colonization, the number of entrepreneurs who profited financially from their settlement activities can be counted on the fingers of one hand, and the number of private fortunes lost or badly damaged in the maw of such adventuring was considerable. Part of the answer is that financial profit from settlement was not what was really at stake for most promoters. They often sought other advantages with the government at home, and were prepared to pay this price for concessions or favours elsewhere. Moreover, it was no accident that semi-feudal grants tended to attract middle-class merchants with money, and many of the individuals involved would find their social status considerably – and rapidly – enhanced by their settlements. Not all men were prepared to wait patiently for the many generations normally required in Europe to achieve landed or aristocratic status. Even for those who did seek immediate financial profit, there was usually an air of romantic adventurism attached to the operation. In short, in the pre-industrial age, when men sought wealth, power, and status in land, wilderness territory held a substantial appeal. Pecuniary profit, social advance, and utopian escapism combined in an extremely heady brew. Not surprisingly, islands – then as now – brought out both the best and worst in men's fantasies. Islands had a fatal attraction, producing all the ambivalences explored by Shakespeare in *The Tempest* or Defoe in *Robinson Crusoe*.

The company organized by the comte de Saint-Pierre sent three ships to Île Saint-Jean in 1720 under the command of the Sieur de Gotteville de Belleisle. On the Island, the expedition quickly established itself at what the French called Port La Joie, later the site of Charlottetown, producing buildings that survived in various states of repair until the Americans destroyed them in 1745. The French sent back to Europe encouraging reports on the resources of the Island, and built three ships intended for use in the fishery, which was to serve as the main source of revenue for the venture. Jurisdictional disputes led the French Crown to separate the Island administratively from Île-Royale through appointment of a subdelegate of the intendant of New France. The Island's isolation not only led almost inexorably to separate government, but also to its becoming a haven for debtors and other fugitives. But the Saint-Pierre venture had collapsed by 1724, when crops were destroyed by a plague of field-mice, for its head had anticipated immediate profits and was not prepared constantly to sink capital into the operation. Nevertheless, settlers from France and Acadia were attracted to the Island, and some remained despite this failure and constant threats from the English, which led to the stationing of a tiny French garrison there in 1726. A missionary soon followed.[5]

A census in 1728 showed 297 persons resident on the Island in fifty-four houses.[6] Besides being the year of the first serious attempt to enumerate a small but growing population, 1728 was also distinguished for another plague of field-mice. Mice and forest fire would continue to be the main threats to agriculture until well into the nineteenth century. The mice were not an annual event, disappearing often enough to produce constant hope that they had been eliminated, and then returning to devastate another harvest. Despite such problems, by 1730 a fresh census showed 325 persons in residence, plus another 140 in the fishery. Much of the population probably combined agriculture and fishing, and indeed, without the fishery the people could not have survived the destructions of their crops.[7]

The grant to the comte de Saint-Pierre was revoked by the Crown in 1730, and a year later most of the Island was granted to a "Company of the East" on terms similar to the Saint-Pierre allocation. The company was to provide settlers – eighty the first year and thirty each year thereafter – and hoped to profit from the fishery. One of the partners of the company, Jean-Pierre Roma, actually took up residence on the Island. Roma had some experience in the West Indies, and by all accounts was a hard-driving imperious individual who fought with virtually everyone. He was later described as having "so much causticity" in his character "that it is to be feared he could not reconcile himself to anyone."[8] Such a personality (one is reminded of Captain John MacDonald later in the century) was perhaps uniquely suited to wrestle with the peculiar conditions of early settlement on remote islands. While both Roma and MacDonald would ultimately fail in their ventures, they came closest of any of their contemporaries to fulfilling their visions.

Jean-Pierre Roma fought with the Church, with his partners, and with his settlers, but he plainly had an epic vision of settlement and the energy to move his dream toward reality. The site of his operation was Three Rivers, at the confluence of the Montague, the Brudenell, and the Cardigan, on the eastern tip of the Island. Beginning in June 1732 at Brudenell Point, Roma had a pier and wooden bridge erected, cleared over 200,000 square feet of land by cutting trees and digging out over 6,000 stumps, and built nine substantial buildings. Subsequently he constructed roads, included one to the garrison at Port La Joie fifty miles westward. The financial basis of this colony was to be commerce with Quebec and the West Indies arising out of the fishery, but as might have been expected, Roma's partners were not happy with his expenditures and refused to advance additional money. Such reluctance to invest without immediate return would be endemic throughout the period of settlement, whether French or British. It was a principal disadvantage of colonization by private enterprise. Only the state or an unusually well-financed capitalist could find it possible to supply the vast sums of money required to develop an isolated wilderness without some evidence of immediate profit. Roma managed to wrest total control of his venture from his partners, but after surviving a series of minor misfortunes in the late 1730s and early 1740s, his settlement succumbed to Yankee raiders sent out from Louisbourg, who destroyed it in June 1745. At this point Roma abandoned Three Rivers, although after the British takeover, others would conjure up similar visions about constructing a commercial entrepôt based upon the fishery.[9] Roma was clearly a tenacious colonizer prepared to devote his considerable total energy to his venture, but individual will and leadership – however inspired – had less effect on the future of the Island than the sum total of thousands of decisions made without a trace upon the historical record by countless anonymous settlers.

By the early 1740s, Acadian families had begun to immigrate to the Island from the mainland. We do not know their precise motives in coming, but it seems likely that the pressures of international rivalry combined with word of bumper harvests on the Island to produce the movement. Despite the spillover of New England military activity from Louisbourg after 1745, the Acadian population of Île Saint-Jean grew from 440 in 1740 to 735 in 1748. Only lack of transportation had prevented Rear-Admiral Peter Warren from evacuating the inhabitants in 1745, forcing him instead to arrange for the neutrality of the people. Another proposed evacuation was postponed later in 1745 because transports were needed elsewhere and the Islanders were regarded as a "poor miserable inoffensive people."[10] To everyone's surprise, the Treaty of Aix-la-Chapelle, which ended the war between France and Britain in 1748, returned both Louisbourg and Île Saint-Jean to the French. For the moment, the Acadians were heartened. Despite the setback, however, the British in North America were learning several important lessons, and they would not hesitate the next time to clear the land permanently of Acadians.

France responded to the 1748 restoration of territory in the Gulf of

St Lawrence by encouraging the resettlement of Acadians on French lands, notably on Île Saint Jean, while the British finally began their own scheme of colonization at Halifax and attempted to secure the loyalty of those Acadians in British territory through administration of ironclad oaths of allegiance.[11] In the short run, the two national policies complemented one another. While many Acadians were apparently convinced that the British insistence on oaths in Nova Scotia was pure bluff and bluster that could be avoided, many others found the pressure sufficiently serious to encourage them to migrate to Île Saint-Jean, where the French insisted they would be welcome. Especially vulnerable and susceptible were those Acadians who resided on lands along the border between French and British territory. This "grand dérangement," which had begun in 1749, picked up impetus in 1750 and then slowed in 1751. On the Island, a population of less than 800 in 1748 had become one of more than 2,200 by 1752. As was typical of such periods of rapid growth in wilderness regions, this one was accompanied by considerable suffering and hardship. While the French government spent what at least one official regarded as a substantial sum on goods and provisions, there was never enough.[12]

Settlement in these years was concentrated in the Port La Joie area, on the Northeast River, and in the Pownal/Orwell region along the south coast. The newcomers located by waterside and did not venture inland, except along major rivers, although they were indisputably agriculturalists rather than fisherfolk. Easy access for humans and stock combined with transportation requirements to produce the locations, for there were virtually no roads anywhere on the Island. Moreover, the relatively large amounts of livestock possessed by the new settlers required forage and pasturage, and marshland was confined to water's edge. Like most immigrants from more established jurisdictions, the Acadians did not like to clear trees and did so only reluctantly on small amounts of land. Given the lack of markets for crops and a relative shortage of seed, too much ought not to be made out of the slowness of clearing, however. Although the newcomers did not settle in nucleated villages, as families they seldom moved far beyond their neighbours and the existing limits of settlement. Such patterns would persist under British rule until well into the nineteenth century, and it is worth emphasizing that they were less culturally or politically than environmentally induced.[13] The system of land tenure had little influence on early settlement patterns. The French experience is a useful control against the tendency to ascribe too much importance to the uniqueness under the British of the landholding system of the Island. From the outset, the isolation and geography contributed far more than did institutional arrangements to influencing migration and settlement patterns.

Life on the Island posed considerable hardships upon the Acadian refugees of the post-1748 period. At least one historian has argued that their suffering was "quite as acute and widespread as those of their countrymen after the Expulsion of 1755."[14] Such an assertion constitutes to some extent special pleading in exculpation of subsequent British policy toward the Acadians; the implication is that the Acadians suffered under both British and French. It also represents the typical treatment of early settlement on the Island as an unending story of victimization of helpless colonists. It was true that the Acadians on Île Saint-Jean were often short on supplies, notably seed; that many were dependent on the king's bounty; and that all were uncertain of their land tenure, since an organized land system had not been created. Those at Malpeque, moreover, had experienced in three consecutive harvest seasons an invasion of field-mice, a plague of voracious locusts of a "prodigious size," and wheat scald.[15] At the same time, too much can be made of such hardships among a pioneer population.

The census of 1752 showed a population of 2,223 apart from the garrison, with 368 heads of families.[16] This population, much of which had arrived since 1748, possessed 98 horses, 1,259 cattle, 799 oxen, 1,230 sheep, 1,295 pigs, 2,393 hens, 304 geese, 90 turkeys, and 12 ducks; it had seeded 1,490 bushels of wheat, 129 of oats, 181 of peas, 8¼ of barley, 8 of rye, 1 of linseed, 1 of sprat, and ½ bushel of buckwheat. Land had been cleared for the sowing of nearly 3,000 bushels of wheat, but shortage of seed prevented the full capacity from being planted. At potential average yields of even three or four bushels for each one seeded – typical for the eighteenth century – the Acadians would have been able to harvest between 5,000 and 6,000 bushels of wheat, or nearly three bushels per inhabitant. Not surprisingly, there was a direct correlation between numbers of livestock, acres seeded, and length of time settled. Many of the newly settled areas had been unable to plant, but the St Peters district and that on the north bank of Northeast River had done reasonably well. One family on the Northeast River, for example, had eight children, four oxen, four cows, three heifers, two bulls, four sows, two pigs, and three fowls. Possessors of their own corn mill, they held land four arpents by forty arpents, and had cleared for the sowing of twenty-eight bushels of wheat and peas, although they had sown but ten of the former and two of the latter.[17] Concern expressed by some commentators about the small numbers who had cleared large amounts of land or the holding of considerable livestock misses the point about the nature of Acadian agriculture, and indeed, about the nature of most early subsistence farming in wilderness North America. For most farmers, livestock pasture was more important than arable land, and cleared acreage was not held at a premium, since an absence of market restricted the scope of planting.[18]

By 1753 the French were beginning to feel more confident about the future of Île Saint-Jean. The crops did extremely well, and four priests were assigned to join the chaplain at Port La Joie, to be based at Malpeque, St Peters, Northeast River, and Point Prim. Immigration had intensified in 1753 – over 400 people journeyed to the Island that year alone – and again in 1754, and then at the close of 1755 really exploded, because of the British attempt to remove forcibly the Acadian population of Nova Scotia. More than 2,000 refugees arrived over the winter of 1755/6, and more than 1,400 stayed on, totally dependent on the king's bounty. The colony was not able to adjust rapidly enough to feed these new arrivals, who had nearly doubled the population. The Expulsion of 1755 greatly intensified the problems of Île Saint-Jean, upsetting the process of orderly development and expansion of settlement. Seed had to be consumed as food, and while a refusal to slaughter livestock – especially horned cattle – to meet the immediate crisis may have been a mistake given subsequent developments, the general acquiescence of the population in the official decision to preserve stock indicates that it was a popular one.[19]

The Island was planning for a future which was not to be, however. On 26 July 1758 the fortress of Louisbourg surrendered to beseiging British troops, and under the third article of capitulation, any soldiers on Île Saint-Jean were to be removed as soon as the victors provided transport. Subsequently, it was decided by the British to evacuate not only soldiers but the entire population of the Island, and Lord Rollo was sent there on 8 August with 500 men on three ships of war to manage the removal. French officers accompanied him to confirm the surrender. The population – Acadian and Micmac – offered no resistance to evacuation, although the most energetic managed to escape to Miramichi, Quebec, or the French islands; the numbers who got away are impossible to estimate. Some of the people did attempt to petition the British to be allowed to remain on their lands, even sending a delegation to Louisbourg, but the British command had learned its lesson about Acadians and refused to consent.[20]

The British command had also learned of the potential agricultural value of the Island, initially receiving quite inflated reports from the French on this subject. Admiral Boscawen wrote to William Pitt in mid September that Île Saint-Jean had been the major supplier of beef and corn to Quebec. It was alleged to possess 10,000 horned cattle, and many habitants boasted of substantial cereal crops, as much as 1,200 bushels of "corn" (or grain) annually.[21] Such statements were both exaggerated and misleading. The thousands of cattle on the Island were present only because of a conscious policy of conservation, not as a source of supply. As for the alleged crop yields, they bear no relationship to the available census returns of the French government. The Island had not been a great exporter of foodstuffs, but had consumed more than it was ever able to produce. At the same time, the important point about such information was not that it was misleading, but that it was in circulation among British officers at Louisbourg. As we shall see, the British officer corps, especially those who had served in the Gulf of St Lawrence area, were among the most active petitioners for land on the Island of St John when it was taken over by the British.

The misapprehension of the British regarding the state of development of the Island was further increased by the number of Acadians evacuated from Île Saint-Jean in the autumn of 1758. While exact numbers are unobtainable, approximately 3,500 people were removed by the British, who were aware that the population of at least one parish (Malpeque) had been left behind and others had escaped to French territory.[22] Much of this evacuated population had only recently arrived on the Island, which had served as a refugee camp for displaced Acadians, and the numbers did not reflect the true state of orderly colonization. Nonetheless, the British assumed a far more substantial settled population than ever had existed, and were also led to believe that the Island was ultimately completely depopulated. A mop-up squad arrived early in 1759 to remove stragglers, but was informed that they had all gone off to Canada. Several hundred still remained in hiding, to serve as the basis for the subsequent francophone population of the Island.[23] But for all practical purposes, the Island was deserted, and the British conquerors could dream of how such a fertile and prosperous territory could best be repopulated.

The French had not left a substantial imprint upon Île Saint-Jean, but their experiences ought to have been more instructive than turned out to be the case. Private settlement under semi-feudal arrangements had not worked. The Island was fertile but extremely isolated, making it difficult if not impossible to integrate its agriculture into a larger market economy. Nevertheless, the British proceeded to replicate the French mistakes, partly under the misapprehension that the French farms were ready – as in Nova Scotia – for fresh immigrants.

CHAPTER ONE

British Colonial Policy and the Island of St John, 1763–1767

The early history of the Island of St John under British rule has long been surrounded by an air of confusion and misunderstanding, particularly in terms of the background to the decision of the Privy Council to parcel the Island into 20,000-acre townships, which were allocated to applicants by lottery on 23 July 1767. This action, of course, constituted the beginning of the complex land question on the Island, which saw the proprietors battling with the residents until well into the nineteenth century. Two factors have hampered a proper understanding of the "lottery" of 1767. In the first place, the hostilities of later generations of Islanders toward landlords have been read back into historical accounts of the origins of the land system.[1] In the second place, the early history of the Island has been usually viewed either in splendid isolation or at best in comparison with the development of other Canadian provinces, rather than within the framework of Britain's vastly expanded American empire of the 1760s.[2] Placed in its proper context, however, the decision to distribute the Island to proprietors in 20,000-acre parcels – perhaps a mistaken one in the long run – ceases to be arbitrary and ill consider-ed, and becomes instead a perfectly comprehensible and even liberal move on the part of a British government, which could hardly be expected to predict the later stormy history of the colony. The complicated manoeuvring that led up to the lottery of 1767 highlights some of the principal divisions of the time in Britain regarding policy toward America – and especially new settlement in the territory taken from the French.

With Île Saint-Jean virtually depopulated in 1758 (perhaps 200 French and 200 Indians remained), the next step very much depended upon the peace negotiations that culminated in the Treaty

of Paris in 1763. In the preliminary discussions for the treaty, the
Island was conceded to the British without debate. While the French
did hold out for fishing rights in the Gulf of St Lawrence – ultimately
winning concessions in Newfoundland as well as regaining possession
of St Pierre and Miquelon – Île Saint-Jean was specifically excluded in
the final treaty from any fishing concessions to the French.[3] Its only
appearance in the public eye during the peace negotiations came
when the double agent Thomas Pichon, writing as "an impartial
Frenchman," published in London a treatise entitled *Genuine Letters
and Memoirs, Relating to the Natural, Civil, and Commercial History of the
Islands of Cape Breton and Saint John* (a work originally written in
French and printed at Paris).[4] While Pichon's real focus was on Cape
Breton, he managed to wax lyrically about St John as well, describing
it as "the largest of all the islands in the gulph of St Lawrence, and [it]
has even the advantage of Cape Briton [*sic*] in point of fertility. Its
length is twenty leagues, and circumference about fifty. It has a safe
commodious harbour, with plenty of wood, and as great a convenien-
cy for fishing as any place on the coast."[5] Pichon then described the
Island's coastline in some detail, based upon a trip he claimed to have
taken around it in 1752, emphasizing its natural advantages for the
fisheries. He concluded his work with an imaginary conversation
between an Englishman and the author (as "impartial Frenchman")
regarding the merits of these islands to each side. As befit the work of
a double agent, it was impossible to discern which nation Pichon felt
should possess them; the discussion revolved around their great
economic and strategic value.

Although it could hardly be maintained that the Island of St John
had a high profile in Britain in the early 1760s, the occasional
references to it suggest that – at least in some informed circles – it was
seen as a very desirable piece of real estate. One description in the
Hardwicke Papers in the British Library, prepared by an anonymous
officer who had in 1762 "run over" the Island in a whale boat with a
French pilot and thirty men, concentrated on the sites of the former
French villages and their prospects for settlement by the British.
Emphasizing the rich meadows and cleared lands, this brief survey
emphatically made the Island sound ready for immediate recoloniza-
tion with minimal effort.[6] Prosperity would be based on agriculture
and fishing. Certainly those Britons initially most attracted to St John
were a handful of Anglo-American merchants with their eye on the
Gulf of St Lawrence fishery, a few land-hungry Nova Scotians, and a
large number of military officers who had served with the British
forces, especially the fleet, in the reduction of French America. Many

of these officers had been involved in the capture of Louisbourg – or knew someone who had – and they had obviously heard promising words about the Island.

Even before the British ministers had decided on policies for the newly acquired territories, applicants for land grants on St John were making their appearance. On 3 June 1763, the Commissioners for Trade and Plantations (the Board of Trade) received a memorial from Colonel Alexander MacNutt, generously offering to transport foreign Protestants to the Island in return for a grant of fifty acres for each settler so transported. The commissioners replied that they were willing to consider the proposal if MacNutt had in mind a limited operation, but not on St John; MacNutt shifted his attention to what is now New Brunswick.[7] Despite their response to MacNutt, on 18 November 1763 the commissioners heard another memorial from Hutcheson Mure, Robert Cathcart, and George Spence – all London merchants – offering to settle villages and carry on a fishing trade from the Island in return for a large grant of its land.[8]

Between the MacNutt and Mure memorials the government had finally made a public announcement of its intended policy for the newly acquired American territory. On 7 October 1763 the king had issued the famous Proclamation of 1763, a product of months of high-level deliberation over the best policies to adopt not merely toward the new possessions but regarding North America in general.[9] From the standpoint of the Island's future, three features of the complicated discussion over American policy were important. First, there was the oft-expressed concern that the American colonists were becoming entirely too insolent and independent; they needed to be brought under "due subordination" by a variety of new strategies, including the nurture of a colonial aristocracy and landed interest. Many observers were convinced that the absence of a proper aristocratic element in American society was a critical factor in the rambunctiousness of the colonies. Second, North America would require a large permanent military establishment, partly for protection against hostile Indians, partly to occupy and defend territory populated by former enemy aliens, and partly to keep the Americans in line. Finally, the administration and defence of the vastly expanded American empire would be very expensive, and insofar as possible should be financed out of American revenue.[10] These concerns about a landed interest, military protection, and American revenue led directly, of course, to the policies of George Grenville that culminated in the Stamp Act and its resistance in the American colonies. But they also led somewhat more circuitously to the procedures ultimately adopted by the government for the settlement of the Island of St John.

While the king's proclamation established at some length a basis for four new colonies – Quebec, East and West Florida, and Grenada – it merely annexed St John and Cape Breton to the existing colony of Nova Scotia. Nevertheless, one clause of the proclamation was of critical importance for the future development of the Island. All reduced officers in both navy and army, as well as private soldiers who had served in America and resided there, were promised substantial land grants "without Fee or Reward" and free from quitrents for the first ten years. The amounts of land offered ranged from 5,000 acres for field officers to 50 acres for private soldiers. This promise of land had been personally added by the king to the proposed proclamation prepared by the government, and would undoubtedly further encourage officers to apply for attractive American land.[11] A few days later, advertisements appeared in the *London Gazette* offering townships of 20,000 acres in East and West Florida to any proprietor who would settle foreign Protestants or British-Americans on the land at his own expense.[12] Nova Scotia was not similarly advertised at this time, but the announcement indicated the general thinking of the Board of Trade regarding the best process for the settlement of the conquered territory; the main outlines of these advertisements would be ultimately applied to the Island.

In early 1764, however, the board had under consideration a proposal for the Island's development from the earl of Egmont.[13] Not long after the publication of the proclamation, a syndicate of distinguished military officers, politicians, and merchants headed by the earl had submitted a memorial to the king asking for the grant of St John to be held perpetually in fee from the Crown as one entire county with "all manner of Rights, Royalties, Privileges, Franchises, and Appurtenances whatsoever; with all the Civil and Criminal Jurisdiction, with all manner of Courts as in England, and with Power to appoint or commission from time to time all manner of Officer for the Exercise of the said Jurisdiction, and for ordering the Government thereof.[14] Egmont was an outspoken opponent of the Whig ministries of George II and a close friend of the present monarch's father (Frederick, Prince of Wales); he had come to prominence and power with George III's accession to the throne. Created an English peer in 1762, Egmont served briefly as paymaster general, and then in September of 1763 was appointed First Lord of the Admiralty. A learned man of great ambition, he was a staunch advocate of the reinstitution of feudal tenures and traditional ways. At Enmore he built a residence that was to be defensible with crossbows and arrows, "against the time in which the fabric and use of gunpowder shall be forgotten."[15]

Egmont's efforts to obtain St John Island (in all, he prepared three memorials) have received rather a bad press from historians, chiefly because they were based on the institution of military feudalism in America and came from a man apparently so out of step with his time. Since the beginning of the nineteenth century, for example, the story has been repeated that Egmont sought to make himself "Lord High Paramount" of the Island, although this high-sounding title was never used by him and was apparently first invented by John Stewart as part of an attempt to blacken the Earl's proposals and British policy generally.[16] Both because of such inaccurate treatment and because they greatly influenced the Board of Trade's final arrangements for the Island, Egmont's plans are worth examining in some detail.

As the text of the memorials and their supporting documentation make quite clear, Egmont was not engaged in a single-handed, naked, and idiosyncratic land grab, but was acting on behalf of a large number of influential men who felt they had some legitimate claims to land in North America and had deliberately left the complex question of distributing the land in the proposed grant to him. In 1765, when the Egmont scheme was again brought before the king after its rejection by the Board of Trade and Privy Council, its supporters emphasized that Egmont was only the "Nominal Grantee," holding the land "in Trust ... for a due Division, Subdivision and Distribution thereof between him and your Majesty's Petitioners."[17] At the outset, the earl's colleagues were mainly senior-rank naval and army officers who had served in North America and were familiar with the reported agricultural and commercial possibilities of the Island. On the basis of the king's proclamation, they were entitled by their rank and service to substantial amounts of American land. A few merchants were also part of the original group of petitioners, but at its inception the proposal was largely backed by military men. It was a mark of the credibility of Egmont's memorial as initially presented – both in terms of the influence of those involved and of the perceived good sense of their plans – that most of the other groups seeking Island land chose to withdraw their applications and join the Egmont syndicate. Thus three other major groups of petitioners – one of seven career officers headed by Charles Saunders, one of twenty-one reduced officers organized by Colonel Charles Lee, and one of four merchants already active in the fisheries – had themselves added to the Egmont ranks by mid-January 1764.[18]

The numbers in the Egmont syndicate were subsequently increased as twelve more senior officers and fifteen "gentlemen" (including three members of Parliament, a number of Crown officials in Britain and America, and several Perceval relations of Egmont) signed on. Those who were to receive major subdivisions from Egmont were carefully distinguished, and while they included all members of the three competing groups who had merged with the earl's, very few of the latecomers expected to benefit directly. They were simply adding their weight to the proposals. In any event, the final list of seventy-five names signing Egmont's first memorial included eight members of Parliament, two peers, four admirals, and three generals. There would be considerable continuity between this initial list and the final one approved by the Board of Trade in 1767. Egmont's colleagues were not only of impressive combined political influence, but they also represented individuals entitled, in terms of the king's proclamation, to hundreds of thousands of acres of land in North America.

If, given the ground rules of the time, most of the members of the Egmont syndicate had a proper claim on land in America, so too their proposals for the settlement and governance of that land had a certain legitimacy as well, As First Lord of the Admiralty, the earl was well aware of the discussions within ministerial circles over American policy, and he had even participated in them himself. His proposed grant of the Island of St John was an ingenious attempt to provide due subordination, a military presence, and self-financing, not only for the Island but by extension for all of newly-conquered North America. The scheme's drawback was not that it was completely out of step with the direction of some British thinking, but that it was too close a reflection of the ideas of those who were calling for the firm reassertion of Crown sovereignty in America and the establishment of a standing army to force due obedience from the colonials.[19] As such it was open to criticism from those who were not prepared to support any thoroughgoing reorganization of North American administration. It is worth emphasizing that the scheme was not merely a personal whim of the earl of Egmont, for most of those military men associated with him resurrected it without his active support in 1765.

At its outset, Egmont's first memorial made quite clear that his proposal would result in a government by "Persons who will have a permanent and common Interest in the Prosperity of those over whom they are to preside, and a great Stake at home to pledge for their good Behaviour abroad, either to the People or the Crown — Without the Expence of One Shilling to the Public."[20] Not only was there no mention of any "Lord High Paramount," but the Island would remain firmly under the direct control of the Crown. The common and statute laws of Britain (except those relating to land tenure, game, and taxes) would be in force; the king's assent would be required for criminal executions (except those for mutiny) and for the appointment of officials, who would be removable by the king in council. In short, Egmont was asking for far less political autonomy for himself than had been given to earlier large proprietors such as William Penn – or was ultimately allowed to the government of the Island. He proposed to hold St John as "Earl of the whole County" in return for providing 1,200 soldiers within ten years for its defence upon demand of the king or his governor. The basis of the complex system of landholding and land tenure, therefore, was to be military obligation. An eclectic scheme, it was based on a number of models, including the grant of Carolina in 1663 and several for settling West Indian islands. One proposal that anticipated many of Egmont's arrangements had been made in 1728 by the Duke of Montagu in a petition for the Island of Tobago.[21] Not surprisingly, Montagu's proposal was in 1764 again before the Board of Trade at the same time as Egmont's.[22]

The plan for St John called for the Island to be surveyed into fifty parts of equal extent, each of which would be called a "hundred." Forty of these hundreds would be let to major tenants and ten set aside for the earl, who would provide land for a capital town. The hundreds would in turn be divided into twenty manors of 2,000 acres each (with court baron, court leet, and hundred court), ten of which would be granted to Lords of the Manor and ten reserved to the Lord of the Hundred, who would set aside 500 acres for a town. Each holder of 2,000 acres would establish two freeholds of 200 acres and set aside 100 acres for a village. No individual could engross more than a single hundred, and each was obliged to re-grant half of his holding. Through a complicated series of obligations on the part of tenants and subtenants, every hundred would be able to furnish thirty men for military service. Land would be granted on the basis of a quitrent of one shilling per 100 acres to the Crown and one shilling per 100 acres to the landlord, payment to commence ten years after the institution of the grant.

In a lengthy footnote, Egmont observed that his proposal for the Island could serve as a pilot plan for settling all the conquered territory in America, which could be subdivided into 62 provinces of 18,000,000 acres each and then granted to "the Peers, great Commoners, eminent Merchants, and other Gentlemen of Distinction" in Britain according to the scheme for the Island of St John. This policy, he maintained, would provide 744,000 soldiers for the British army.[23] Left unsaid, of course, was that these soldiers could be employed against any American uprisings, which were feared by some private advisers of the great ministers.[24] Indicating the extent to which he was thinking of the Island in West Indian terms, Egmont noted that he

had expectations from the earl of Egremont for a grant on Domi-
nique, and was prepared to take land in the Caribbean if St John fell
short of the 2,000,000 acres required for his plan. In conclusion, the
memorial proposed the allocation of the hundreds to the syndicate
members by setting up a ballot box at the Board of Trade filled with
fifty tablets corresponding to lot numbers on a map.[25] Here was the
origin of the subsequent lottery.

The Board of Trade's response to Egmont's memorial was almost
immediate – and very critical. At stake was not simply the Island of St
John but overall British policy for America. In the behind-the-scenes
struggle over the question of American policy, the members of the
board were opposed to any efforts for grand colonial reform or
intimidation of the Americans.[26] The board reported to the king on
Egmont's scheme on 12 February 1764, less than a month after it had
been received – a remarkable feat of alacrity for any eighteenth-
century government body. It criticized the proposal for its reinstitution of ancient tenures, arguing that they were designed more for
military discipline than to encourage trade and commerce. Such
tenures were totally averse "in their Principles to that System of
Settlement and Tenure of Property, which have of late Years been
adopted in the Colonies" with much advantage to the kingdom.
Emphasizing that its principles of settlement were economic rather
than political, the board opposed any burdensome and unnecessary
services that hampered commerce and industry. America was flourishing and held a "due Dependence ... upon the Mother Country," an
obvious reference to the implications of the Egmont plan. Grants to
high persons with elaborate schemes of government – however much
based upon study and reading of the wisest and most learned
philosophers – checked and obstructed the settlement of the country.
Noting the similarity to the seventeenth-century Carolina grant, the
board emphasized that Carolina had succeeded only when taken back
from proprietors and reinvested in the Crown.

The Board did not even bother to take legal advice on the Egmont
proposals because they were so unacceptable. Contemporary gossip
reported that the problems of the Isle of Man, then before Parliament, were also an important factor in the reaction to Egmont's
memorial. As Captain William Owen noted, it had become necessary
"to purchase the right of the Athol family to that Island, and to subject
it to the same regulations in trade as the rest of the Empire." He
continued: "If Man was a nest and nursery of smugglers and
smuggling, a pest to the society of fair-traders, and a diminution of
the legal revenues of the State; is it not more than probable, that St.
John's would have stood in the same predicament with regard to her

neighbouring colonies in America?"[27] Owen's emphasis upon smuggling, trade, and autonomy in the Isle of Man situation ran counter to the main thrust of the Board of Trade's critique of Egmont's scheme. But although the board did not mention Man specifically, it undoubtedly realized that the ministry could produce its own illustrations of the dangers of ancient tenures.

In reply, Egmont prepared a second memorial withdrawing the requests for special tenure and extraordinary jurisdictions that had been so criticized by the Board of Trade; this memorial was apparently never submitted to the government.[28] A third memorial, however, was sent to the Privy Council on 8 March 1764, asking for the Island in free and common socage as part of Nova Scotia, with settlement terms and quitrents to be decided by the Crown after ten years.[29] The Board of Trade responded to this proposal even more swiftly than to the original memorial, drafting an answer on 23 March 1764. Admitting that settlement and cultivation in America might be expedited if persons of rank took the lead and that military officers deserved to be rewarded, the board recommended distributing the Island to the earl and his associates upon "those *Principles of Settlement, Cultivation, and Government, which have been adopted for many Years Past,* and are founded upon the Experience of former Times." Obviously pressed to spell out how these principles applied to St John, the board offered an alternative scheme for dividing and allocating the Island lands, based, it insisted, upon the proposals of Egmont's associates that had been withdrawn in favour of his arrangements. This plan called for a survey to divide the Island into 500,000 acre counties, 100,000 acre parishes (with church glebe and school site) in each county, and townships of 20,000 acres each. No one but the earl himself would get more than one township, but he could have ten (one for himself and each of nine children) at his majesty's discretion; the board would undertake the allocation of the townships remaining. It again maintained that every condition of landholding, other than cultivation and settlement, "only ... embarrass the settlers, and ... delay and discourage, or altogether prevent the Settlements." Egmont's military conditions were thus "impolitick, inexpedient, and anti-commercial." Significantly, the board did not consider a quitrent to be one of those unnecessary conditions of tenure. It emphasized that – because of the Island's value – it had even before the appearance of Egmont's proposals been contemplating the institution of a quitrent of three shillings per hundred acres in allocating the townships.[30]

Egmont responded to this report with a trenchant critique of the board's position. Although it wanted the nobility and upper classes to lead in America, it sought to reduce everyone in practice to the level of the "low and unhappy People" transported to Nova Scotia. If the Board could point to Carolina as an example of the foolhardiness of Egmont's schemes, he in turn used Nova Scotia as a club to beat the board's principles. Despite government expenditure in excess of £600,000 in Nova Scotia, Egmont observed, the province had attracted only 1,400 families. He blamed this failure on the want of "*that Order, and that Protection, that Care and individual Patronage*" embodied in his proposals. The board's plans were totally contrary to his, since they were based not on "British liberty" but the notions of the actual occupiers of land, the "most indifferent and wretched of mankind, quite hostile to men of rank, distinction and property.[31] On 9 May 1764, the Privy Council approved the board's report and directed that "no grants of land in the Island of St. John be made upon other principles than those contained in the Board's representation."[32] Instructions for the laying out of counties, parishes, and townships were given to Samuel Holland, whose proposal for a survey of the Island had been earlier approved by the Privy Council. On 14 May 1764, a petition from twenty-five of Egmont's colleagues prayed that since the earl's scheme was unacceptable, they could receive 20,000 acre townships under the Board of Trade's proposals.[33]

Despite the apparent rejection of his scheme, Egmont's memorials had produced a considerable impact on British policy for the Island. Most obviously, they forced the Board of Trade to bring forward a plan of its own for the systematic and total allocation of land on the Island; grants would not be considered piecemeal, but 20,000 acre townships encompassing the entire land area of the Island would be awarded simultaneously. Moreover, the Egmont memorials had collected many of the grantees who would subsequently receive land under the final Board of Trade lottery. As well, there were some less apparent implications of the Board of Trade's response to Egmont. It had accepted the principle of quitrents, both as a condition of tenure and as a means of financing whatever form of government – yet undecided – was instituted for the Island. Egmont's emphasis on the self-financing aspects of his scheme made it politically impossible to implement any plan of settlement that would involve public expenditure of money, as had been done in Nova Scotia. Finally, although the point was not underlined in 1764, Egmont had suggested the mechanism for the final allocation of unsurveyed townships to the grantees through his proposal for a lottery. These influences upon policy were by no means negligible. But Egmont was not quite finished with the Island in 1764.

While Samuel Holland was off in America surveying, any controversy over the Island's future remained in abeyance. But in late 1765, rumours that the survey was nearly completed combined with the latest news of resistance from the American colonies to the Stamp Act and the vagaries of British politics to produce one final attempt on the part of the Egmont syndicate to overturn the Board of Trade's plans for the Island. By this time the Grenville ministry had fallen, and had been replaced by a Whig administration headed by the Marquis of Rockingham. In the new government, Egmont continued as First Lord of the Admiralty, and several of his principal associates in the Island of St John memorial, especially Sir Charles Saunders and Augustus Keppell, had been appointed to the Admiralty Board. The political strength and influence of the memorialists was greatly enhanced, and they decided to exhume their rejected proposal. On 8 October 1765, Egmont wrote to Captain Holland:

I think it proper to let you know that a petition will be again presented to His Majesty in a few days for a grant of the Island of Saint John, upon the very same plan as that proposed before, which I have now reason to expect will meet with better success than the former. The same persons very nearly will be concerned, those only excluded who were drawn away by proposals and grants elsewhere by the Board of Trade, in order if possible to defeat my scheme ... Whether the grant may be made before the arrival of the survey or not I cannot certainly say, but we wait patiently for it, and hope it will be done accurately as to Hundreds, Manors, Freehold Villages, Towns and Capitals, that a moment's time may not be lost afterwards in proceeding to draw the lots ...[34]

In the end, Egmont did not associate himself directly with the new petition, headed by the names of Admiral Sir Charles Saunders and Admiral Augustus Keppell, asking the Lords of the Committee of Council for Plantation Affairs for a reconsideration of Egmont's scheme with a clause that if after ten years "any ill consequence shall be found to have arisen therefrom," the king in council on address to Parliament "may change the Jurisdiction in such manner, as experience of the use or abuse thereof in the course of time, may then dictate or demand."[35]

The new memorial of 1765 rehearsed the previous history of the attempt to gain the grant of St John, concluding this account by asserting that the Board of Trade had insisted upon employing the "System upon which *Nova-Scotia* has hitherto been conducted," declaring it the one system they always "intended to adopt for the future Settlement of America." In the wake of the Stamp Act controversy, the Board of Trade's sanguine philosophy for American settlement was obviously impeachable, and the memorialists proceeded to attack it vigorously. Referring to their own proposals, they insisted that they had "*an absolute Certainty, that they are able, upon this Plan, speedily and at their own Expence to compleat the Settlement of the said Whole Island, to maintain the said Settlement so made, and to support the Government thereof, without the charge of one Shilling to the Publick, and that the like Benefit to this nation, respecting either Policy or Commerce can be attained by no other Means in this or any other part of America.*" The memorialists further charged that obstruction to their proposal had come from "private and secret" interests either desirous of choice locations in the old French settlements or anxious to maintain the old mode of loose and partial grants in the colonies. The Egmont scheme was less improper "from the distracted State of many of Your Majesty's Provinces at this time, proceeding plainly from the Want of a regular Division and Subdivision of Lands, with proportional Powers annexed thereto; and of that Connection, Order, Gradation, and Subordination which may be naturally produced thereby." They continued: "For a Plan adopted to diffuse a legal Authority through a whole People (where little or none seems now to be maintained) and in the Consequence thereof, to prevent, correct or controul, a licentious Spirit, might not be considered or conceived a necessary Measure then (in 1764), and yet be judged (from a Change in the State of things) a wise Expedient *now*." In conclusion, the memorialists asked that "this important *Experiment* on this small Portion of Your Majesty's immense Empire ... be permitted to them."[36]

The Privy Council on 19 November 1765 referred all the documents in the case to the English attorney- and solicitor-generals for an opinion on the legality and constitutionality of the Egmont scheme and ordered them to recommend any alterations necessary to enable the king to comply with the memorialists in a way "as may best agree with their intentions, but in strict conformity with Law."[37] The Egmont proposal was clearly not yet dead, and although the earl's name was not signed to the November 1765 memorial, he was still observing a great interest in St John. In April 1766 he wrote Attorney-General Charles Yorke requesting a speedy legal opinion, since the capital of many of the "most deserving adventurers" was being consumed during the delay.[38] Soon afterward, the Board of Trade received the official Holland survey, and forwarded the documents to the king.[39] On 1 August 1766, the Crown lawyers finally made their report on the Egmont plan.

According to the lawyers, the king had the legal power to make the grant requested by Egmont, although the matter of its constitutionality was a complicated business.[40] The Egmont scheme, observed the lawyers, did not accord with any modes of the constitution either at home or abroad. The plan was well formulated and peculiarly adapted for the Island to effect settlement without cost to government while avoiding the usual inconveniences of granting land in America. It clearly maintained a "regular Subordination" with "great Ability and ingenuity," but it posed some tricky legal problems. Military requirements of tenure and limitations on alienation of land had to be reconciled with conflicting English statutes. Moreover, the plan made no provision for liberty of fishing on the coasts of the Island, and did not spell out either judicial or legislative powers. The report concluded, "Perhaps the peculiar Circumstances of some part of His Majesty's extended Empire in *America* may demand new Establishments deviating from those already formed upon that Continent, but preserving always the Trade and Navigation of the Mother Country in view, as the great essential Object."[41] Local circumstances called for different arrangements, opined the lawyers, and Egmont's proposals were certainly legal and with alterations constitutional.

At this point, except for several petitions for land on the Island submitted to various authorities, the documentary record becomes exasperatingly silent until 23 May 1767, when the Lords of the Commmittee of Council for Plantations referred applications for land to the Board of Trade to "proceed upon the plan approved by His Majesty On the 9th of May 1764."[42] Obviously the resurrected Egmont memorial had failed, and in the absence of concrete evidence we can only speculate about the reasons. Undoubtedly the principal factor was the fall of the Rockingham ministry in July 1766. Although Egmont remained as First Lord Of the Admiralty in the Chatham (Pitt) government, he soon resigned on 13 August 1766 for reasons completely unrelated to the Island. No longer in power, Egmont had no hold upon the government, which could then find several cogent reasons for rejecting his proposals.[43] In the first place, the legal officers, in questioning the military requirements of tenure, had probably cast considerable doubt upon what its supporters regarded as the central ingredient of the scheme. Moreover, the Holland survey, which had been very costly, had been based upon the Board of Trade's plan, and Holland had either not received or not heeded Egmont's pointed advice to revise his results. The board had undoubtedly hurried Holland off to America with detailed instructions to help prevent any change of policy. Finally, the new Chatham government had no wish to pursue any program, however obscure, that might bring the "American problem" back to the fore. In the end, therefore, the last gasp of the Egmont scheme had merely delayed final action on allocating land in accordance with the 1764 proposals, although only the rapid shifts in British politics prevented Egmont and his associates from gaining their objective. The "liberals" had won the round.

Unlike the tale of the schemes of the earl of Egmont for the Island, the story of its ultimate allocation by lottery has often been told, and need not long detain us here. Advertisements were placed in the *London Gazette* that the Board of Trade would receive applications for St John lots at the end of June and the beginning of July 1767.[44] The earl of Egmont was – by the king's instructions – offered an entire parish of 100,000 acres, but quite properly responded that under the board's plan he "could not now do credit to himself or service to the public by an undertaking there."[45] Egmont had intended a major colonial experiment, however utopian, not merely a land grab. On 8 July, lots 40 and 59 were reserved in advance for those merchants who had been active in seeking Island land since 1763, "in consequence of Assurances given to Messrs. Mure, Spence, Mill, and Cathcart in the year 1764, that they should have the choice of situation," and lot 66 was set aside for the Crown.[46] A list of approved applicants was prepared by the Board of Trade for the forthcoming lottery, and a number of conditions were attached to the grants. Quitrents were to be "proportional to the value of the lands" as assessed in the Holland survey, ranging from six shillings per 100 acres for twenty-six prime lots, to four shillings per 100 acres for twenty-nine average lots and two shillings per 100 acres for eleven poor ones, to be payable on half the acreage in five years and all in ten. The grantees had ten years to settle one person per 200 acres, the settlers to be either European Protestants or individuals resident in America at least two years before the date of granting.[47]

The board's final list of applicants included forty names from the ninety-eight that had appeared on the various Egmont memorials. These forty were to receive twenty-seven lots among them (many were granted half and even one-third lots). Thus Egmont's associates accounted for just over 40 per cent of the sixty-six lots allocated in 1767. Thirteen of the seventeen reduced officers in the Egmont group were included in the final list of individuals whose names were to be written on a piece of paper and put into a ballot box for draw by an "indifferent person." On 23 July 1767, the balloting was carried out and the Island finally allocated.[48] The stage was now set for its subsequent development and the ensuing controversies over land.

The ultimate arrangements for the allocation of the Island of St John were, of course, the responsibility of the Board of Trade. But there was considerable overlap and personnel and detail between the board's scheme and the various proposals advanced by Egmont and his associates. To a great extent, the board's hand had been forced by the earl. The Island was totally granted at one time, and the quitrent figures were much higher than usual in British North America in order to assure that under the board's plan – as in Egmont's – the Island would provide a sufficient revenue to finance its as yet unspecified governance. What the board's policy would have been without the pressure from Egmont is uncertain, although it likely would have preferred making purely ad hoc grants as suitable applicants for land on the Island appeared before it. Whether such a procedure would have proved more satisfactory than the one adopted is a matter for speculation and no more. What is demonstrable, however, is that the question of land granting on the Island of St John received considerable attention from the British government between 1763 and 1767, and that the final arrangements were decided against the background of British politics and in the context of general policy toward North America. The lottery of 1767 was not some offhand decision taken without consideration by a British government. The eventual system implemented represented a victory of sorts for the relatively liberal attitudes of the Board of Trade regarding American policy, and while the allocation of the Island may have been greatly influenced by the nearly successful schemes of the earl of Egmont, it was hardly arbitrary.

Finally, it must again be emphasized that there was nothing peculiar or distinctive about the allocation of large tracts of land on the Island of St John to proprietors, subject to conditions and quitrents. The history of the preceding settlement of North American offers numerous examples of similar policy.[49] The "parent" colony of Nova Scotia was at the same time being similarly granted to large proprietors.[50] The only distinctive feature about the St John situation was the resurrection of earlier British practice of expecting that the quitrents could both be collected and could serve as an immediate revenue, one that would very quickly be taken as sufficient to support a colonial administration. In the long run, what would be different about the Island was that its proprietorial system remained in place well into the nineteenth century. Why the continuation of the system should occur is one of the principal subjects of the pages that follow.

CHAPTER TWO

The Organization of Government, 1767–1775

Unlike the various proposals for the Island associated with the earl of Egmont, spelling out complex and ingenious – if semi-feudal – arrangements of governance for the area, the plans of the Board of Trade concentrated upon the allocation of land and little more. All mineral resources were reserved to the Crown, and within each township granted by the 1767 lottery were reservations to the Crown of any parts needed "for erecting fortifications, building wharfs, inclosing naval yards, or laying out highways for the communication between one part of the island and another," as well as 100 acres for a church and glebe "for a Minister of the Gospel" and 30 acres for a schoolmaster. In townships along the coast, all subjects of his majesty were given liberty to fish and to erect stages and other buildings within 500 feet of the high-water mark. Details for the laying out of towns were equally minute. The number of lots was at the surveyor's discretion, but care was to be taken to reserve land for "church, town house, market, and other necessary buildings." House lots were not to exceed 60 by 100 feet; a common was to be marked out; and the remainder of the land was to be placed in pasture lots, one acre of pasture for every ten feet of town-lot frontage. If land still remained, it was left in the royal demesne. The town and pasture lots were to be granted in fee simple under the seal of the Province of Nova Scotia; they were to be improved within a reasonable time; and they were subject to a ground rent of one penny per foot of frontage for town lots and a quitrent of three pence per acre of pasture lot. No person was to receive more than one town and one pasture lot.[1]

In its own way, the Board of Trade's scheme was as unrealistic as that of the Egmont syndicate, making its own assumptions about how uninhabited islands ought to be developed, particularly in its provisions for towns. The board took for granted that the inhabitants would reside in a nucleated centre of house lots and employ commons and pasture land in standard medieval village fashion. That no resident needed more than one small town lot and a proportional amount of pasturage flew in the face of all North American experience with respect to the acquisition of land, not to mention agricultural practice. Moreover, the Board of Trade dealt with government only indirectly, specifying that the land was to be granted under the seal of Nova Scotia.[2] If Egmont's proposals for administration were too complex, the board's were far too simple, indeed non-existent. The Island was to be governed by Nova Scotia, but the details of that administration were not spelled out.

The government of Nova Scotia and its leading politicians were, of course, quite happy to step into the breach and extend their activities to the Island of St John. Nova Scotians had long cast covetous glances at the Island, and several of them had applied for land grants there even before the Egmont consortium had moved into action. Charles Morris, the provincial surveyor, had seen the possibilities of a whaling station and fishery, although he thought the soil "generally poor and Hungry" and noted that the Island "lacked one good safe Harbour of safe Entrance on all the north side."[3] Despite these problems, the possibilities for Nova Scotia were too considerable to be ignored. In May 1768, Lieutenant-Governor Michael Francklin of Nova Scotia received a dispatch from Secretary of State Hillsborough detailing the plans for settlement and requesting suggestions for the civil establishment on the Island.[4] For a colony suffering from economic depression and for an acting governor desperately in need of patronage, the dispatch was a godsend. Francklin did not hesitate for an instant. Instead of responding with a plan for administration, as Hillsborough had obviously intended, Francklin made eight official appointments among his cronies and political supporters. The total salary bill was £1,028 per annum for a list including Isaac Deschamps as chief justice and Jonathan Binney as naval officer. Almost immediately a government was rushing off to the Island, expending the entire Nova Scotia contingency fund in the process. Charles Morris, the chief surveyor, was ordered to proceed directly to the Island to survey the towns reserved to the Crown, which following the Holland survey were to be named Charlottetown, Georgetown, and Princetown. Francklin not only provided an expensive corps of officials, he also managed to spend over £3,000 supplying them, with profitable contracts for many of the leading merchant firms in Halifax.[5]

Francklin's precipitate actions, proudly announced to the Board of Trade, annoyed the British and distressed the new proprietors of the

Island. They provide a perfect illustration of the way in which historical process may be influenced by wilful short-sightedness. Francklin may have alleviated pressing political and economic problems in Halifax by his response to Hillsborough's dispatch, but he also threw away Nova Scotia's opportunity to take over the Island of St John. Annexation to Nova Scotia would ultimately become a continual theme of those seeking reform of the Island's administration, but it would have been unnecessary had Francklin acted with more caution and good sense in 1768. As it was, he would be told his actions were "highly disapproved" by the king, although he was excused for his rashness. Called to England to explain his conduct, Francklin left his successor to undo all the orders as his first act of administration.[6]

At about the same time that Francklin was opening his dispatches from Hillsborough, the Island's proprietors began meeting to decide on the matter of government. They have been subjected to criticism from later historians for putting their energies here instead of into settlement, but such attacks are quite ill founded.[7] The Board of Trade had provided no outline of administrative structure, beyond the vague notion that Nova Scotia would provide supervision, and the actions of Francklin demonstrate quite conclusively that the concerns of the proprietors were legitimate. On 13 May 1768, a group of thirty-two of the leading proprietors petitioned the king, pointing out the economic potential of the Island, adding "the settlement of this Island will be very much retarded by its Dependence on the Government of Nova Scotia, as no legal decisions can be obtained, nor any matters of property determined without a tedious and expensive voyage to Halifax," which was "impracticable during the winter months because of the ice." Settlement would be "rendered speedy and certain," concluded the petition, "if it should please Your Majesty to form the Island into a separate Government.[8] Nova Scotia had in one sense obviated these arguments by its rapid expansion to the Island, but one major point that Michael Francklin had overlooked was the concern of the Board of Trade to govern the new territory at no expense to the Crown. This requirement was certainly not met by Nova Scotia's actions, which had involved considerable expenditure for salaries and supply contracts, and which had blithely assumed that the British government would foot the bill.

The greed of the Halifax merchant oligarchy played into the hand of the proprietors, for the hazard of winter ice was not really a sufficient argument. Aghast at what Francklin had done, the Lords of Committee of Council for Plantation Affairs reported on 21 June 1769 on the proprietorial petition of 1768. It found the petition "useful" if the business could be managed without expense to the government. The Board of Trade was asked to find a revenue, and it consulted some of the major proprietors, who offered to forego their five-year freedom from quitrents, paying half of the amount due in 1772 from 1 May 1769, to provide a fund for civil government; the other half was now deferred for twenty years. After several consultations, all but eight of the proprietors agreed to the scheme. No record survives of the arguments used to convince the large majority of proprietors to support a separate government, but the spectre of rapacious Nova Scotians running over the Island must have been a considerable inducement. The Board of Trade emphasized to the proprietors that the whole point was to establish a government that would not burden the kingdom. Should the revenue fall short, the salaries and allowances of the officers would be reduced "and no demand whatever brought either upon Parliament or upon the Treasury to make good such Deficiency."[9] Estimates and quitrent revenue and expenses indicated that the plan was feasible, and the newly appointed governor of the Island was to convene an assembly as soon "as the circumstances of the People will admit" to provide a permanent revenue by taxes or proper duties; no one anticipated that the quitrents would suffice for very long.[10] The Privy Council approved the scheme on 28 June 1769, and the Island had its own government, separate from that of Nova Scotia.

A number of points are worth noting about these proceedings, again executed unusually swiftly by Whitehall standards. In the first place, the alacrity with which the Island was granted autonomous status and separate government owed as much to the concern to staunch a potential drain upon the Treasury (which Nova Scotia's profligate spending obviously represented) as it did to the influence and machinations of the proprietors. A self-financing government had not been suggested when the proprietors had requested separate administration, but echoes of the Egmont scheme – which had promised such a result – combined with the concern to keep American revenues to a mimimum. The trade-off was one the proprietors were willing to accept. But the records make clear that the proprietors had not initiated the financing scheme ultimately accepted. In the second place, the proposed estimates for expenditures and revenues included a total figure of £1,470 in income, the maximum figure that quitrents could produce under the revised understanding, and expenditures of £1,330 for official salaries and £140 for contingent expenses. Clearly, the expenditures were adjusted to fit the income, and there was no margin for error, much less money for development. The Island's budget included nothing for capital expenses, apparently on the assumption that the officials would find adequate public buildings on the spot, built by the Nova Scotians. Such an assumption was, of course, ludicrous.

Because it has been so often overlooked in discussions of the founding of the early government, it must be stressed that neither Whitehall nor the proprietors expected the quitrents to provide a permanent, or even long-term revenue, for the Island's government. The quitrents were to provide seed money to get the enterprise off the ground, and as the Island prospered it was to find other sources of revenue through taxes and duties. The quitrents were to be collected in perpetuity, but they would ultimately return a revenue to the British Treasury, not directly to the Island. However chimeric may have been the notion that the Island of St John could be self-supporting within a few years, it was a guiding principle behind the granting of separate government, and followed naturally from the concept that private proprietors would develop the Island out of their own pockets and turn a profit in the process. Had the proprietors fulfilled the terms of their grants, it may be argued, the Island would have become sufficiently populated and prosperous to pay for itself. Few on the Island were ever prepared to make such an argument, however. Later critics of the proprietors complained that their failure hampered Island progress, but it was never suggested that the Island, even if wildly prosperous, should pay its own way. Finally, the early officials appointed under the 1769 arrangement and budget were either proprietors or hungry office-seekers (or both). If the former, they were parties to the undertaking of the proprietors to fund the government and develop the Island through private means. If the latter, they ought to have foreseen the difficulties. In either case, the first appointments to the Island's government were not innocent victims, but willing accomplices who went in with their eyes open.

The acceptance by the Privy Council of the arrangement between the Board of Trade and the proprietors to fund a separate government was quickly followed by the appointment of its first officials, including the governor. The responsibility of leading the infant colony was given, on 14 July 1769, to Walter Patterson, a reduced army officer and co-proprietor of Lot 19, probably one of the major figures behind efforts to obtain separate administration for the Island. Patterson was Irish-born, emerging out of obscurity to become a junior officer in the final war against New France, serving in the eighteenth-century equivalent of a commando regiment. He had come to Lord Hillsborough's attention in the course of a land grab in New York after the war, and undoubtedly owed his appointment to Hillsborough's support. Patterson's credentials were no better and no worse than those of countless other colonial appointments in the British Empire.[11] He was an original proprietor himself, a fact he would later attempt to bury and which has often been forgotten by those who have defended him. By the time of the drafting of his instructions as governor, dated 4 August 1769, Thomas DesBrisay had been appointed lieutenant-governor and secretary/registrar. He was another reduced Irish army officer, with a large family, and was also a proprietor.[12]

Patterson's instructions were in most respects consonant with those to other eighteenth-century British governors in North America, modified only by the colony's infancy and peculiar temporary system of revenue.[13] He was to constitute a council similar to that in other colonies, establish courts of judicature with the advice of the chief justice, and institute English law. An assembly was "a consideration that cannot be too early taken up," for it was essential to complete the constitution of any government as Britons understood it in the century. But Patterson was warned not to allow the Lower House to assume unwarranted powers and privileges – the conflict with the American colonies to the south was still simmering – and no laws respecting private property were to be passed without a suspending clause. The instructions emphasized that the quitrents were to support the civil establishment for a maximum of ten years, that any failure of the quitrent revenue would diminish the salaries of the officers, and that the inhabitants were expected to provide as quickly as possible "a proper revenue arising out of the duties and taxes granted ... by act of Legislature." Salaries were to be paid only to officials in residence. Liberty of conscience was to be granted to all ("except Papists"). but the Church of England was established by law.

Even before Patterson's appointment, the Earl of Hillsborough had acted to eliminate the Nova Scotians. On 7 July he wrote to David Higgins, another proprietor who had entered into partnership with Scottish Lord Advocate James Montgomery to develop lots 59 and 51 as a fishing, lumbering, and mercantile centre.[14] Hillsborough observed that the Island would be erected into a separate government within a few days, although the new administration would probably not take up residence until the spring. In the meantime Higgins – who was soon departing for the Island – was entrusted "with the care of such stores, provisions, and materials, now lying within that Island, as are His Majesty's property," according to an enclosed list from Michael Francklin. Higgins was to keep the stores and turn them over to the governor when he arrived.[15] The actual transfer was made on 24 September 1769, when Francklin's storekeeper John Moreau handed over the remaining supplies shipped by Nova Scotia and departed the Island. Very little was left, Francklin was informed by Moreau – an observation born out by the detailed receipt signed by Higgins – and the wharf upon which much money had been expended had been swept away by ice.[16]

In December 1769, Higgins reported to the Board of Trade that Patterson would be most disappointed by the returns Higgins was enclosing, for he was expecting "good houses provisions many utensils boats etc." The five boats were "all in bad repair and not fit for use." As for the dwelling house erected by Francklin's order (and glowingly described to the Board of Trade), the cellar was "much hurt by water the windows much out of repair and the house in general damaged." Another house was not finished and was weather-damaged; it was "no way habitable." Higgins could find no evidence of the wharf supposedly carried away by ice, and "most of the stores and tools [were] rendered unserviceable by rust and damage."[17] Nova Scotia was leaving behind little of value to be salvaged from its efforts.

Before leaving England, Patterson established that proprietors need not apply to Nova Scotia for land patents, but could obtain them from himself, subject to the usual conditions.[18] It was probably also Patterson who organized a petition to the Lords of the Treasury dated June 1770 and signed by twenty-two proprietors (including Joshua Mauger and James Montgomery requesting financial assistance for the construction of a church, courthouse, and gaol building.[19] The colony's budget did not allow for such luxuries, and the government would be supportive if slow in responding to the request.

Walter Patterson landed at his "capital" on 30 August 1770, apparently expecting to find a flourishing community, fields in crops, and suitable provisions in store. Certainly he was too late in the season to undertake any planting himself. What greeted him instead was a few Acadians and a handful of British officials, inhabiting some huts set against a timbered wilderness as far as the eye could see. He was personally welcomed by Nova Scotia lawyer John Duport, who had been appointed as chief justice, but Duport would soon depart the Island to winter in Nova Scotia because there were neither provisions nor accommodations for him. The governor's first problem was to house and feed himself and his entourage, which consisted of Mrs Patterson, as well as one Susanna Torriano and her maid, seventeen servants, and two artificers. Hester Warren Patterson was an Essex heiress who had married the governor in March 1770; she would later claim that her husband had spent her fortune in attempting to tame the wilderness.[20] The principal house erected by the Nova Scotians was fitted out against the forthcoming cold as best it could be, and Patterson and his household, unable to find a single loaf of bread or flour to bake one, turned to lobsters and oysters – "neither very good," pronounced Patterson – for their sustenance. Nevertheless, he was optimistic. The soil looked promising, although agriculture had been neglected, with mice devouring what few crops had been planted, and bears eating the sheep.[21]

Despite the primitive shabbiness of it all, Patterson maintained appearances in proper imperial fashion. Producing and reading his commission on 19 September 1770 in the presence of Duport, William Allanby, and David Higgins (the only members of his council actually resident on the Island), and "several resident Gentlemen and Inhabitants in and near said Town," Patterson then appointed four of the auditors – Phillips Callbeck, J.R. Spence, Thomas Wright, and Patrick Fergus – to the council. Patterson opened "his doors," presumably of his house, to those outside so they could hear articles six to fifteen of his instructions read aloud. The council established "His Majesty's Supreme Court of Judicature" as the court of record that same day, and then adjourned. The government of the Island of St John was formally in being. Becoming more than a mere formality would take a little longer.

The first ordinance of the council of the Island was one to regulate the sea cow (or walrus) fishery, undoubtedly because Lord Hillsborough had discussed this subject with Patterson at length before his departure.[22] The matter was not quite as esoteric as might first appear, since the infant colony obviously needed a marketable export commodity, and the regulation incidentally asserted Island sovereignty over the Magdalene Islands, which were not attached firmly to any government and would be claimed by Quebec. On 11 October, the councillors appointed Samuel Smith as colony agent, and discussed the thorny question of currency, a far more pressing business than sea cows. Most colonial governments found it advisable to set a premium on the most respected money, such as the English pound, to offer some encouragement to keep it within the colony. The council deferred action on the currency question for the moment, but in subsequent meetings in the autumn of 1770, it did pass ordinances regulating the liquor trade and requiring those departing the Island to have a licence to do so.[23]

The liquor ordinance, which limited sale of more than two gallons of spiritous beverage without permission from the governor, was intended to protect the "constitutions and morals" of the "lower orders," for employers often paid servants and labourers in rum at inflated prices, so that despite ostensibly high wages the workers ended up drinking much of their pay.[24] The licensing scheme for departing residents would prevent debtors and indentured servants from leaving their creditors and masters behind on the Island. In a society perennially short of a circulating medium of exchange, and in which most business transactions were conducted on credit, the problem of absconding debtors was a serious one.[25] The Island would, over the years, receive many fugitives from other jurisdictions both in North America and Great Britain, and it would lose much population for the same reasons. Indentured servants, of course, represented capital investment, for they were brought to the Island at their master's expense in return for their labour. Indentured servants were arriving on the Island by 1770, although the inability to control them soon became obvious. How the government intended enforcing either of these regulations is not clear, and they had virtually no practical effect either on alcoholic consumption or population movement.

In a series of dispatches to London, Governor Patterson began pressing for public buildings and roads. The colony still required a gaol, a church, and a courthouse. Not even a barn existed in Charlottetown in which the inhabitants could assemble for public worship. All transportation was by water. The cost of improvement would be considerable, Patterson warned, because labour was scarce and expensive. To assist in the public construction, especially of roads, the governor requested five companies of soldiers, who could be barracked at Fort Amherst, abandoned by the British after the war. A garrison was necessary to prevent privateering plunder and raids by Indians from Nova Scotia, although Patterson was never clear how the soldiers would defend the isolated and embryonic settlements scattered across the Island if based in Charlottetown, and evidence for Indian threats was non-existent. More to the point, the garrison would "bring a little money among us."[26] The problems of building a colony in North America on the basis of the budgets projected in Britain were undoubtedly daunting, and Patterson's pressures upon the ministry understandable. Lord Hillsborough responded sympathetically to Patterson's requests. He would try to find some money for buildings in the Nova Scotia estimates. As for the soldiers, he was not hopeful.[27]

The problem of money was a serious one from the standpoint of capital construction. Defence was not provided for from the colony's only available revenue, the quitrents to be paid by the proprietors. There was also the question of the dependability of that quitrent revenue itself, upon which the officials of the colony depended for their salaries. As any investigation of the history of quitrents in North America would have demonstrated – and the device had been instituted time and time again – collection was a difficult matter.[28]

Actual settlers could not afford to pay in the first years of pioneering, and land speculators refused to pay before their property had real value. The lands of the Island of St John were not at this period regarded as valueless, for lots and shares of lots exchanged hands at high prices frequently over the early years, often as collateral for debts. John MacDonald of Glenaladale purchased lot 36, generally regarded as one of the Island's choice properties, for £600 in 1770 from James Montgomery. Like MacDonald, Montgomery had serious intentions of improving his Island lands, seeing them as fertile, "in an Island of a good Climate, for Grain, fortunately situated for a Market."[29] Many of the active proprietors would purchase their property from the original grantees, and there was considerable willingness on the part of many to fulfil their obligations. Curiously enough, more money was paid in quitrents over the years by the proprietors of the Island of St John than in any contemporary British colony in North America.[30]

Unfortunately, the colony's revenue did not depend upon *some* quitrent payments by *some* proprietors; its annual budget in fixed official salaries demanded the full payment of quitrents by every proprietor, and the government had made quite clear that while it might provide some capital grants, it was not responsible for the civil list. Any shortfalls meant salary arrearages. By the spring of 1771, the colony's agent was already pressing the Lords of Trade about the quitrents, undoubtedly in response to queries from the Island by its officials about their salaries. In April 1771, Chief Justice John Duport complained to Lord Hillsborough that he was unable to obtain his salary from agent Smith "occasioned by the backwardness of the proprietors in paying their Quit Rents," to which Hillsborough responded with regrets, but a firm reminder that he "cannot, however, on any account at present recommend any Payments beyond what the Quit-rent will answer."[31] The great quitrent chase was already begun.

Over the winter of 1770/1, Walter Patterson and his government continued to develop – at least on paper – the details for a colony that would, in a sense, catch up with its pretensions. An Irish lawyer who had arrived with the governor, Phillips Callbeck, was appointed attorney-general, surrogate-general, and judge of probate. Justices of the peace were appointed in each county. Thomas Wright prepared "A Plan of Charlotte Town the Capital of the Island St. John Delineated by Order of His Excellency Walter Patterson Esq.," detailing the proposed development of the 7,300 acre town site. The town proper was to occupy 270 acres, with 565 acres reserved for a common and expansion. Roads to St Peters and Princetown were thirty feet wide, others twenty feet wide, with sixty-four acres consumed by the proposed highway system. The remaining 6,401 acres were divided into 544 pasture lots of 12 acres each, to match the number of town lots 84 by 120 feet. The five principal streets fronted the Hillsborough River, and were to be 100 feet wide. Obviously the prime town lots would be in this area.[32]

Patterson forwarded this plan to Lord Hillsborough in July 1771, noting that he had altered it to give every house a southern access and to allow every back lot access to the street. He had enlarged the town lots to 108 by 140 feet, adding that not all applicants would receive an entire lot. The size of the pasture lots, twice that which his instructions had specified, he justified because every resident must "be something of a Farmer to supply his Family with Milk, Butter, Roots, and all other Vegetables." The governor was also able in this letter to thank Hillsborough – whom he had earlier described as "Father to this Infant Colony" – for a £1,500 parliamentary grant (on the Nova Scotia estimate) for public buildings to make his government more respected. Many had said, Patterson observed, "that the Government was formed rather by way of experiment, than with any fixed intention of being supported or carried into execution," and the grant indicated British support.[33]

By summer 1771, the problem of quitrent arrearage was obvious and pressing, and the council dealt with it by passing "An Ordinance and Act of Council for the effectual recovery of certain of His Majesty's Quit Rents in the Island of St. John." Noting that many proprietors who had signed the petition for a separate government had not paid their quitrents, the ordinance authorized the receiver-general of quitrents to enter and distrain lots upon which the rents had not been paid by 1 November 1772.[34] In short, the land was to be seized for non-payment of rent, and sold by public auction on the Island after six months' notice. The act contained a suspending clause, and it would be years before legislation would be properly in place. But subsequent legislation would follow the principles of the 1771 ordinance, and it is worth noting that as early as 1771, there was no concept of executing the distraint proceedings in England or auctioning the distrained properties there, where St John's lots might fetch a sufficient price to assist the revenue. Instead, the lots were to be distrained in the Island courts, and sold locally in a small closed market not likely to provide much in the way of cash payment or high prices. What the intention of council was at this stage is not clear. Perhaps it only meant to frighten the proprietors. It was true that distraint might have been more difficult in England, where proprietors might oppose the action in the courts. But it is equally true that the purchasers of distrained land on the Island were likely to be a limited crew, consisting largely of the Island's official class, most of whom sat on the council.

Governor Patterson forwarded the quitrent ordinance to Lord Hillsborough on 3 September 1771, commenting that he had tried to make it "mild and equitable," but adding that government officials laboured under hardship due to proprietorial backwardness.[35] In a letter to Hillsborough dated the same day, John Duport wrote that he doubted the quitrents – already three years in arrears – would serve as a revenue. He had experienced several protests of bills of exchange, and recommended a fund, presumably from parliamentary grant, to provide salaries until the quitrents could be regularly collected, an occasion still far in the future.[36] Duport's suggestion was eminently sound, but could not be taken up by a British government still committed to financing a government out of revenue that could only – if at all – be collected in the long run.

The Island's first grand jury was assembled in Charlottetown on 12 August 1771. The governor had reduced the Island to a single county and lowered jury qualifications in order to convene this body, with David Higgins as foreman. The qualifications Patterson had ignored were undoubtedly confessional, as several Roman Catholics were among the jurymen. As Patterson would observe a few months later in reporting the death of councillor Patrick Fergus and the appointment of George Burns and John Patterson to the council, although the latter was not a resident, "I am obliged as yet, to catch people as I can, for these purposes."[37] While settlers were arriving on the Island in some numbers, few of them were the substantial citizens (or of Protestant persuasion) required for public office. Patterson was understandably reluctant to enforce laws without juries, but assembling them would remain a problem for years, both because of the scattered nature of settlement and the fact that many of the inhabitants, as Roman Catholics, were technically ineligible.

Patterson began to plan to spend the parliamentary building grant, receiving permission to import hewn stone from Cape Breton Island, although he was denied access to material still at Louisbourg. Lord Hillsborough made it plain that there would be no more money for construction until there was something to show for what had already been advanced.[38] The proprietors petitioned the British government early in 1772 for money to cover 100 miles of road construction, essentially for major arteries linking the shire towns and principal settlements.[39] Although they did not make the case, water transportation was difficult and dangerous, as was demonstrated by the deaths of councillor Fergus and his family in a shipwreck off the Nova Scotia coast while sailing from Three Rivers to Charlottetown. The response of the Board of Trade to the road petition was simply to note that the sum voted by Parliament for the Island had been labelled "the last."[40]

Not surprisingly, concern for the quitrent revenue became an obsession of the Island government. To Patterson's surprise, Lord Hillsborough responded to the council's ordinance on the quitrents and other regulations without enthusiasm, observing that "these Ordinances appear to me in no other light than as Regulations having, in the present state of the Island and under its present Constitution of Government, no other Effect and Validity than what they derive from the Voluntary Consent and Adoption of the Inhabitants."[41] Hillsborough's comments reflected both practical and constitutional considerations. If Patterson had no means to enforce his laws, given his problems in assembling even a grand jury and his admitted difficulty in constructing local ones, then the laws obviously had no more effect than the population would permit through their own acceptance and observation of them. On the constitutional level, of course, at issue was the absence of an elected assembly, that essential of proper British colonies, without which all legislation passed by an appointed council was of dubious validity.[42] Hillsborough's successor, Lord Dartmouth, reiterated the point upon assuming office later in 1772.[43]

Patterson and his officials were caught in a cruel dilemma. Unable to assemble even juries to enforce their ordinances, they were now being told that nothing they legislated was constitutional without an assembly. At particular issue were not regulations about sea cows and even absconding debtors, which required wide-reaching power in order to be effectual, but the pressure upon the proprietors that the quitrent ordinance represented, and which required for execution nothing more than an Island Supreme Court with one justice sitting on it. The quitrent legislation was, in a sense, enforcable, either requiring the proprietors to pay up or permitting the local officials not paid to reward themselves with proprietorial land obtained through local auction of distrained property. Patterson and his council did not hesitate.

Within days of receiving confirmation from Dartmouth that Hillsborough's views of the ordinances were not idiosyncratic, the council unanimously agreed on 17 February 1773 to call an assembly of eighteen "representatives of the people." Seven plus a speaker would constitute a quorum, and the only qualifications were that the candidates be Protestant and actually resident on the Island at the time of election. The religious qualification probably eliminated at least half the adult male population of the Island in 1773, if it were strictly enforced.[44]

Voting was to take place at Charlottetown on 4 July 1773, and voters were required to vote for all eighteen members or their ballots would be rejected. This last curious provision was explained by Patterson in a letter to Dartmouth a few days later when the governor observed that no more than eighteen "respectable" persons could be found to serve, who would make a "very tolerable appearance."[45] Patterson did not attempt to justify the haste in institution of an assembly here, although a letter later in the spring implicitly dealt with the question. The governor pointed out that most settlers suffered great hardship because they lacked capital upon their arrival. As for the Island's officials, they were deprived by their station of the "advantages of peasants" and were "obliged to support the appearance of Gentlemen without the Means." Patterson had advanced them money at his "own risque" out of the parliamentary building grant, and no one could hold out much longer. In five years, only enough quitrent revenue had been collected to "pay the establishment (low as it is) for one year."[46]

The first assembly of the Island of St John was duly elected at Charlottetown on 4 July 1773, meeting three days later at the tavern/house of Alexander Richardson – there still being no public buildings – for the transaction of business. On that occasion, the doorkeeper was alleged to have muttered it was a "damned queer Parliament."[47] There is no evidence of any political activity on the part of the eighteen legislators, who appear to have been nominated or recruited by the governor and elected unanimously on a single ballot. The personnel of the assembly, as has been suggested by Patterson's discussion of "respectable people," was no gathering of "peasants." The legislators may have been impoverished, but then, who on the Island was not? At least half a dozen resident proprietors were among those elected, and most of the remaining figures were either large tenants and agents of major proprietors (such as the Lawsons) or shopkeepers and merchant adventurers. One legislator, George Burns, was also a member of the council, a practice discouraged in more settled colonies.[48] While these men may have been angry at the failure of the absentee proprietors for failing to develop the Island and to pay the quitrents, and while they may have been in financial difficulties, they were hardly a cross-section of the population or representative of popular feeling among the average inhabitants, who were probably content enough to be left alone by an impotent government. In short, the first Island assembly represented resident

landholders, and for them the quitrent issue had enormous significance, partly because the absence of revenue and development hurt
the Island, but also because distraint raised the prospect of the
redistribution of Island land into more deserving hands.

One of the most important effects of the "experiment" on the
Island of St John, it must always be remembered, was that the total
land surface of the Island, less the towns, had been spoken for in
advance of the arrival of settlement. One of the major attractions of
any wilderness colony was the opportunity it afforded for ambitious
men without capital to acquire both large tracts of unsettled land for
speculative purposes and land upon which to expend their energies
in improvement. This process had been short-circuited on the Island.
In theory, the proprietors were supposed to move there and assume
their rightful places as leaders of government and society. Unfortunately, all too many of the original proprietors had no intention of
leaving their comfortable niches in Britain. Some of those men who
did come in the early days, like Captain George Tead or the
MacDonald brothers, bought land in Britain from the original
holders in advance of immigrating. Tead had been involved in the
reduction of the Island and had lost his chance to become a charter
proprietor because of a posting to remote Florida. He had become a
proprietor, he observed with some acerbity, "by purchase only."[49] But
many other leading citizens, like Chief Justice Duport, Attorney-
General Callbeck, and Surveyor Thomas Wright, had no stake in the
land when they first arrived. Not only were their official salaries
critical to such men, but so too was the acquisition of property for
economic and social reasons. The quitrent legislation thus assumed
enormous significance for both the officials of the Island and other
ambitious newcomers.

The first assembly swiftly re-enacted all the ordinances of the
council, including the quitrent one, plus a few new items, and was
then dissolved, ostensibly because the influx of new settlers would
make it rapidly unrepresentative.[50] Patterson forwarded the legislation to Lord Dartmouth, and waited a reply, which was penned in
Whitehall on 1 December 1773. Dartmouth was pleased the assembly
had been called, and was not much concerned with its informalities of
election, observing that such procedures "must, like everything of the
same nature adopted only on a Plan of Experiment, be in many
respects imperfect." He hoped the assembly "will be induced to adopt
such a Plan, for enforcing the payment of the Quit Rent, as may
render that Fund effectual to the purposes for which it was allotted,
without inducing the disagreeable Dilemma of either, on the one
hand, burthening the Kingdom with the Civil Establishment of St.

John's, or what may otherwise be the case, of revoking those Establishments that were adopted, only upon the Condition of the Proprietors' bearing the Expence."[51] Curiously, Dartmouth did not reprimand Patterson for using the parliamentary grant to pay salaries, but he was upset over the question of reallocating it for road construction. Lieutenant-Governor Thomas Desbrisay, not yet in residence, had written that the British would allow the reallocation, and Patterson had received council approval to make roads on this authority, thus providing employment and meeting an obvious need. Calling DesBrisay's remarks unauthorized, Dartmouth insisted the funds should not be transferred from one purpose to another. This incident marked the beginning of hostilities between Patterson and Desbrisay that would become quite serious after 1780.

Despite Dartmouth's seeming approval of the actions of the first assembly, the Board of Trade was not satisfied with the resultant legislation, especially the quitrent bill. The acts were sent to veteran colonial agent Richard Jackson (friend of Benjamin Franklin) for vetting, and that worthy reported in March 1774 that the Quitrent Act was improper because it authorized the sale of lots without providing any criteria for the action beyond the recommendation of the receiver-general to the Supreme Court of the Island.[52] Such an opinion failed to observe that the legislation also neglected to provide for the advertisement of the sales or for the sales themselves to take place off the Island, although Jackson presumably intended some more complex legal mechanism than was provided before sales could actually occur.

While Patterson waited to hear the results of the Board of Trade's deliberations on his legislation, he attempted to get on with building construction and reorganization of his government. It was impossible to get any contractor to bid on the public buildings because of the unknown costs of labour and materials on the Island, he had earlier insisted, and he would have to supervise matters himself.[53] Although doubtless correct in his assessment of difficulties in obtaining bidders, there was enormous opportunity for graft in the procedure he suggested. Phillips Callbeck, when acting governor a few years later, would exploit the system with considerable success. The governor also vacated a number of seats on his council for non-attendance, including that of David Higgins, who had earlier been responsible for licensing all departures from the Island. Higgins himself had disappeared to the colonies to the south without permission late in 1772.[54]

The governor also began pressing for a resident clergyman. One Ernest Caulfield had been appointed at the time the colony was organized in 1769, and put on the civil list, but had made no move toward the Island. Pointing out that settlers abandoned the Island for want of religious services, including christening, Patterson requested that Caulfield either take up his post or be replaced.[55] Lord Dartmouth acted swiftly on this point, writing Caulfield angrily that his "neglect of Duty ... will not, as it ought not to be, passed over." Although Caulfield had been appointed for life and could not be easily fired, Dartmouth would recommend an assistant who would receive the entire salary.[56] The question of who would become the assistant took several years to settle, and once again Patterson and his lieutenant-governor came into conflict. The governor recommended a Mr Edward Patterson, obviously a kinsman, but Dartmouth responded that while he found Edward acceptable, "I had, before I received your letter, yielded to the Solicitation of Mr. Desbrisay on behalf of his son who has lately taken orders."[57] Theophilus Desbrisay did come to the Island, serving as resident Anglican clergyman for the remainder of his long life.[58] Patterson had many grievances accumulating against the elder Desbrisay, who was still in Britain, but there were obviously advantages to having immediate access to Whitehall, and the governor began to consider a visit to England for himself.

The Island's officers continued to turn over rapidly. John Duport, the chief justice, died of gout early in 1774, and Patterson was forced to put the office in commission, since the attorney-general was the only lawyer on the Island. Adrian Van Brankle arrived as the Island's first resident clerk, having purchased the office from the original incumbent, who languished in an Irish gaol.[59] As Patterson pointed out in a 1774 report to the Board of Trade, his government was immature and unsettled, and "kept in motion only with great difficulty, so that great regularity cannot be expected in the offices, nor have I thought it just, to insist on it, considering the hardships the officers labour under for want of their salaries."[60] He subsequently requested leave of absence for himself, arguing that he "could be of more service to the Island by spending a little time among the proprietors than by remaining at home."[61] While Patterson waited to learn of British response to his various entreaties, he received the revised Quitrent Act from the Board of Trade, and immediately called for another election of an assembly.

The second assembly, elected at Charlottetown on 1 October 1774, and beginning its deliberations on 4 October (simultaneously with the Supreme Court sessions), had a substantially different composition of personnel than the previous one, although there was still apparently a single slate of eighteen candidates. The eight new members, all recent arrivals to the Island, included Van Brankle, Benjamin Chappell (an indentured servant and Methodist lay preacher lately settled at

Elizabethtown), and Cornelius Higgins, a kinsman of the departed David; other new members were Charlottetown merchants and shopkeepers. The returning members included at least three proprietors and two proprietor's agents. While the assembly's popular base was broadened, it still underrepresented the rural settlers and hardly constituted a cross-section of the Island's population. The amended quitrent act was swiftly passed and sent off for royal assent, the major item of legislation. While the assembly was meeting, the council distributed a number of unallocated small islands to petitioners. Assemblyman David Lawson and proprietors George Burns and Robert Stewart all received islands, as did Attorney-General Callbeck, Dugald Stewart, and Susanna Torriano, Patterson's mulatto mistress.[62] Patterson also granted a few town and pasture lots in Charlottetown, with Susanna Torriano again a prominent recipient.[63] What little land was available was to find its way into the hands of the elite.

By 1775 the government of the Island of St John was firmly in place, however uncertainly. There were resident officials, although they were a constantly changing lot disgruntled over their situation. An assembly had been created and a court system established, at least on paper. Charlottetown had been planned and surveyed, although there was not as yet a single public building in the capital, unless one counted the houses of the governor and the chief justice, both constructed with public funds. Patterson had spent £358 of the parliamentary grant on building materials, but had advanced most of the money to his officials for salary arrearages. The earl of Dartmouth had promised to "attempt to obtain some allowance in the next Parliamentary Estimate" for relief of the officers, and while Patterson had misdirected funds, he would not be heavily criticized in Britain for his actions.[64] He was readily granted leave to come home. As the governor prepared to embark for England in August of 1775, he could be optimistic. The Island had succeeded if not prospered as an independent government. The question of revenue was a thorny one, but to this point the emphasis had been placed upon the failure of the proprietors to fund the civil list through quitrent payments, rather than upon their failure to live up to the remainder of the terms of their grants. In truth, while the record of the proprietors regarding settlement was spotty, up to 1775 the Island did enjoy a substantial influx of people. As newly founded colonies went, the Island of St John had not done badly in its earliest years.

CHAPTER THREE

Settlement, 1769–1775

The establishment of an autonomous administration for the Island of St John had not been a matter of high priority for the British government, whose real concern was to populate the Island at no expense to itself. The ministry had been forced to deal with the question of governance by the behaviour of Nova Scotia, but both Walter Patterson's administration and the future of the Island were ultimately dependent upon the men who had received land in the lottery of 1767. These proprietors were not only required to pay quitrents, but to finance settlement. The terms of their grants called for the establishment within ten years of one settler per 200 acres of lot, or 100 persons per township. Moreover, the settlers could not originate from the British Isles and had to be Protestants. They could come either from Europe or from the existing American colonies if they had been resident in the New World for at least two years.[1] Had these terms been fulfilled, the Island would have had a population of nearly 7,000 by 1777, and at least theoretically, such a number could have afforded to pay taxes providing a revenue to support the government, rendering quitrent collection irrelevant. Reality was a quite different matter.

Much has been written of the failure of the proprietors to fulfil the terms of their grants, and that fact is indisputable. The question of the reasons for failure is more complex than usually admitted, however.[2] The problem did not initially reside solely in the apathy, inactivity, or cupidity of the original proprietors, although undoubtedly there were some who had accepted land with no intention of doing anything except watch it increase in value as others invested in improvement. The real difficulties lie in the failure of either the British government or the proprietors to comprehend the obstacles to speedy settlement of such an isolated area, and in the lack of consonance between the restrictive terms of the settlement provisions and unfolding events in Europe and America. The first problem was perhaps inescapable, while the second was unpredictable. But combined, they produced far less population growth than had been anticipated, and that growth mainly consisted of officially unacceptable settlers.

The source for settlers was a crucial matter. The prohibition on inhabitants of the British Isles was totally consistent with the British government's growing hostility to emigration, especially to America.[3] A rapidly modernizing economy required a labour force, and the escalating conflict with America made the transference of that labour force to the New World even less desirable, given mercantilist assumptions of the day. The insistence on Protestants was equally consistent and comprehensible, both because of the religious assumptions of Hanoverian England and because such a restriction would help prevent losses of population from Catholic districts of the United Kingdom – Scotland and especially Ireland – which were particularly susceptible to removal. The preference for Americans is also understandable, part of a government policy which went back to the Proclamation of 1763 in hopes of deflecting surplus American population away from the transappalachian west to the territories newly acquired from France.[4] Such a policy was given additional impetus by the developing hostility of the American colonies to Britain in the 1760s; far better to relocate potential dissidents under loyal governments than to keep them under their own or have them off in the west organizing new colonies, which – because illegal – could hardly be controlled by the mother country.[5] Americans were unfortunately not eager to head north. Thousands of New Englanders attracted to Nova Scotia after 1759 were by the early 1760s returning, complaining bitterly of conditions in "Nova Scarcity." There was no reason to assume that Americans would fare better on the Island of St John. While talk of "foreign Protestants" to people America was endemic, and Nova Scotia had received a fair number of settlers from the king's German territories in the 1750s, little ever came of such schemes.[6] The net result was that the most likely sources for settlers willing to chance a territory as remote as the Island of St John were the poor and oppressed regions of the British Isles, where Irish Catholics, Scottish Highlanders (often Catholic), urban artisans often converted to dissenting sectarianism, and displaced farm workers formed a potential population for an uninhabited island.

The twin goals of economic advancement and liberty, frequently religious, had always been the mainsprings of North American settlement activity, and the Island of St John would be no exception.

As an island it tended to attract those who sought to promote particular visions for the oppressed. The religious inspiration of much of the Island's early settlement has been largely overlooked. The leaders of the Scottish Catholic Church certainly had hopes of turning the Island into a haven for the disinherited and persecuted members of their faith, especially from the remote corners of the Highlands.[7] A Quaker visionary attempted to use the Island to become a second Penn, intending to establish a settlement of pietists based upon principles of religious toleration, with personnel recruited chiefly among the urban workers of London.[8] Combined with the hope of freedom from persecution was the expectation that the like-minded could be moulded into a coherent group, or at least kept from disappearing individually into the wilds of the New World. Here the concept of "island" was crucial.

The government's insistence on American residents would bring those who had some experience with the problems of subsistence farming in a wilderness situation. The experienced also knew better than to attempt such a settlement, however, for the main problems confronting the newcomer on the Island of St John went well beyond adjusting to a new environment and conditions of life, albeit those difficulties were real enough. Far more critical was the matter of beginning afresh on an isolated island with no existing economic infrastructure and no easily available source of supply and provisions. Whether eighteeth-century Americans were any better equipped than Scottish Highlanders or Irishmen to deal with these obstacles is a moot point. It was virtually impossible to reach the Island from Europe early enough in the season to clear land and harvest a crop, and so most settlers had to be prepared to live off the supplies of others for at least a year. Even had there been financial resources to buy the necessities of life, or someone willing to credit, such supplies were not locally available before 1775 or for many years thereafter. Such problems had faced the first American settlers in the early years of the seventeenth century, and few survived as well as did the *Mayflower* passengers of 1620, fortunate enough to find land already cleared by native peoples and sustained by their religious beliefs. Even the Pilgrims had no easy time, however.[9] Comparisons between the Island of St John and early Virginia or Plymouth make far more sense than visualizing the Island in the context of late eighteenth-century American expansion into Kentucky or the Ohio Valley, or even in the context of the Loyalist colonies in New Brunswick and Upper Canada.

After initial footholds had been gained – at enormous expense in terms of human suffering – the basic American pattern of settlement was to expand gradually outwards from a flourishing base, which could supply a new community until it had become established. Successful settlement was thus more a gradual process of concentric growth rather than a series of thrusts into total wilderness hundreds of miles from a base of supply. The history of early colonization in America is littered with the many failures, commonly characterized by an inability to accept that settlers could not live off the land, however bounteous, but required a lifeline to commodities and markets that they could not themselves be expected to provide or generate. Yankee settlement in Nova Scotia after 1759 had not worked because of the supply problem, and settlements on the Bay of Fundy were far less isolated than the Island of St John.[10] Supplies very nearly defeated the British resettlement of the Loyalists, and the British government spent millions of pounds on that occasion.

To some extent the British government had some vague notion of what was required for successful settlement: hence the proprietors, who were expected to provide initial financial backing and resources. If the settlement of the Island of St John were to be organized, some institution such as the proprietors was necessary. The alternative was to allow the Island to populate itself without planning or supervision, permitting a series of individual decisions to govern those who came to the Island, and producing a series of individual instances of immediate suffering (which would have gone largely unrecorded and could not be blamed upon anyone). Ultimately the process would have produced the organic growth of the infrastructure necessary to sustain steady development. Such a process would have taken years, many false starts, and might have produced a quite different result. But planning was too great a temptation, particularly given the insular nature of the territory and the problems the British government was facing with those pesky American colonists who were viewed as the products of a cumulative lack of forward calculation on the colonial front.

As for the proprietors themselves, few had the slightest notion of the problems to be faced in fulfilling the terms of their grants, and it should be again emphasized that a number of the early proprietors began with the best of intentions. Quite apart from the question of finding settlers, given the restrictive provisions of the grants, there was the matter of sustaining them. Here two points are extremely important. First, the proprietors had been gravely misled about the cultivable state of the lands, and even where not misinformed, were overly sanguine about the ease with which wilderness land could be brought into production. The general understanding, fuelled by information from those involved in the reduction of Louisbourg in

1758, was that the Island had been the granary and livestock centre of Acadia. Dispossession of thousands of Acadian residents therefore should have made plenty of cleared land ready for cultivation. It was not clearly understood in Britain how much of that Acadian population had literally camped in the forest, too recently arrived and too quickly dispersed to have had much impact on the landscape.[11] The survey of Samuel Holland further contributed to the notion of available fields ready for the plough. Whether Holland had exaggerated the extent of clearing is uncertain. Quite possibly he had not, but neither he nor a group of British proprietors could appreciate the speed with which cleared land hacked out of forest could return to its wilderness state. In five to ten years of neglect, a field would almost certainly disappear. Holland had not stressed this point sufficiently in his optimistic account of the state of the Island.[12]

Moreover, neither British gentlemen nor prospective settlers could be expected to appreciate that an abundance of natural food resources – game, fish, fruit – could exist at the same time as starvation. Here the failure to comprehend the nature of the Island's geography and climate was critical, for it could not be judged in Old World terms. The Island of St John, while in latitude to the south of the British Isles, enjoys what has come to be called a "continental" climate, consisting of cold, harsh winters with much snow and ice and a warm, pleasant (but by English or even American standards short) summer season. Spring comes late and autumn arrives early; the growing period is relatively brief. In winter the Island became virtually isolated from the outside world, for Northumberland Strait froze in the winter months, too solid for boats but often too unstable for foot traffic; winter deaths from attempts to walk the strait were common until well into the 19th century. The open side of the Island has few harbours and treacherous winds, as more than one early settler discovered to his dismay. During these winter months when the Island was dependent on its own resources, fish were unavailable, game scarce and hard to hunt, and the trees were bare. Heavy snows made food foraging difficult, and few Europeans had the necessary skills to shoot game birds on the wing on a regular and consistent basis, even had many wintered on the Island. The natural resources, in short, would not supplement the food supply in the critical winter season when links were cut with the outside world. Hunting and fishing were not year-round activities, and their seasons overlapped those for other business. Winter was a particularly hard and discouraging season in the early years of settlement.

As has been observed, the allocation of the land surface of the Island to proprietors was intended largely to overcome the difficulties of early settlement without cost to the British Treasury. The proprietors were not intended to become absentee landlords or land speculators, but they *were* intended to finance the settlers during the critical first years, providing them with capital and much-needed supplies. Although the proprietors were slow in moving toward fulfilling their obligations, a number of them had become active in the years before 1775, when the American rebellion effectually shut down settlement activity. Most of the resident population on the Island in 1775 owed their presence to a proprietor, although few showed any signs of gratitude. In the absence of any detailed statistics – the first Island census was not taken until 1798 – early demographic growth cannot be discussed with any precision. The number of incoming settlers may be calculated with some accuracy, but many soon departed for other jurisdictions. Several boatloads of immigrants were recruited by shippers rather than proprietors, and there may well have been a trickle of independent settlers (including some Acadians) whose arrival is quite impossible to document. By examining the various early ventures, however, we can piece together a fairly accurate picture of settlement before 1775.

One of the first proprietors to attempt to fulfil his grant was Captain Robert Stewart, whose family had received a half share in lot 18 on the east side of Malpeque Bay.[13] Sensibly, Stewart came to the Island in advance, arriving in 1769 to examine conditions and prepare the way. Apparently he did little more than to construct a house for himself before returning to Scotland to recruit settlers. He probably decided it was not possible to clear land or begin planting in advance of a labour force, a circular problem that remained throughout the early period. In 1770, Stewart sent a number of Scottish families – chiefly Highlanders from Argyleshire – most of whom paid him for their passage in return for gifts of land. The party of eighty, mainly children, left Glasgow about 1 August 1770 aboard the *Annabella*, arriving at Malpeque Harbour around mid September. The vessel ran aground off Princetown for want of a knowledgeable pilot, and most of Stewart's supplies were lost.[14] Although Princetown was one of the Island's royalty towns, it existed only on paper. "Instantly a dissatisfaction arose among the immigrants against the proprietor," tradition tells us, and that malcontent was undoubtedly fostered by the subsequent winter of starvation, heightened by the loss of the cargo from the *Annabella*. Unhappy with the heavily wooded terrain, which would mean considerable clearing before a crop could be planted – perhaps delaying the achievement of subsistence another year – the people took matters in their own hands and moved in the spring of 1771 to lot 13, where there was an abandoned French settlement that could be brought under more expeditious cultivation.[15]

Little more detail is available for this earliest of ventures, but the existing information suggests a not uncommon pattern, especially for smaller proprietors who were often half-pay military officers like Captain Stewart. Such men were searching for a more satisfactory retirement than their homeland could provide and hoped to reconstruct a semi-feudal situation on the Island with extremely limited capital. Stewart had undoubtedly made the Island sound more attractive than his people found it, and he had the misfortune of losing his supplies, not only his personal investment in the venture but his settlers' lifeline. The scattering of his people seems to have discouraged Stewart, and he never actively sought to replace them – perhaps he could not afford another effort – although a party of seventy did arrive on lot 18 on their own account in the autumn of 1771, again experiencing a winter of starvation.[16] As Chief Justice Duport observed, sending settlers so late in the year was a disastrous error, but one difficult to avoid, given the difficulties of recruiting them and organizing transport on the other side of the Atlantic.

Unlike the Stewart venture on lot 18, those sponsored by James Montgomery on lot 59 and especially on lot 34 were well-funded operations. The Stewart and Montgomery efforts shared little in common but failure. James Montgomery was lord advocate for Scotland from 1766 to 1775, and was thus perfectly placed politically to participate in the lottery of 1767. By 1770 he had acquired lots 30, 34, 51, and 36 in addition to the lot 7 he had initially drawn in 1767, and he would subsequently add more land to his holdings. A self-made man, Montgomery based his growing fortune upon legal and political activities, an astute marriage, and progressive management of landed estates in Scotland.[17] The Island of St John was part of a diversified investment portfolio, giving Montgomery "80,000 Acres of good land, in an Island of a good Climate for Grain, fortunately situated for a Market," which cost little more than "the Fees of Office in passing the Grants."[18] A hard-headed businessman not given to foolish speculations, Montgomery's willingness to invest in the Island demonstrates the extent to which those in Britain were misled by its ostensible promise. He did expect his Island property to become quickly self-sustaining, the usual mistake of those investing in early colonization in North America. Montgomery projected two separate operations: a commercial one in partnership with an American merchant on lot 59, and a large flax farm on lot 34 supervised by an experienced farmer and worked by indentured labour recruited in the Highlands.

The commercial venture was planned in collaboration with David Higgins, a mariner related by marriage to the Prince family of Boston and a man who claimed experience on the Island from earlier fishing operations in the Gulf of St Lawrence.[19] Most of Montgomery's favourable opinion of the potential of St John undoubtedly came from Higgins, whose unbounded enthusiasm for its possibilities was that of the born promoter. In 1769 Montgomery sent Higgins to the Island to take charge of lots 59 and 51. The partners hoped to attract German settlers from the territories of Hesse to these lots, and negotiations were set afoot in Germany. Higgins brought with him a shipload of trade goods supplied by Montgomery, as well as an open letter of credit from the lord advocate to Job Prince in Boston.[20] The plans for the Hessians fell through, but Higgins over the years granted leases to thirty-two small tenants on lot 59, most of them Scots but perhaps one-third of Acadian origin.[21] Higgins kept a store at Georgetown, cleared thirty acres for "St. Andrew's Farm," and built a sawmill and gristmill. He managed to send twenty-two shiploads of Island timber to Britain in the early 1770s, although because of depressed prices they barely cleared the expenses of preparation and shipment.[22] Higgins was ahead of his time, which would bring him little consolation.

David Higgins had no difficulty in disposing of trade goods on the Island. Indeed, his acquisition of provisions in New England on the strength of the Montgomery letter of credit on several occasions helped to save many newcomers from starvation. The problem was that Higgins dealt with his customers almost exclusively in terms of credit. Most of those resident on the Island in the early years were on his books – including many Crown officials – but some would leave and others go bankrupt. Higgins could not collect his debts, and his business was based on advances of over £4,000 from his partner in Scotland. Montgomery finally called Higgins home for an accounting in 1774. Patrick M'Robert, who visited the little settlement at Three Rivers that same year, reported, "The land that has been cleared here is good pasture, the soil pretty good; here are about forty families, Scots and French settled."[23] The dream of Jean-Pierre Roma about Three Rivers was not yet dead.

For his agrarian project, the lord advocate secured the services of a Perthshire flax farmer, David Lawson of Callendar, a widower with five children. Lawson was empowered to deal with prospective servants on his silent partner's behalf, procuring about fifty males on four-year indentures, who were at the expiration of their terms to have from Montgomery on 1,000-year leases 2 to 500 acres of uncleared land rent-free for four years, then at low rents rising progressively, as well as stocking and cash advances on four-year bonds. Lawson was to depart for the Island with the servants in the spring of 1770, where he would oversee development of the farm (named Stanhope Farm) for seven years, in return for half the profits remaining after the lord advocate's total advances had been set against the improved value of the property.[24] This agreement was based on Scottish experience rather than North American conditions. While such leases (known as "Kames leases" after that notable improver) were typical between progressive landlords and their chief tenants in Scotland, it was absurd to expect any profits within seven years of beginning an agricultural operation in the wilds of America. Lawson would have been much better advised to undertake the assignment on a salaried basis, rather than a profit-sharing one. To complicate further the arrangement, it was based upon the supposition of careful bookkeeping that was well beyond Lawson's capacities. He was a working farmer, not an estate manager.

Almost from the beginning Montgomery was unhappy with the Lawson operation, partly because he was not really comfortable in his role as emigrant promoter, partly because the expenses quickly outran his expectations, As lord advocate, Montgomery was uniquely placed among Island proprietors to appreciate the British government's lack of enthusiasm for peopling St John with workers needed at home. Moreover, Montgomery doubtless shared the hostility of the landed classes of Britain to North American emigration. He self-consciously referred to his servants as "White Negroes," and ordered his Edinburgh "man of business" to manage the affair "in such a manner as to incur as little Observation as possible."[25] Lawson succeeded in recruiting more labourers in Perthshire than Montgomery had anticipated – it was the beginning of the movement of Scots to America, and the labouring poor were anxious to sign on – and as the lord advocate complained to a friend, "the expense is enormous, and above double what it should have been, and I have acted like a good natured Fool, that attends not to his affairs or situation."[26]

According to Montgomery's later calculations, he had advanced over £1,200 to get Lawson, the "White Negroes," and a shipload of supporting supplies to the Island in 1770.[27] Even if the lord advocate was correct in his assertion that the venture was badly managed, the figure gives some idea of the capital cost necessary to begin settlement on the Island in the early days, perhaps around £25 per settler. Such sums were not available to many, and fewer men still could afford to expend these amounts without receiving any return on their investment. If Robert Stewart's initial outlay was on a similar scale, it is hardly surprising that he did not try again after his first debacle.

Montgomery would have been astounded had he known that James MacGregor would be told twenty years later that Lawson's people "were decoyed out by one of the great proprietors to settle his land. They were to pay a shilling rent per acre, and they thought it cheap till they came out and saw it; but then they found it dear enough."[28] He would have been even more astounded at the remark of a later historian of the Island that despite "much praise for his early interest in the settlement of his lots, it must not be supposed that he himself contributed towards the emigration expenses of the settlers. He merely directed them to his own lands and offered to lease them wilderness land at one shilling per acre."[29] Hostility to the proprietors runs long and deep in Island mythology.

For his part, David Lawson faced the incredible problems of beginning life in a total wilderness on a virtually uninhabited island. However arduous his travails might sound, they had to be faced by all early settlers, and there was no viable alternative to suffering. When Lawson's vessel put down the party in Stanhope Cove on 8 June 1770, he had no dwelling house, no food except oatmeal and no beverage except salt water, and upwards of fifty servants "who expected better provisions than oat meal and salt water."[30] A shipload of provisions finally arrived from Three Rivers, but Lawson did not receive the bullocks, horses, and farm implements he had been expecting, and none were available on the Island. He eventually found livestock, but later claimed he was forced to make all his own farming equipment. He could obtain no seed grain for the first two years, and even if he had, lacked sufficient cleared land to plant it. Lawson was quite proud of his achievement in clearing enough land to support his many dependents by the harvest of 1772 – more than two years after his arrival – and well he might be.

In the summer of 1772, Lawson freed a river of debris and built a dam for a gristmill that was in operation by 1773. But both dam and mill burnt in summer 1775 when they were engulfed in a runaway fire begun to burn off woods on a tenant's property; fires were a constant danger in the early years, many begun by careless farmers anxious to clear their lands.[31] Lawson rebuilt the mill in 1776, but it burnt down the very day it was completed. Only on the third attempt in 1777 did he appreciate the value of wide clearing around the millsite to protect it from fire, but at this point he had trouble obtaining millstones, and kept losing the dam to floods.

Lawson had problems with the indentured servants as well. In his first year one man was killed when crushed by a large pine he was felling, and two others were drowned bringing a cargo of rum to the tiny settlement.[32] The first requirement for survival was self-sufficiency, and at the very point at which the servants could be fed from the farm and could settle down to the business of a flax plantation, their indentures expired. Most scattered across the Island and even off it, and those few Perthshire men who took up farms demanded their promised stock, weakening Lawson's efforts to build up breeding herds. In June 1774 he gave to former servants sixteen milch cows, and by 9 August of that year, forty-five head of cattle were in possession of the tenants, and only fifty-three remained with Lawson.[33] Since cows were worth £6 on the Island in 1774, those who remained with Montgomery were substantially subsidized for their loyalty.[34] Such rewards were forgotten, as were the initial agreements with the lord advocate, in the stories of early suffering.

Despite all obstacles, Lawson did remarkably well in his first years at Stanhope Farm. He, his family, and the servants constructed a large seventy-by-twenty foot dwelling house, cleared over 100 acres, and built a substantial barn and byres with breeding herds of cattle, sheep, horses, and pigs.[35] To Lawson's efforts could be attributed much of the praise of traveller Patrick M'Robert for the Island's livestock: "There cattle are of a very good kind, and neat; some of them weigh from seventy to eighty stone; their horses are the Canadian breed, about fourteen hands high, very handsome and mettled; they have pretty good sheep and plenty of swine."[36] The farm was not only self-sufficient in terms of foodstuffs, but was even producing a surplus, although Lawson complained he was forced to distribute precious seed grain to needy settlers in 1774, the "year of the mice," when only his carefully tended crop remained unravaged. He had a grain mill in operation, at least after 1777. He had experimented with flax cultivation with some success, and had demonstrated that hemp (another of those raw materials that Britain needed and hoped to acquire from every new colony) did not prosper in the soil of the Island.[37] As for the soil, Lawson shipped one-foot-thick samples home to Montgomery in boxes, enabling the lord advocate to have it carefully analysed. If Montgomery found it less rich than earlier reports suggested, that was not David Lawson's fault.[38] What Lawson could not do, of course, was to demonstrate that his efforts and improvements could be appraised at a value exceeding Montgomery's cash advances.

While James Montgomery was establishing the first major settlement of Protestant Scots Highlanders on the Island, a few miles to the east a substantial party of Highland Catholics also attempted to put down roots. The venture had its origins within the leadership of the Scottish Catholic Church, although it has always been associated with the name of John MacDonald of Glenaladale, who became the proprietor of lot 36 and ultimately himself settled on the Island. The Scottish Church by the late 1760s was becoming increasingly concerned about religious persecution of its adherents, especially in the Hebrides, by Protestant landlords. The one practical response to this "general design ... to root out Religion by discouraging the Catholics all they can" was to encourage and assist those being oppressed to emigrate to America.[39] Such emigration would not only remove the people from persecution but would also threaten a depopulation of estates, thus improving the attitude of the landlords, who were seeking to maximize revenue by raising rents, cutting costs, and utilizing extensive labour wherever possible.

The leaders of the Church found a layman in the person of John MacDonald to take charge of the first exodus. Head of the senior cadet branch of the Clan MacDonald of Clanranald, John had been educated in Germany and was an ardent, if somewhat imperious, Catholic. As Clanranald's chief tacksman, MacDonald was finding himself squeezed between higher rents and an increasing tendency of the landlords to eliminate the tacksmen as a mediating class in the Highlands. He was casting around for alternatives to his own precarious situation. The motives of the Glenaladale family (John's brother Donald was also associated with the project), chiefly socio-economic, must be carefully distinguished from those of the Church, which saw the scheme principally in religious terms. While the Glenaladales were solely responsible for the tactical execution of the project, both its strategic and financial aspects were shared with men of the Church.[40]

In summer 1770, Donald MacDonald was sent to America to survey the land situation there, while the Church negotiated with James Montgomery for land on the Island of St John, a territory about which all Scotland was then hearing very favourable – if exaggerated – reports. Through the unofficial offices of the Church, John MacDonald was able to obtain lot 36 from Montgomery, a township generally regarded as one of the best on the Island. It cost £600, although the transaction involved no immediate cash and an open-ended understanding about repayment. This price, at the time regarded as a bargain, indicates the value with which Island property was then regarded. Having obtained his land, MacDonald sent brother Donald again to the Island in spring 1771 with a small contingent of settlers to prepare the way for a larger body the following year.

Glenaladale became increasingly reluctant to become involved with any "threadbare Scheme of Emigration," particularly since those the Church sought to assist were extremely impoverished and he wanted only emigrants in "good circumstances."[41] MacDonald may also have become suspicious of the visionary nature of the Church's intentions, described by Bishop George Hay: "The plan proposed is to make an entire Catholic Colony to keep up a constant Intercourse with this Country, to have Schools there in common for boys from this and which plan if it could be brought to bear might turn out to our great mutual advantage, and it would be a constant asylum for all our distressed people."[42] But when the Church raised funds for transporting thirty-six oppressed tenants from Uist, MacDonald agreed to include them in his venture, keeping the source of the money a secret.

As Glenaladale began to make his final preparations, it became increasingly clear that expenses would be high. Information from Donald, lately returned from the Island, indicated the need for proper supplies of food, clothing, seed, tools, and farming implements. Provisions were virtually unobtainable on the Island, and Donald reported that most of the early arrivals spent their time "in procuring and wanting for those Necessarys at extravagent rates." As a result, Glenaladale attempted to equip and supply the 1772 party as adequately "as the frugality we had in view would admit," carrying tools and sufficient meal for a year.[43] The details of the financial side of this emigration give some additional idea of the amount of capital required for early settlement on the Island of St John.

In spring 1772, 210 emigrants departed on board the ship *Alexander* for the Island. The cost of passage was £3.12.6 per person above the age of seven, for a total of just over £600. Were a return cargo available on the Island – of course it was not – 2.6 shillings of the passage money would have been refunded. A full year's provisions of meal cost £500, and clothing and utensils added another £400 to the bill. Of the grand total of £1,500, about half was born by the Scottish Catholic Church as loans and grants to Glenaladale, and the remainder by the emigrants.[44] Even more detailed figures are available for the eleven families from South Uist whose expenses were totally absorbed by the Church and for whom an itemized account survives.[45] Glenaladale provided axes, spades, hoes, scythes, saws, files, and nails at a cost of £1.16.4¾ per family. One hundred and fourteen bolls of meal (and barrels to keep them in) to feed the families for a year cost £110.8.7, or just over £10 per family. Incidental expenses (porterage, cartage, freight) added another £1.10 per family. The full bill of £256.15.9 for thirty-five full passengers worked out to just over £9 per person, tallying almost exactly with the amount per person for the entire ship.

A reasonably well-equipped settlement venture to the Island of St John would cost a minimum of £30 per family at an average family size of four persons, and could go higher for larger families. Cost of transatlantic transportation would be high from any point in Britain or Western Europe, since a vessel would have to be chartered that had little hope of acquiring a return cargo on the Island. This estimate of £30 per family does not include £5 for local purchase of a cow (which Glenaladale regarded as a minimum for each family), nor local transportation costs on either side of the Atlantic; the *Alexander* sailed straight from the Highlands to MacDonald's Tracadie location. Because few families could raise £30 or more in cash – the amount was considerably in excess of the average annual income of a farmer or an artisan – many were undoubtedly deterred from emigration, or (like the ill-fated *Hector* passengers landed at Pictou, Nova Scotia, in 1774) went seriously underprepared, with resultant great suffering.[46] Reports of such disasters would, in turn, deter further settlement. Few emigrants received the sort of financial assistance provided by the *Alexander's* poorer passengers by the Scottish Catholic Church. In short, settlers coming from Europe to the Island of St John had to be relatively prosperous, or dependent upon a proprietor, or doomed to face extraordinary privations. As the fate of the *Falmouth* and *Alexander* passengers made clear, even a relatively well-planned and well-financed settlement venture to the Island of St John faced considerable local difficulties.

The *Alexander* made a surprisingly easy passage to the Island, the only noteworthy incident on the voyage being the death of a child. But from their arrival in June 1772, the settlers – especially those from Arisaig and Moydart who had paid their own way – were restive. In Scotland, Glenaladale and the Church leaders carefully studied the letters sent home, concluding there was "no other cause for their discontent but the Inconveniencies inseparable from such an Affair ... that the seeing and trying of any Country produces a different Effect from the reading a description of it, and that our Cropt [*sic*] last year, excepting the Potatoes and Garden Stuffs, was exceedingly bad."[47] Glenaladale blamed the agricultural problems on bad tillage procedures and old seed that had not germinated. Even the malcontents, he reported, had to admit the Island favourable for raising cattle, but all doubted that their traditional grains would flourish. Acadian experience before 1760 and subsequent experimentation demonstrated that the Island was not well suited for grain, although changing farming patterns would take generations.[48] Advance talk of extraordinary yields was, of course, not borne out by reality, and the ubiquitous presence of primary-growth forest over much of the Island was forbidding to anyone from Europe. Many of MacDonald's people came to doubt they had sufficient resources to subsist and improve their lands, although they were far better prepared and supported than most early arrivals.

Discontent seemed to cluster around Father James MacDonald, the Scottish priest who had accompanied the settlers. His friends and relations came from the mainland districts of the Highlands rather than the Hebrides. The settlers talked eagerly of Nova Scotia, where they had heard they might obtain lands already cleared and ready to plant. Whether Nova Scotia was really an improvement was debatable, but the people could see daily their existing problems. In late May 1773, Father James travelled to Quebec, partly to see the bishop and receive both the sacraments and his local authorizations, but also to look into the possibility of new lands in Catholic Quebec for his flock, who were, he wrote, "in a most miserable condition" likely to continue while they remained on the Island.[49] "There is," he insisted, "no money, no Cloathes, no meat to be met with there without paying four times the price of it, and it gives me a heart break that my poor friends who were in a tolerable good condition before they left Scotland are now upon the brink of the greatest misery and poverty."[50] Father James was obviously not referring to the Church-sponsored people from Uist, but to those from the mainland who had originally financed their passage and now found themselves with insufficient resources to withstand the first difficult years of settlement. Because their expectations were initially higher than those of impoverished Hebrideans, their sense of disappointment was far greater. Significantly, they lacked the capital to bring themselves "out of their Captivity," wrote the priest, and would need financial assistance to leave the Island.

The use of rhetorical flourishes such as "misery" and "captivity" demonstrates the difficulty of interpreting complaints about the early days on the Island. No one at Scotchfort starved – unlike settlers on other parts of the Island – and only a few indentured servants among the party were tied to it. As many observers would later comment, Highland settlers in America always had a tendency to moan and complain.[51] While Father James undoubtedly accurately reflected the feelings of those he spoke for, their responses were not entirely to be taken at face value. Perhaps equally important is the fact that most of the malcontents had been prosperous in the Highlands. The Uist people did not complain, and appear to have flourished. As was so often the case, the settlers everyone desired were the very ones who would find pioneering most uncongenial.

One point on which all settlers could agree was that Glenaladale should come himself to the Island to take charge of the tiny settlement establishing itself around Scotchfort. By April 1773 he had arranged the sale of his Highland estate to cousins.[52] Delaying his departure for America by waiting for cash payment on the estate transaction, MacDonald missed direct connections to the Maritimes and was forced to sail for Philadelphia, where he intended to winter. Rumours among Scots merchants in Pennsylvania of starvation conditions on the Island pushed him on to Boston, where he learned the earlier rumours were greatly exaggerated. None had starved in his settlement or elsewhere; despite great troubles with seed, Donald had planted seven acres of wheat and had continued good success with potatoes and garden produce. Nonetheless, MacDonald in Boston collected a schooner-load of Indian corn, rye, and molasses to take to the Island to see his people through the winter, paying for these goods with a draft upon the Scottish bishops.[53]

Glenaladale was undoubtedly accurate in his assumption that the bishops would honour his draft, for a disaster among Highland Catholics upon the Island would have spelled the end to any strategy of employing emigration as a threat against persecution. By the autumn of 1774, however, the Church could rejoice that letters from the Island "give sufficient room to hope that the undertaking will thrive well enough."[54] Father James, although "near destroying the affair," had become reconciled to the Island, and the bulk of the settlers had become established. John MacDonald and his people had many trials and tribulations yet to experience, but they had survived the initial relocation.[55] Highland Catholics would continue their movement to North America, and the Island of St John – although never the Catholic colony at first envisioned – was always one of their preferred destinations.[56]

Although the Scotchfort immigrants had received some unofficial assistance from James Montgomery, the British government did not regard such settlers as either desirable or as fulfilling the terms of the grants to the proprietors. For the most part, a blind eye was turned to the recruiting of Island settlers in the British Isles, but the government could and occasionally did take offence at such activities, especially when done in the backyard of government ministers. The principal target for the complaints in the early years was Lieutenant-Governor Thomas Desbrisay, a part proprietor of lots 31 and 33, in central Queen's County. Desbrisay had not only been recruiting among the tenants of the earls of Hillsborough and Hertford in Northern Ireland, but had done so publicly, with newspaper advertisements that employed his Island appointments in a prominent way. The Board of Trade wrote Desbrisay to desist from such activities, and while his response was to protest – "I think it hard I should be the only person debar'd from sending people to America" –he had too much at stake to defy the ban.[57] Some of the settlers sold lands by Desbrisay in lot 31 did come to the Island in 1774, only to discover that the lieutenant-governor had mortgaged his holdings and could not convey title to them.[58]

Desbrisay also negotiated leases with a number of Irishmen, mainly from County Antrim, involving land in amounts from 50 acres to 200 acres. The leases were to be progressive in terms of rental, the tenant paying 2d. per English acre the first year, 4d. the second, 6d. the third, and 1s. per acre by year four. Of the thirty-seven known lessees, twenty-five actually took up their lands on lots 31 and 33, probably eventually moving to other land on or off the Island, for Desbrisay's terms were extortionate and the size of the holdings small.[59] So far as is known, the lieutenant-governor provided no assistance to the settlers, many of whom were quite discontented upon arrival. The survival of copies of Desbrisay's leases does give some glimpse of the sorts of Irish attracted to the Island in the early years. Of the twenty-three occupational designations given on the leases, eight were farmers, eleven were skilled artisans (six weavers, three carpenters, one tailor, and a smith), two were retired soldiers, one a mariner, and one was an innkeeper.[60] All must have been reasonably prosperous, since they would have to finance their own passage to the Island. The situation of those who actually settled Desbrisay's lots was complicated by the matter of ownership, and the record is not clear whether that problem was ever sorted out. Desbrisay subsequently attempted to recruit German settlers in place of Irish, but his schemes never came to fruition.[61]

Two passenger lists for the *Lovely Nelly,* which departed Scotland in 1774 and 1775 for the Island of St John, provide another fascinating glimpse into the sorts of people attracted to the Island in the early period.[62] The lists indicate that the typical Island immigrant came from one of two social groupings: first, heads of families around thirty years of age, with an average of three small children, usually unemployed or underemployed artisans unable to support their families or see any future for their children at home, and second, young single males, usually around twenty years of age, who had no stake in society and no prospects for improvement apart from what they could gain by their own labour. The appeal of the Island among older artisans and young labourers meant that the new settlers were not, by and large, experienced farmers accustomed to operating their own farm enterprises. Insofar as the Island provided a challenge for farmers, in which the old techniques and mindsets of the mother country were not valid, the absence of experience probably was not a disadvantage. At the same time the fact that few Island settlers had ever managed a farm was a distinct liability. The absence of American pioneers who did have experience in beginning farms under wilderness conditions undoubtedly contributed to the slowness with which agriculture on the Island developed. All the mistakes had to be made again, and the learning experience was slow and painful.

The attractiveness of the Island – and any wilderness territory in North America – for European artisans and young labourers is shown by the settlement of New London on lot 21, which was begun in 1773 by Robert Clark in partnership with another Londoner, Robert Campbell, who died on the Island sometime in the early period. A Quaker clothier, Clark had some notion of founding a religious haven for Quakers and other sectarians. According to a hostile Governor Patterson, Clark "really thought himself a second Penn and believed he would transmit as great a name to Posterity. From being a Methodist, he had turned Quaker a little before he left England, and to give his change the appearance of real conviction, he outdid his whole Fraternity in Sanctity."[63] Clark did his principal recruiting among the young of London, both those of the artisan class and of the idle better sort, the latter of whom he hoped to reclaim through commitment to his vision of New London as a "place for recovering of Sinners."[64] Arriving on the Island in 1773 with a cargo of merchandise, Clark began planning his township of Elizabethtown around his "large magazine of universal stores," most of which were stored on the open beach and available to anyone who chose to take them.[65] He had brought a number of artificers from London as indentured servants, to serve as a labour force in the lumbering operations he hoped would be the basis of economic success. But Clark had great difficulty in managing this cadre of settlers, surrounded as they were by young idlers from London and "all the Vagabonds of the Island," who consumed food and drink and "did as they pleased."[66] Governor Patterson, who disliked Clark, maintained that he was very susceptible to flattery and extremely proud of his "powers as a Preacher, and the purity of his Figure." Clark returned to England in autumn 1773, convinced that he had set his enterprise afoot, although Patterson – who visited the settlement before Clark's departure –opined he was "ruining himself, by expense and want of care."[67]

Upon his return to London, Clark leased lot 49 to John Adams and Joseph Smith, Jr, who sent Quaker Edward Allen to Derbyshire to recruit settlers for their land. Adams and Smith, with Allen as supercargo, came to the Island with their settlers in 1774 aboard the brig *Lovely Kitty*, but the new arrivals thought the terms proposed by the partners for subleasing land exorbitant, and they scattered to other property.[68] Quaker missionaries as well as Quaker proprietors were active on the Island before 1775, however. Clark himself organized a second shipload of settlers on a similar basis as his first. These settlers arrived aboard the 200-ton snow *Elizabeth* in 1774. Recognizing the need for proper management of his settlement, Clark had the good sense to secure as agent and supercargo a London wheelwright named Benjamin Chappell, who had earlier been drawn to the preaching of the Wesley brothers and had travelled extensively with them as an itinerant preacher.[69] Chappell had married in February 1774, and was attracted to the Island by Clark's descriptions of its riches and promise. The sales pitch undoubtedly was little different from that given Thomas Curtis in 1775. The proprietor waxed rhapsodic about well-stocked timber land, available at "4d per Acre, for Life, or 1s per acre freehold," where the "Captain's or masters of Ships which were frequently coming in, would purchase all" one "could cut for Ship or House Building, & that Sawyers were better paid for their labour, than in England, that the Rivers abounded with fish and the Country with game Which were free for any one, that Deer and Turkeys were so plentiful that a person might shoot them from the Windows, and when at work in the woods might shoot enough to serve his family without loss of time – in short any man could live more comfortable there, than in England."[70] The *Elizabeth* carried another cargo of goods: Clark had imported from Quebec a separate cargo of cows, sheep, and horses, which he supplied to indigent settlers on the Island. According to John Cambridge, by the end of 1774, Clark and Campbell were £14,000 to £15,000 "in advance to their concern" on the Island, partly in unrecoverable expenses and partly in advances of goods to the settlers upon credit.[71]

Benjamin Chappell's diary, begun on the 19th of January 1775, records the rapid demise of Clark's substantial investment. The diary begins in midwinter, the settlers huddled together in a few hastily constructed log houses. The Chappells shared their dwelling with "three gentlemen" and their cookroom with seventeen people, including "eleven strangers." Elizabethtown was obviously still harbouring others besides its own people. Timbering was made impossible by the shortage of horses, hunting was hampered by the snow, fishing by the ice. Most of the men refused to work through illness or idleness. Food was virtually impossible to obtain, and the people became very restive. On 18 February, Chappell reported, "Very short of provisions. No rum, no bread, no meat, no beer, no sugar in the stores." He attempted to ration what little remained, but the settlers threatened to raid the storehouses. Occasional supplies dribbled in from other settlements, but by the end of March a large part of Chappell's men, "outrageous through want of Provisions," formed a plan to "surprize Charleytown." The coming of spring sent folk to their gardenplots and made shellfish available. Chappell and his wife considered leaving, but on 9 May "Concluded not to remove but to trust to God for food."[72] The same sad story had over the years been recorded in countless journals by numberless newcomers to America. The unhappy fate of Elizabethtown had not come about through the deliberate neglect by proprietor Robert Clark, or as a result of a lack of financial commitment to the settlement. Indeed, Clark's mistake was overgenerosity, not the reverse.

As the settlers at Elizabethtown, and elsewhere on the Island, turned with eternal optimism to the spring planting of 1775, they could not know that events to the south would greatly affect their already precarious existence. In the small Massachusetts villages of Lexington and Concord, the opening shots of the War of the American Revolution were fired in April 1775, and the Island of St John– like all of North America – would be greatly influenced by the lengthy military and political conflict that ensued. As of spring 1775, the Island of St John was still very much a fledgling colony, although its progress since 1767 had not been inconsiderable in terms of settlement, as well as political development. While it is impossible to offer precise figures, the population of the Island by 1775 had reached approximately 1,500, and at least a few of the tiny settlements were moving out of the first stages of rudimentary foundation. The proprietors had not fulfilled their promises, but by comparison with the development of other new colonies before and after, they had not done badly in the initial decade. Perhaps as much as £40,000 had been invested by individual proprietors in the settlement process, little if any of the capital ever recovered. Quitrent payments were not up to date, but that they were paid at all was unusual within the British Empire at the time.

In 1775, the Island of St John appeared to be teetering on the brink of success. The American rebellion changed the picture rather dramatically.

CHAPTER FOUR

The Years of the American Revolution, 1775–1780

After years of conflict with the mother country, the thirteen American colonies rose in open rebellion in April 1775. Of the long-festering disputes with Britain in which the Americans had engaged even before the signing of the Treaty of Paris in 1763 and which gradually escalated in armed revolt, the Island of St John remained largely ignorant and innocent. As a newly acquired territory that had received a formal government only in 1769, with a small population drawn almost entirely from the British Isles, the Island simply was not part of the conflict. It had little interest in the issues, and the Americans made no attempt to draw the Island into them, partly because few in the thirteen colonies were aware of its existence and those who did know it wrote it off as either too small or too dependent upon Britain. Even after the Island had established an assembly and representative government in 1773, the assembly did not receive any correspondence from its fellow legislatures to the south that were most active in attempting to organize American resistance. Nor is there any evidence that Islanders had any clear understanding of the extent of the tensions that were building in the American colonies. Had he appreciated the situation, for example, Walter Patterson might well have postponed his leave of absence. But little outside news came to the Island, dissemination of information was difficult, and most connections were with the mother country rather than the Americans.

At the same time, the American Revolution and the wartime conditions prevailing between 1775 and 1783 were absolutely critical for the Island of St John. The disruption of commercial and maritime activity brought about by the emergence of privateering in the Gulf of St Lawrence combined with British restrictions of emigration and the uncertainties of prospective immigrants to halt the settlement process, which had been gradually building. Population growth was not only arrested, but the number of inhabitants actually declined during the wartime years. Even those few who were active proprietors deferred investment in the Island for the duration of hostilities, and almost all ceased paying their quitrents. The conduct of government was interrupted by a privateering raid on Charlottetown late in 1775. The later years of the war would bring some prosperity to the Island in the form of military subsidies from the British government, but in the disorganized state of affairs, the money had little impact on development.

Perhaps most importantly of all, the isolation of the Island during the wartime years bred a peculiarly insulated perspective among its residents, and especially among its official elite. Always slightly off the beaten track at the best of times, disrupted communications forced the Island and its people to make do as best they could during the war. Those who remained battled to survive economically by any means possible. For ordinary inhabitants, the struggle manifested itself outwardly in a failure to fulfil obligations to their landlords. For ordinary inhabitants and elite alike, earlier understandings were negated by emergency conditions, and if the proprietors neglected the Island, their agents in turn ignored the proprietors. For the elite especially, a conviction grew that they deserved some reward for their troubles. They easily persuaded themselves that their travails bordered on martyrdom and entitled them – rather than any group of comfortable absentee landlords in Britain – to assume control of proprietorial assets, including the undeveloped lands of the colony. The end product was not only a hiatus in orderly development but also an encouragement to disorderly development that teetered precariously on the brink of impropriety.

War between Britain and her colonies was bound to affect immigration adversely. Most settlers had been coming to the Island from the British Isles, particularly from Scotland. On 21 September 1775, the Scottish Board of Customs began to implement a policy of refusing to clear ships carrying emigrants to America. This action was probably less important in stemming the stream of settlers from Britain than was news of American civil war. As early as July of 1775, Peter Stewart, newly appointed chief justice of the Island, reported that Highlanders were being put off emigration by reports from America.[1] Americans had never begun moving to the Island in substantial numbers, and they were not now likely to begin. For most prospective settlers, however, the most effective bar to the Island of St John was the emergence of a fierce naval struggle in the Gulf of St Lawrence between the royal navy and colonial privateers. The privateer was a pirate legitimized by government in time of war. Given a licence – called a letter of marque – to prey upon the enemy, privateers acted in the name of booty and profit, and seldom made fine distinctions. They were a particularly favoured device of belligerents without an adequate regular navy, and the American colonies were enabled by this convention to convert hundreds of commercial vessels and fishing boats into instruments of war at little expense. Privateers specialized in operations against the weak and defenceless at sea and ashore. The Gulf of St Lawrence was especially attractive because it was not a major commercial area and was thus not extensively patrolled by the Royal Navy. For the Island, dependent as it was on maritime commerce for settlers, foodstuffs, and other necessaries of life, the success of the privateers was little short of a disaster.

A few vessels with passengers did manage to arrive on the Island in the summer of 1775. The *Lovely Nelly* brought eighty-two Lowland Scots, and the *John and Elizabeth* unloaded another fifty-two settlers for lot 57 on the Orwell River, the proprietors of which were Samuel Smith (a London merchant and Crown agent for the colony) and James Smith (a royal naval officer). According to Walter Patterson, writing years later, the proprietors refused to continue responsibility for provisioning the settlers when their supply ship was carried off by American privateers in November 1775. The newcomers were reduced "to such extremity that it is said they eat their own children, the report of which hath prevented hundreds from coming among us."[2] While cannibalism was an exaggeration, the plight of the settlers was severe. The passengers aboard the *Lovely Nelly* who had arrived in 1774 survived an infestation of field-mice that reduced them to subsistence on shellfish for the summer months, but were unable to withstand the plundering of their stores in autumn 1775 by American fishermen returning to their home base. According to the later accounts collected by Dr George Patterson,

From scarcity of food the men became reduced to such a state of weakness, and the snow was so deep, that they became at last scarcely able to carry back provisions for their families, and when with slow steps and heavy labor, they brought them home such was the state of weakness in which they had left their children, they trembled to enter their dwelling, lest they should find them dead, and sometimes waited at the door, listening for any sound that might indicate that they were alive.[3]

Not surprisingly, these settlers left the Island for Pictou in 1776.

Yet another venture affected by privateering was that of David

Higgins on lot 59 at Three Rivers. Higgins attempted to return from Scotland to the Island in the summer of 1775 with another load of trade goods and an elaborate outfit for distilling molasses, still hoping to employ Three Rivers in a triangular trade with the West Indies. His vessel was captured by privateers on the voyage out, however, and Higgins was able to ransom himself and his cargo only at great expense. The still would be eventually carried off by American raids on Three Rivers later in the war.[4] Given the scarcity of provisions on the Island in 1775, exacerbated by the work of the privateers, the wreck of the *Elizabeth* off the uninhabited sand bars near Princetown late that year was a double disaster. The ship's cargo was almost entirely lost, representing the demise of another infusion of supplies from Robert Clark for his Elizabethtown settlement, where Benjamin Chappell was still desperately holding on.[5]

At about the same time that the *Elizabeth* went aground on the north shore, Yankee privateers raided Charlottetown. Little permanent damage was done, but the vulnerability of the tiny capital had been exposed. The Americans threatened a pregnant Mrs Anne Callbeck, wife of the acting governor, plundered some houses and stores, and carried away Phillips Callbeck with several of his fellow officials.[6] This raid of November 1775 removed most of the colony's leading officials for over six months, perhaps no major disaster. More significantly, it had taken away provisions that were much needed and it demonstrated just how easy it was to attack the Island. Callbeck would later employ this raid as evidence to obtain a considerable British military presence in Charlottetown. But over the winter of 1775/6, no one on the Island could foresee the good that would come from such depredations. Several attempts to supply the Island had failed, and the marauders were subtracting provisions from a limited supply. The winter was an exceedingly difficult one for those residents remaining, probably the hardest of the wartime period. The people at New London, for example, began the winter with little but salt cod and potatoes in their larders. Three barrels of flour had to suffice for forty people. As for the cod, it was sandy, and alternating hot and cold fish and potatoes three times a day was not very stimulating.[7]

We owe much of our detailed descriptions of the personal hardships of the winter of 1775/6 to Thomas Curtis, one of the passengers aboard the *Elizabeth*. No unbiased witness, Curtis felt he had been badly misled about the potentiality of the Island by Robert Clark. In fairness to Clark, he did not know the American war was about to begin. After listening to the Quaker proprietor describe his settlement, Curtis noted, "such a favorable Accc't from so respectable a man I suck'd like Sack, Nay Don't think if any one would have given me £500 I should have been Satisfied to have stay'd in London."[8] In New London, where he ultimately wintered, he found sixteen log houses, and "came to the determination of leaving this place as soon as possible from the first View."[9]

Curtis found food in short supply, and discovered that the depths of the snow made hunting virtually impossible for anyone not experienced with snowshoes. He complained that many nights he was "to Cold to Sleep," and like other settlers was too fatigued by cold and bad diet to work hard collecting more firewood to keep warmer. Temporary additions to food were initially made possible by collecting oysters from under the ice, but as the ice froze harder and thicker even this operation became impossible. Curtis was convinced that the severity of the climate would render the Island "not agreeable to an English constitution," and he described in detail one housemate in bed with – on his blanket – "a large fleak of Ice that reach'd from his mouth as near as I could gues about 16 or 18 Inches long and about 4 inches Wide [which] seem'd thin at the farthest End and apear'd about 2 Inches thick near his Mouth."[10] But in this unremitting and sometimes exaggerated litany of hardship and woe, Curtis did not witness anyone actually starving or without food.

Thomas Curtis had no stake in the Island, and he did not hesitate to leave it at his first opportunity in spring 1776. Even his departure was made difficult, however, both by government policy and the uncertainties of wartime conditions. Curtis was forced to pay eight shillings for a certifcate granting him permission to depart, adding that "Others said if they was Out of debt they would go too & was very Sorry they Were so Situated. Their is but little chance for a person to go off this Island if in debt one Shilling." This statement is the only evidence suggesting that legislation preventing the unauthorized departure of debtors was at all effective. At the same time, Curtis was offered steady employment and some attempted to persuade him to remain.

Even after getting away aboard a brig at Malpeque, Curtis was not yet safe. His captain, he observed, "scarsely new how to Act for the best, Being as it Were in Prison for Six months, new not what Turn Affairs had taken in America." Word at Canso, the Nova Scotia fishing station, that "a War was carried on between England & America very hot" was hardly reassuring. Fortunately, the vessel met with only British ships and was able with difficulty to satisfy them that it was not "Yankey." It eventually arrived safely at Newfoundland.[11]

Curtis's account communicates the paranoia and anxiety of any maritime travel in those days of active privateering. No ship was safe, and either belligerent was a potential enemy.

To the other problems of dislocation and disorganization during the first year of the American war was added a serious shortage of leadership, both for the colonial government and in the outlying settlements. On the level of the colony, Governor Patterson was in leave of absence in England, Lieutenant-Governor Thomas Desbris-ay had not yet taken up his appointment in person, while acting governor Phillips Callbeck and several other senior officials were making their way back from captivity in New England. Chief Justice Peter Stewart and his family arrived on the Island late in 1775 aboard the ill-fated *Elizabeth*; Stewart spent his first weeks on the Island in a tent on the beach near Princetown. If Thomas Curtis is to be credited, Stewart's selfish concern for his own well-being and comfort un-doubtedly rendered him unsuitable to assume leadership in a time of crisis and suffering. He did not do so on the beach and he did not do so in Charlottetown in the months that followed. In June 1776, the assembly was forced to pass an act legalizing the failure of the Supreme Court to sit the preceding February, rehearsing the loss of officials and public records (including those of the court), and blaming the hiatus on the "distracted state" of the Island.[12] The council remained short of members during this period and for most of the war, and the source of continual aggravation and complaint.

The tiny settlements were in no better shape than the colony's government. Except for David Higgins, who arrived back on the Island late in the year, and Robert Stewart, there were no proprietors resident on the Island over the hard winter of 1775/6. John and Donald MacDonald had both departed for military service with the British, taking some of their tenantry with them. Scotchfort and Tracadie were in the hands of the MacDonald sisters, and while they did their best to keep affairs going, they did not have the same authority as the males of the family. The Clark settlements were gradually disintegrating, not aided by the loss of most of the *Elizabeth's* cargo in the shipwreck. Of the major settlements, only that at Covehead had some vestige of authority in the person of David Lawson, but he was technically only an employee of James Montgom-ery, and his term was about to expire. The problem of local leadership would be exacerbated as the war wore on, since even the few people in authority in the countryside gravitated toward Charlottetown, which offered both security and some prosperity after Phillips Callbeck had succeeded in gaining British military assistance. David Lawson, David Higgins, the MacDonald sisters, and even Benjamin Chappell were by the end of the war more or less permanent residents in the tiny capital.

That the Island survived at all – politically or economically – during the war was a product of two factors. First, Parliament did respond in 1777 to a proprietorial petition (initiated by Walter Patterson) by voting £3,000 for the Island's administration in the forthcoming budget, an annual grant that soon became automatic, despite continual disclaimers to the contrary from British officials.[13] There were some obvious dangers to such grants, because they encouraged proprietors to delay paying their quitrents. But the British government patently felt that during the crisis period of war, proprietors could not be expected to maintain their obligations. Arrearages of quitrents quickly increased, and would become a future bone of contention. While £3,000 per year did little more than pay the salaries of the major officials, it did represent some infusion of income into the Island economy.

More significantly from the standpoint of prosperity, acting governor Phillips Callbeck did eventually succeed in persuading the British authorities that the privateering raid on Charlottetown in November 1775 constituted evidence of a desperate need for improved military defences at British expense. Callbeck had been carried off by the invaders and presented to General George Washington at Cambridge, Massachusetts. Washington received Callbeck and his fellow captives politely but without interest, and immediately returned them to Halifax on board what the acting governor indignantly described as a "foul-smelling coastal vessel." The American general's response indicated that the rebels had no formal territorial designs for St John's Island, but Callbeck played heavily and with Irish bravura upon his experiences.

He got much of the mileage out of the sufferings of others, especially Mrs Callbeck. His wife, the acting governor wrote Lord Dartmouth from Halifax early in 1776, was left with child "in so wretched a Situation that I am to suppose she is barely breathing the breath of life, without a neighbour, or person, capable of soothing the Afflication natural in a young Wife on the Absence of her Husband, Father & Friend, who has been torn from her."[14] Subsequent events would demonstrate that the Island had no shortage of men prepared to sooth the afflictions of damsels in distress, and so perhaps Callbeck had a point. But his rhetorical flourishes and evidence of further freebooting enabled him ultimately to acquire his own volunteer company, a garrison of four (later six) provincial companies from New York, and even some Hessian soldiers. Callbeck exploited the diffuse command structure of the British military with either Irish luck or sheer genius, employing an offhand commitment in principle to a limited force from Lord George Germain and an absence of any military district willing to claim primary responsibility for protecting the Island to promote a major assignment of troops by Sir Henry Clinton in New York. Perhaps significantly, in the Island records for the war Callbeck preferred to style himself "Commander in Chief" rather than "Acting Governor."

While Phillips Callbeck was coping with the local situation, Governor Walter Patterson was safely ensconced in England attempting to persuade the proprietors to accept an alteration in the structure of the colony's government. By February 1776, he had organized a minority group of proprietors, few of them active colonizers, to petition the king for a revised relationship with the mother country. The petition emphasized that the Island had enormous potential, despite its immediate problems in supporting its civil administration. It insisted that "no other Colony belonging to your Majesty" had ever "been established on a Similar Plan," and went on to maintain that the initial arrangements were merely a "public Experiment, rather than a mere bargain with Individuals" that had not worked. Nevertheless, the Island was loyal – "it can never be dependent on the Temper & Proceedings of the Continental Colonies, but being an Island must ever continue in peaceable Subjection to the Mother Country" – and deserved public support. The petitioners suggested an abatement of quitrent increases for those fulfilling their engagements, and action against defaulters.[15]

Attached to the petition was a document entitled "Observations on the Island of St. John in the Gulph of St. Lawrence – briefly setting forth the Advantages which must arise from the Settlement of it to Great Britain, and offering some Reasons why at this Juncture it may prove particularly advantageous to give it extraordinary Encouragement &c."[16] Like the petition itself, this document was undoubtedly penned by Walter Patterson. It pointed out the attractiveness of the Island as a Loyalist refuge if under proper British protection, adding that few would risk their property and labour in a remote jurisdiction likely to be deprived of its own government. Moreover, it argued, prospective settlers judged a new country by the extent of public commitment to it. Patterson was walking a tightrope in these submissions, for he needed to appeal for British support without leading the government merely to abandon the Island to an existing jurisdiction such as Nova Scotia.

On 4 March 1776, the Lords of Commerce of the Council for Plantation Affairs discussed the Island's situation, deciding to use existing quitrents for public roads for ten years, while abating the increase in quitrents specified in the original grants for those who paid their present levys by 1 August 1776. Thereafter, the council added, "Levys may be made on Defaulters for Arrears by publick sale agreeable to a Law on the Island."[17] This statement, minuted by the Treasury, would serve as the ostensible basis for the land sales of 1781 on the Island. For the moment, the petitioning proprietors opposed the transfer of the fund to road building, apparently out of concern that salary arrearages would not be paid. Patterson met personally with Board of Trade officials over the matter, and on 7 August the government agreed to apply all quitrent arrears and payments to 1 May 1779 to back salaries, any surplus going to roads, and requested the Board of Trade to prepare an estimate for a parliamentary grant for one year; Patterson had already submitted such an estimate in March 1776. The receiver-general of Quitrents was instructed "immediately to take all proper Steps for recovery, and enforcing payment of the Quit Rents and all arrears thereof."[18] The Board of Trade's estimate for one year's establishment was ready in December 1776 to be laid before the Commons in January 1777, where it was accepted. The colony had made the Civil List, however precariously. Patterson could congratulate himself on some success, although he perhaps overestimated the government's sense of urgency about collecting the back quitrents.

As for the military situation, Lord George Germain, who had replaced Lord Dartmouth as the British minister in charge of the war effort, first acknowledged the Charlottetown raid in a dispatch of 1 April 1776. He observed that the Newfoundland fleet had been augmented and would protect the Island, but insisted that in the main the inhabitants must rely on their own devices against what would be "sudden insults" rather than full-scale invasion. He reiterated that the Island had a separate government only because the Crown had been assured that there would be no financial demands made upon it, adding that the proprietors had been "greatly deceived in their Expectations, and I see nothing between a revocation of the whole system, or a temporary grant of Parliament to support the Civil Officers."[20]

From New York, Lord Howe had responded more positively to the military danger. He agreed to send arms and ordinance to the Island, and agreed to the suggestion that Callbeck raise his own company of volunteers locally, to be paid for at the full rate for king's troops. Because the Island was not within his command, he could not offer financial assistance but he was certain Callbeck would be reimbursed by the government.[21] In a letter to Germain in May 1776, Callbeck pressed again, on the grounds that there were disaffected French on the Island, a full 250 "half breed Savages" ready to collaborate with the Americans. The acting governor was beside himself when he received a further communication from Howe noting that a sloop had been sent from Quebec with a frigate to follow for temporary protection of the Island. Howe was removing the cannon he had sent since it only posed "a Temptation to the Rebells to disturb the peace of the Island." Given the naval support, he concluded, Callbeck's company of soldiers would be unnecessary.[23]

Phillips Callbeck did not give up easily. He encouraged the council and assembly to memorialize Howe "at this calamitous period of Rebellion & War" with the insistence that the Island could not even repel a force of a few Indian canoes or whaleboats, and to request that Callbeck complete recruiting of his volunteer company.[24] All rumours of American activity were assiduously collected and forwarded to Whitehall.[25] Germain responded to this flurry of activity by ordering Howe either to send a detachment of 100 men or to authorize a local company.[26] Even before receiving this dispatch Callbeck had acted, continuing to recruit his company, building fortifications, and erecting barracks for the anticipated troops. He emphasized that no commander was willing to assume primary responsibility for the Island, maintaining that four to six companies of infantry and some artillery men were necessary for its defence.[27] Eventually Sir Henry Clinton ordered companies of provincials from New York to the Island; they arrived in July 1778.[28] Late in 1779, those companies were inadvertently augmented when a troop transport ship carrying 200 Hessian soldiers from New York to Quebec put in at Charlottetown and was declared unseaworthy. The Hessians were ordered by the ship's captain to be quartered on the Island, ultimately remaining there until spring 1780.[29]

Improvising and learning as he went along, Callbeck quickly grasped the essential points of the situation. The British authorities were not and could not be properly co-ordinated, and a rejection from one quarter meant nothing. In this time of emergency, local officials could act with relative impunity, secure in the knowleqge that government in Britain would ultimately support them and honour their expenditures. The secret was to act first and seek reimbursement later. This insight worked wonderfully well for Callbeck and the Island during the period of hostilities, although it undoubtedly left the acting governor and his colleagues with a false impression of the ease with which the British authorities could be manipulated.

Callbeck had first proposed that he raise an independent company of 100 volunteers to Lord Howe in January 1776, while he was still in Halifax.[30] By June of that year he had raised twenty men, despite Howe's ultimate disapproval, and he continued recruiting on the strength of the support he had received from the assembly and council.[35] The assembly that met in July 1776 passed a lengthy statute providing for the construction of roads, but an act organizing an Island militia had to wait until 1780; Callbeck wanted no local competition for his volunteer contingent. From the outset he had emphasized that he could not personally afford to support the company, pointing out that officers on the Island had not been paid in recent years.[32] By 1 July 1777, Callbeck reported to Germain that he had enlisted, clothed, and armed sixty to seventy able men, and he was claiming over eighty in September of that year. He drew continually upon the British Treasury to pay and victual these troops. One estimate of provisions to supply them for twelve months included 22,000 pounds of pork, 40,000 of bread or flour, 1,800 gallons of pease, 1,800 pounds of butter, and 344 gallons of rice. With pork at 6d. per pound on the Island, fresh butter at 1s 3d. per pound, and a 31/2 pound loaf of bread at 1s. 3d. per pound, the bill was considerable. The estimated annual expense of supporting the company at full complement – including salaries – was £3,555.3.10.[33] Despite the expenditures, the acting governor had trouble in maintaining his force, and at one point sent a recruiter to Newfoundland to fill his ranks.[34] Nevertheless, the company was seldom at full strength. On 10 December 1779, an official return showed it consisted of four officers, two sergeants, two corporals, one drummer, one fife, and thirty-eight privates.[35] Callbeck never billed the government for less than a full complement, however.

The acting governor did not merely draw Treasury bills for support of his volunteers, but also for the construction of fortifications and for barracks to house the troops. The barracks were begun in summer 1777, in anticipation of future manpower augmentation, and were never satisfactorily completed.[36] Callbeck himself was the principal supplier of building material, having accumulated most of the lumbering operations in the colony into his hands. He had taken over supervision of the Clark settlement, giving him access to a sawmill, and his employees cut timber off Island lots with virtual impunity. Who would prevent them? Benjamin Chappell appears to have supervised much of the timbering operation.[37] According to Chief Justice Stewart, the acting governor even timbered off land ostensibly under agency. Callback had made an arrangement with David Lawson to cut spruce and pine on James Montgomery's lots for shipment overseas, but when the ship failed to arrive, he threatened to prosecute Lawson for non-delivery unless allowed to timber at will. Much of the wood cut for Callbeck in these years doubtless ended up in Charlottetown in the colonial fortifications and barracks.[38]

In Whitehall, Lord George Germain had hoped that taking the

Island's officers off "the precarious Fund of the Quit Rents" through the transfer to the "generous" protection of Parliament would satisfy the leaders of the tiny colony.[39] To his dismay, demands for further expenditures – and a continual flow of bills drawn upon the Treasury – came from the Island of St John. The provincial troops from New York required supplies, estimated in early 1780 at 200 blankets. 200 rugs, Osnaburg linen for 400 pair of sheets (one to use, one for change "when foul") at ten yards per head, 2,000 weight of candles, 40 pots, 40 hatchets, ticking for 200 beds and bolsters for the beds at ten yards each. The annual expense here was calculated in July 1780 at £11,009.8.9.[40] Germain had long since ceased attempting to refuse the requests, and was reduced to pleading with the acting governor not to build anything unnecessary.[41] In May 1779, Germain wrote Callbeck noting that the Treasury Lords had questioned his bills for construction and troop maintenance. While these bills were being paid, there would be no more funds.[42] This advice got Germain nowhere.

A year later Germain was still calling Callbeck's attention to his insistence that all further expenditures would have to be paid by the American commander-in-chief. Even without this directive, Germain continued, "you must have been sensible" that accounts had to be furnished for bills drawn on the Treasury. He observed that no proper returns for Callbeck's company had been received since it was raised, and there was some reason to doubt that his numbers were accurate. The secretary of state requested vouchers and accounts, particularly since Walter Patterson was returning to resume his governorship. "Notwithstanding the want of regularity," Germain concluded, he was certain that Callbeck had been a faithful servant. But, he made abundantly clear, he was relieved that Patterson would soon be back in control.[43] It would not be long before the government in Britain would regret even this pleasure. When he had received all the bills, Germain could only expostulate that he had intended a detachment of no more than 100 men commanded by a captain and could not conceive "by what accident the garrison has been composed of six companies."[44] General Henry Clinton, who had sent the companies, resolutely denied any responsibility for their support.[45]

However the substantial garrison had come into being, its presence had a major economic impact upon the Island. Provisioning the troops, who were nearly as numerous as the inhabitants, was beyond the capacity of Island agriculture. When a transport brig loaded with provisions was captured by rebel privateers in early November 1779, there were serious doubts whether all the soldiers could be fed over the winter.[46] The result of the shortages of food and goods was inflation and by January 1780, molasses was selling at 7s. per gallon and potatoes at 4–6s. per bushel. The council debated price controls but was unable to agree upon a policy. It finally recommended that the assembly pass legislation regulating prices, especially of liquor at public houses, but the action was doubtless ineffective.[47] Removal of the Hessians to Quebec in the spring of 1780 may have eased the provisioning situation to some extent.[48]

As for Governor Patterson, he had managed to employ the difficulties of transatlantic travel during wartime to stretch a twelve-month leave into one of nearly five years, despite several orders to return to his post and the efforts of Callbeck to claim half the salary of the office.[49] When Patterson finally did appear at Deptford in 1779 to take passage to North America aboard the transport ship *Aeolus*, he attempted to bribe the owner and master of the vessel to assist him to "fill up the ship with what goods he thought proper." Moreover, Patterson insisted the *Aeolus* had been ordered by Lord George Germain "particularly for his use," and, unhappy with his accommodation arrangements, brought his own carpenters on board "to build up cabins between the guns."[50] Self-importance had obviously infected Walter Patterson. When the governor managed to return via Georgia to his Island in June 1780, he found conditions considerably different than upon his departure. The senior colleagues with whom he now had to work were a different breed of men. Callbeck had been replaced as acting governor late in 1779 by Thomas Desbrisay, who had finally decided to take up his residence upon the Island; there was a new chief justice in the person of Peter Stewart; and the principal military officer on the Island (in power if not in title) was Major Timothy Hierlihy. None of these men would take a back seat to Patterson when it came to self-importance.

Like Patterson, Desbrisay was an Irish-born military officer who had a curiously inflated notion of his own competence. He also had an incredible ability to say and do the wrong thing.[51] Severely reprimanded for his immigration recruiting in Ireland in 1773, Desbrisay since his arrival had constantly complained that he had not received most of the back salary due him as secretary of the colony. Simultaneously he refused to serve under Patterson because the governor had failed to support his demand for command of the volunteer company organized by Callbeck.[52] The two Irishmen had jousted for years separated by an ocean, and now they were together. In one of his first letters home after his return to the Island, Patterson apologized for mentioning "so worthless a Character" as Desbrisay, adding "the safest, and best way, with regard to Mr. Desbrisay is to take it as a general maxim, that, he never writes or speaks truth if he has the smallest motive for doing otherwise. And as his first object is to remove me from the Government, he will pay very little regard to what he says if he imagines it tends in the least to that purpose."[53] Co-operation between Patterson and his second-in-command would be strained, at best.

Timothy Hierlihy was yet another Irishman, who had served in North America from 1755, rising to major of brigade in 1759 under Lord Amherst at Ticonderoga and Crown Point, then serving at Havannah in 1762. A year later he retired to Connecticut at half pay, where he ultimately refused to take up arms on behalf of the rebels. Leaving behind a wife and nine children, he fled behind British lines at New York. Subsequently raising 125 recruits at his own expense for one Loyalist battalion, he then recruited the independent companies that were ordered by Sir Henry Clinton to the Island in 1778.[54] Hierlihy sought compensation for lands he claimed to have lost in New York and Connecticut, and quickly fixed his eye on the half of lot 24 that had been (in 1767) granted to General Charles Lee, one of George Washington's officers.[55] Not yet a proprietor, Major Hierlihy soon hoped to become one.

Unlike Hierlihy and Desbrisay, Peter Stewart was Scottish-born. A former law clerk, he was appointed as chief justice thanks to the influence of Scotland's Lord Advocate James Montgomery and kinsmen who were proprietors.[56] Having lost all his possessions in shipwreck at the time of his arrival on the Island, Stewart was further aggrieved that the house promised him as chief justice had been successively occupied "as a Church, a Prison, Barracks for Soldiers, an Assembly House, and a Court House alternately," and was in total disrepair.[57] Worse still, Walter Patterson had gotten his house improved at Crown expense but had refused to support Stewart's requests for similar treatment.[58] Not himself a proprietor, Stewart had rented land from James Montgomery on lot 34, and given "the passion the Lower sort of people ... have for emigrating," he had hoped to recruit subtenants. News of the American uprising postponed these plans, but by 1779 he had several farmers on his land and was writing Montgomery seeking to lease more.[59]

Although Desbrisay had been an original proprietor, his lots were heavily mortgaged by the time of his arrival to take up his duties. For all intents and purposes, he – like Stewart and Hierlihy – was not a landholder. And like Desbrisay (the father of twelve "motherless" children) and Hierlihy (the father of nine), Peter Stewart had a large family of nine offspring. Given the small community of the Island, it was hardly surprising that Desbrisays and Stewarts should begin quickly to intermarry; only the fact that Hierlihy's family was in Connecticut prevented their doing likewise. All three men were understandably land hungry, with large broods to get started in the world, and not favourably disposed to Walter Patterson.

Despite the potential personality conflicts that he faced with men whose egos were fully as inflated as his own, Walter Patterson was initially pleased at what he found upon his return to the Island. He reported to Lord Germain that the population had doubled in the five years he had been away and the people had large stocks of cattle and full tables. Callbeck, he insisted, had done his work well. As for himself, Patterson continued, "I am now, my Lord, at the Summit of my Wishes."[60] At first glance Patterson's statement about the size of the population does not accord with an estimate by Peter Stewart at about the same time that the Island's population had been halved by the war. But the two seemingly contradictory estimates are probably quite reconcilable.[61] The governor's observation was written within a week of his arrival on the Island and before he had much opportunity to travel outside the immediate environs of Charlottetown. The presence of the independent companies, the Hessians – even Callbeck's own volunteer corps – nearly 800 men in all – plus possible visitors in the form of sailors and mariners from vessels putting into the harbour to supply these forces, must have given the tiny capital the temporary appearance of tremendous vitality and bustle. Peter Stewart commented that the Hessians were "full of Money," and the soldiers filled the streets, the shops, and, of course, the grog houses that sprang up to serve them. At the same time, the population in the outlying communities undoubtedly decline during the wartime period, drifting in part off the Island and in part into Charlottetown, where money – the support of the military establishment there was costing in excess of £14,000 per annum – was readily available. If Stewart were thinking of a population of permanent settlers spread over the entire Island, his assessment was reasonably accurate. Were Patterson thinking of a Charlottetown thronged with temporary arrivals, his estimate was equally correct.

While the military garrison undoubtedly deterred further privateering excusions on Charlottetown itself, privateers continued active in the waters off the Island and occasionally made forays against the more isolated communities. The utility of soldiers as a deterrent was clearly limited. But the soldiers did provide other services to the Island, including a much-needed injection of a circulating supply of money. Some attempt was made to quarter a few soldiers in the settlements, both for protection and because of the shortage of accommodation in Charlottetown, and they apparently did assist the local population at peak times of labour need. Nelly MacDonald reported to her brother late in 1779 that the year's crop had been a good one, and that the soldiers had been enormously helpful with the harvest.[62] As a woman, Nelly may have been a particular object of chivalrous assistance, and she was at the time being courted by one of the officers from the independent companies.[63] Her experience may not have been typical. But troops were stationed at Tracadie and St Peters, and besides labour for Island farmers, they were employed on road construction, much needed on the Island in the early years.[64] Finally, the men of the garrison were a potential source of new settlers for the colony. If they were impressed with the possibilities of the Island, if they were offered good land under suitable conditions, and especially if they were locally disbanded, some of the garrison might remain as permanent residents.

For most of the duration of active hostilities, little attempt was made to maintain much continuity of civil administration on the Island. To some extent, problems of personnel and leadership made effective operation difficult. The acting governor devoted much of his time to military matters, the governor's council was seldom quorate, and the dislocations of wartime made it difficult to replace those absent; many had semi-legitimate reasons for not being on the Island or being unable to attend to business. Little was done about the quitrents and the growing arrearages. The addition of the Island to the British Civil List in 1777 removed some of the immediate urgency for action on the quitrents, although collecting back salaries was another matter. Phillips Callbeck concentrated on other sources of revenue. After meeting in 1776, the assembly was not reconvened for several years, and the council met mainly to deal with immediate problems. In March 1778, for example, the council was forced to grapple with the need to find someone to carry out a death sentence imposed upon a black woman convicted of murder. The sheriff had offered a £5 premium to anyone willing to do the job, but found no takers. He sought to evade the responsibility himself, but the council refused to delay until an executioner could be brought from the mainland in the spring, on the grounds that it was against "the polity and Civil Interest of Government." As a result, the sheriff resigned, and the sentence was never carried out.[65]

Thomas Desbrisay ordered a new assembly election in 1779, undoubtedly because of the rapid turnover of population, and called it to meet in early October of that year, mainly to pass enabling legislation extending the existing laws of the Island.[66] The assembly met again in March of 1780, before the return of Walter Patterson as governor. At this time, a number of legislative initiatives were taken, including the regulation of prices at public houses and severe limitations on animals running at large.[67] Perhaps the most important piece of legislation at this session, however, was an act for ascertaining the privileges of the members of the House and for establishing the methods of election. It provided for immunity from arrest for legislators and their servants during the time of assembly, for by-elections to replace absentee members, and made the House the sole judge of questions arising from contested elections.[68] While this statement of legislative privilege was fairly limited, it did mark a potential step along the constitutional road to an independent legislature. The Island had a long way to go, as the next decade would demonstrate. Desbrisay explained the act as necessary to keep the House in "good temper," but it was disallowed by the Crown in 1781.[69]

At the third session of this assembly, held in July of 1780, Desbrisay was more in evidence than the recently returned Walter Patterson. A Militia Act was finally adopted, as well as legislation permitting proprietors to divide lands held in common. The latter act was particularly interesting for its distinction between proprietors who "have never been in the Island, nor appointed Agents or Attorneys to manage their respective Affairs there" and proprietors "as do reside and live in the Island, or in their occasional Absence, have committed the management of their Affairs to Attorneys or Agents."[70] The act also editorialized that the absentees, especially those holding partial lots, had "delayed and impeded ... the Settlement and Improvement" of the Island. The legislation permitted resident proprietors seeking division of commonly held lots to apply to the governor and council, who were empowered to appoint an agent for the absentee in order to effect the division. While the proprietor seeking action was initially obliged to defray all expense, he could subsequently apply to the governor and council to be considered a creditor of the absentee for half the cost plus six per cent per annum in interest. After three years, the creditor could apply to the Supreme Court for a warrant to expose sufficient of the property to public sale – after thirty days' advertisement "in all the usual places" – to pay the expenses. This piece of legislation obviously worked to the disadvantage of absentee landlords, and was highly suggestive of the direction in which Island minds were already working. At issue was not quitrent payment, but expeditious settlement, and the difference between those on the spot and absentees was clearly marked. This act would be employed against the proprietors in a way probably not envisaged by those approving it.

The July 1780 assembly session also saw legislation to prevent the cutting of trees without the permission of the proprietor, noting "the great Waste committed of Pine and other valuable Timber Trees in this Island."[71] This act was passed only after the depredations that had taken place over much of the Island during the war years, and required prosecution within six months of the offence, again penalizing absentees not on top of their affairs. This assembly also attempted to change the name of the Island to "New Ireland," an alteration that would prove unacceptable to the Crown because of plans to create a Loyalist colony on the mainland with that name.[72]

The legislative enactments of 1780 were obviously looking forward to a conclusion of wartime hostilities, to the end of government largesse, and to a return to settlement and development. In anticipation of peace, those resident on the Island wanted the decks cleared and the absentees removed from a position of obstructionism. Had they stopped here, all might have proceeded smoothly. But the officers of the Island were almost without exception extremely land hungry, and the Island – despite its largely vacant state – had precious little land available upon which they could speculate and build. The obvious next step was to turn in a more systematic fashion to the townships being held by absentees.

CHAPTER FIVE

Grabbing for Land, 1780–1783

The period of the war with the American rebels had been a traumatic one for the Island of St John and its inhabitants. Any normal and orderly process of development had been arrested. The Island's absentee proprietors had lost touch with the infant colony, ceasing both their settlement efforts and their quitrent payments, apparently assuming that the normal rules governing their obligations would be suspended by the Crown for the duration of the war. This assumption was not without foundation, but it was not accepted by the Island's officialdom, still claiming large sums in back salaries for the years before 1777 and fully conscious of the legislation approved in 1776 that provided for the distraint and auction of lots upon which proprietors were delinquent. The result was the first attempt by the Island government to seize the private property of the absentee proprietors, thus setting into motion a complex political controversy that would keep both the Island and the British colonial authorities in a permanent uproar for over a decade.

Although Governor Walter Patterson had substantial local support for his campaign against delinquent proprietors, there was a growing faction of opposition within his government to his policies. Upon his return to the Island, Patterson had quickly come to terms with Phillips Callbeck, the two men apparently agreeing that in return for Callbeck dropping his claims to Patterson's salary while the governor was on leave, Patterson would not examine closely the financial operations of his replacement and would write glowingly of Callbeck's administration in dispatches home. Peter Stewart, Thomas Desbrisay and Peter Hierlihy were less easy to placate. Desbrisay was soon after his arrival in 1779 at odds with Callbeck. Even before Patterson's return, Desbrisay had coveted command of Callbeck's volunteer company. Patterson did attempt to arrange a compromise, suggesting that

Desbrisay, who had considerable military experience, surrender some of his civil emoluments to Callbeck, who had none, in return for the military appointment. Desbrisay refused, arguing that he was being asked to surrender too much in return for a post which Callbeck held mainly by default.[1] Any possibility of assuaging the feelings of his second in command was lost when Patterson returned from a brief visit to Halifax in November of 1780 to discover that Desbrisay, acting as governor in his absence, had shamelessly engineered through the council a wholesale distribution of Charlotte-town town and pasture lots. In this action he had been fully supported by Peter Stewart, Surveyor Thomas Wright, and garrison command-er Timothy Hierlihy – all men with families as large as that of Desbrisay himself.

Granting the lots to men attached to the garrison and to members of their own families ("Soldiers, Sailors, and others as Faggotts, purely for purpose of evasion," stormed Patterson), and then buying them up at bargain prices, Desbrisay had acquired 58 town and pasture lots, while Stewart obtained 41, Hierlihy 22, and Wright 7. Patterson observed to Lord George Germain that he had granted a mere 15 lots between 1769 and 1775, Callbeck had allocated 50 from 1775 to 1779, while in a few days in 1780 Desbrisay had distributed 162.[2] The lieutenant-governor insisted that the property had been obtained for his motherless children, pathetically expostulating to Germain "for Gods Sake what business is it of Mr. Patterson's if I procure honestly other people's Grants of Land to make a Livelihood for my dear Children."[3] But although he managed to rake up some earlier evidence of dubious behaviour by Patterson, Desbrisay had been caught sufficiently red-handed as to be reduced to affixing to his signature in frantically defensive letters to Germain constantly larger masonic emblems.[4] Desbrisay's charge that Patterson had misappro-priated the parliamentary grant of 1771 would subsequently become a major rallying cry of the anti-Patterson forces, but the resort to masonry appears to have had little effect.

Major Hierlihy also argued that his lots had been acquired for his large family, insisting that if their title was not good "there is no security for any property on the Island," an assertion that in other contexts perhaps came closer to the truth than its author realized.[5] Stewart's explanation has not survived. In any event, a livid Patterson demanded that the culprits return all their ill-gotten land, including that taken in the name of their children, thus cementing the enmity of Desbrisay and adding that of Stewart and Hierlihy in the process. The parties agreed to leave the final decision as to how the lots should be restored to Lord George Germain and the Board of Trade.[6]

Although the governor's response was hardly unreasonable, it would stand up only if his hands continued to be clean, and it returned to haunt him when he subsequently organized a much larger and even more audacious land grab for himself only a few months later.

To the point of the Charlottetown land transactions, Walter Patterson had behaved well under trying circumstances. Whatever dubious steps he was willing to take over land had been executed off Island, in adjacent Nova Scotia. Most of his activity since returning had involved attempts to maintain the substantial military presence Callbeck had so painstakingly built up on the Island. But within days of the council meeting at which Patterson had confronted Desbrisay and his cohorts, another well-attended session agreed unanimously to implement the hitherto forgotten Treasury minute of 1776 ordering the Island's receiver-general to enforce payment of the quitrents of delinquent proprietors.[7] The minute had been issued, of course, back in the days when the British government had anticipated a speedy victory over the pesky Americans and it had never been formally rescinded or postponed. The Island was too peripheral and the Treasury too busy to pay attention to such minor matters.

According to the council decision, the lots in arrears on the Island were to be sold in June 1781. In preparation for the auction, advertisements were to be placed three times in the *London Gazette* warning the proprietors of the consequences of non-payment, which would be distraint and sale of their property. How the council – given the communications of the day – expected to follow such a tight timetable (allowing only six months for a series of complicated transatlantic transactions) is not clear, particularly since the governor claimed to have obtained permission from Lord Germain in 1778 to collect quitrents only on the Island, where the local administration could monitor the transactions. In any event, the advertisements were never published because they reached the colony agent in London too late to be effective. Need for urgency of action on the arrearages, moreover, had ostensibly been lessened by the parliamentary action of 1777 placing the Island's officers on the Civil List, and the Treasury would doubtless have maintained such action superseded their minute of 1776. Most officers were heavily in debt and pressing for back salaries thar could be recovered only out of the quitrent revenue. Moreover, no one on the Island or in America knew yet what the outcome of the war would be, and the entrance of France into the conflict, especially the French naval presence in the North Atlantic, raised all sorts of spectres.

Why Patterson either acquiesced or took the lead in moving so precipitously is as unclear as the thinking behind the proposed timetable. Both he and his council ought to have realized that their actions were threatening one of the major watchwords of eighteenth-century Britain: the sacred right of property. Any hasty actions were bound to be met with proprietorial protests to a sympathetic ministry. It does seem impossible to regard Patterson as merely an innocent agent, since in September 1780, only two months before the council action, he had appointed his brother-in-law William Nisbett as receiver-general of quitrents and his personal secretary James MacNutt as deputy. Neither appointment had yet been confirmed by the British authorities, and Patterson later became frantic about the slowness of confirmation.[8]

One possible explanation for the dangerously sudden actions is that Islanders had become so inward looking that they failed to appreciate the hazardous course on which they were embarking, although Patterson had only recently returned from London and ought to have known better. But in London he had failed to create any great groundswell of proprietorial support for paying back quitrents. Proprietorial lack of interest could have been interpreted as meaning they did not care about their Island property, although subsequent events would belie such an interpretation. A less charitable but more credible explanation for the actions begun in November 1780 is that both Patterson and the council felt they had a legitimate grievance that would be thwarted if possible, and the very isolation of the Island during wartime would permit the completion of the necessary steps as an irreversible fait accompli before anyone in Britain could learn what had happened or move to arrest matters. Phillips Callbeck, who served as chief political adviser to Governor Patterson in these years, had demonstrated what could be accomplished by acting first and seeking authorization later. Acting to defend the colony, of course, was in a somewhat different category than unilaterally altering its land arrangements, although both were done in equal defiance of official British wishes.

Were Patterson and his colleagues to get away with their actions, two necessary conditions had to be met. In the first place, all the legal niceties would require observance. If the distraint were to be based upon the legislation approved by the Crown in 1776, it would not do to cut any corners, for illegal or improper procedures would raise the possibility that actions would be overturned on technical grounds by the British authorities. Unfortunately, little that was done on the Island followed the legislation to the letter, and the sales of land themselves were shrouded in mystery and inconsistency. In the second place, the Island's officials needed to remain unanimous in their support of the actions taken. Patterson could ill afford to have officers insisting that they were dubious about the policy, and offering information to London and the proprietors contrary to the official explanations he would eventually proffer. With unassailable legality and a common political front, the governor might well have weathered the subsequent storm of criticism. Instead, he gradually came under attack from all sides and was eventually reduced to open disobedience to the Crown.

Whatever the advisability of the council's decision of November 1780 to sell lots after placing advertisements in the *London Gazette*, such proceedings were spelled out in the province's quitrent legislation. In February 1781, however, the council decided to ignore the formalities of the distraint process by moving directly against the "land only."[9] The quitrent legislation called for the seizure of all property on the land and its sale, proceeds to be applied to the delinquent accounts, before distraint actually took place. Such a procedure assumed that property on the land belonged to the proprietor, ignoring the possibility of tenantry. In most cases there was little property on the lots in question, although in several cases, including lot 35, which would become a major bone of contention, settlers were grazing livestock. A number of Captain John MacDonald's lot 36 tenants, practising transhumanist traditions brought from the Highlands, summered their livestock on adjacent lot 35. Subsequent testimony indicated that the government had good reason for not attempting to seize such assets, although some critics did properly note that the legislation was quite clear in this regard.[10]

Observing the precise terms of the legislation, obviously not well drafted, would have been distinctly unpopular, affecting ordinary settlers who had little stake in the larger issues, however technically improper their use of the land was. Attempts to collect an unpopular "bear tax" had met with considerable resistance in the countryside, forcing the presence of soldiers from the garrison to accompany the collecting officer. The governor and council did issue a proclamation in March 1781 forbidding Island residents to use the distrained lots, which it was later charged caused over 100 inhabitants to depart the Island.[11] The rumour of the possibility of the seizure of livestock, which settlers allowed to graze virtually at will over undeveloped land, spread like wildfire across the Island. Many inhabitants talked about abandoning their lands for Nova Scotia.[12] One can thus sympathize with this first contravention of the precise terms of the quitrent legislation that was accepted by Chief Justice Peter Stewart.[13] But Stewart properly ought not to have permitted writs to be issued until the law was observed. The problems involved in observing the details of the act ought to have suggested to someone to go more slowly, but they did not have such an effect.

Having formally distrained much of the land on the Island for non-payment of quitrents in March 1781, the government then paused. Patterson later claimed that the delay was an act of generosity, giving delinquents more time to pay their arrearages. But proprietors did not know their property was in danger, and they would have to make their payments on the Island. At least one proprietor, Captain John MacDonald, at the time serving with the 84th Regiment in Halifax, did make some efforts through his sisters to raise money for the quitrents from his tenants on lot 36. MacDonald wrote to his sisters from Halifax in June of 1781 that he had received a letter from the receiver-general of quitrents declaring the entire amount of arrearages payable in Charlottetown "in hard cash" within six months from 13 March 1781, or his land would be sold. According to private information, he added, "there are people of the first Interest in the Nation whose Lots will also be sold," and no partiality was being shown. MacDonald felt his tenants owed him some assistance, but admitted that they represented their emigration "in a very unfavourable and different light from that which any Knowing us ... should readily believe," adding he was not prepared to throw himself "entirely at the Mercy & Justice of the people fond as I am of them."[14]

If Captain MacDonald's testimony was accurate, the receiver-general of quitrents had set September of 1781 as the deadline for the payment of arrearages. Nevertheless, it would be several more months before the distrained lots were actually put up for auction. A substantial body of evidence dealing with the 1781 sales is available. The Board of Trade collected affadavits late in 1784 in response to the complaint of the proprietors, and a number of local witnesses were examined at length by the House of Assembly in 1786, their testimony recorded verbatim in the minutes of the House. While there are considerable discrepancies in detail, and some key questions that were neither asked nor answered, it is possible to piece together a reasonably satisfactory account of the proceedings.

The first problem the government faced was finding someone to conduct the sales. The provost marshal, who was charged with responsibility by the legislation, was not in residence on the Island, and the individual appointed as his deputy resigned in November 1781. Eventually James Curtis of Stanhope, a strong supporter of the governor, was pressed into service as "Deputy Provost Marshall of the resold lots."[15] A number of witnesses, including Curtis himself under close examination in 1786 testified that the sales were postponed a number of times in October and November before finally taking place at the tavern/house of John Clark on the 13th and 14th of that latter month. Although initial notices of the sales may have been widely disseminated on the Island, the eventual proceedings were advertised only by handwritten bills put up in Charlottetown itself, and one prominent farmer complained loudly in 1786 that he had come to town for the auction on the announced date of 12 November only to miss the actual sale the following day, being told by those present at Clark's tavern that the sale then in progress was one of dry goods.

Only one Island resident seriously claimed to have been prevented from participation, however. Most men who had not been present or who did not bid admitted that they were not interested in making a purchase. Whether – as several later argued – this reluctance was motivated by a suspicion of the propriety of the sales or by a local awareness that the unimproved land on the Island was "no bargain" in 1781 is an unanswerable question. Certainly the governor did try to involve the residents in the proceedings. He offered to accept back pay vouchers in the Volunteer Company as payment for any lots purchased, and he recommended to Captain John MacDonald's tenants that they "make up a purse" among themselves to buy land, presumably either lot 36 where they had their homes or lot 35 where they grazed their cattle.[17] With the one exception, those who later maintained that everyone on the Island was present "who was inclined to and could in point of abilities be a purchaser" were quite accurate.[18] Not surprisingly, the eligible participants were a small crew of the Island's officials, who made up virtually "the whole of the respectable part of the Gentlemen of Station & fortune belonging to the Island."[19] Walter Patterson pointedly did not attend the sales, although his personal secretary James MacNutt was present and an active bidder.

James Curtis brought to Clark's tavern Supreme Court writs of *sciere facias* for twenty-nine full townships and fourteen partial ones, although only seven full townships (24, 31, 32, 33, 35, 49, and 57) and six half ones (17, 18, 25, 26, 48, and 65) were actually sold the first day. The evidence of Patterson and Curtis is at variance on the question of whether all the distrained lots were actually offered for sale. Curtis testified in 1784 that they were, while Patterson wrote to colony agent John Stuart that the lots to be sold were drawn at random on the day of the sale.[20] At the same time, the governor insisted frequently in the years to come that not one lot was sold "in which one Shilling had been expended by way of Settlement, or upon which there had been one settler placed," arguing on at least one occasion that he had intervened to prevent the sale of any lots that had been improved or were likely to be so.[21] Patterson's claim that the lots actually auctioned were totally unimproved by their owner was valid, as the detailed evidence before the House of Assembly in 1786 demonstrated. What improvement and settlement had occurred was without the approval or instigation of the proprietor. At the same time, several of the lots sold in 1781 belonged to proprietors who had been active – especially James Montgomery and Robert Clark – on other of their extensive holdings. Patterson's testimony is more suspect than that of Curtis, since he had far more at stake in explaining his behaviour. What probably transpired was that Curtis did offer all the lots, while the rationale that improved lots should not be sold combined with local knowledge to select certain properties for bidding. Since James MacNutt did most of the bidding – on behalf of the governor – Patterson (despite his absence) did have considerable say in which lots were actually sold.

Whatever the procedures, bidding was not exactly brisk. Chief Justice Peter Stewart successfully acquired half of lot 18, always maintaining that he had done so in partial repayment of a debt owed him by its original proprietor.[22] Thomas Desbrisay purchased lot 33. Stewart and Phillips Callbeck had wrangled in advance over lot 35, but were unable to reach an understanding, and bid spiritedly against one another until Callbeck emerged triumphant. This lot was the only one on which any competitive bidding occurred. All other lots bid upon were knocked down without competition to James MacNutt, who bought three full and four half townships on behalf of Walter Patterson, and another 70,000 acres in the names of friends and associates of the governor.[23] The bidding had been so restrained that Patterson ordered some of the bids reopened on the following day, later claiming that higher prices were thus obtained, although other observers insisted that none had competed against the governor even in the new round.[24] No actual cash changed hands in the course of these sales. All the successful bidders – indeed, all the bidders – were government officials who applied vouchers for claimed salary arrearages against their purchases.

Patterson would subsequently defend the manner of payment by maintaining that a rumour was circulating that the Island would be ceded to France, leading the officers to wish to get their salary arrears settled somehow before the transfer. He further argued that all the purchasers "would much rather have had the money than the land," which was "thought to be of no value at all" at the time of the auction. The prices were quite legitimate given the situation, he claimed.[25] To colony agent John Stuart, the governor later denied the principle that an officer of government was ineligible to purchase land at public sale. If the officers were precluded from "acquiring a little land," he claimed, "it would shut up the Only Channel they can have, of making some Provision for their Families."[26] Those earlier involved in the Charlottetown lot business would clearly have applauded these sentiments, but might understandably have been surprised that Patterson held them.

Having completed the initial round of sales of distrained lots, the council met on 1 December 1781 and agreed to postpone further sales until the following November, in order to give notice to the proprietors. Why this postponement was decided upon is unclear, but if it were on Patterson's initiative (as seems likely), it was a dreadful mistake. While it did substantiate an interpretation of the sales as essentially designed to pressure the delinquent proprietors to pay up their quitrent arrearages, it also suggested that there had been something precipitous about the sales already completed. Moreover, this action (accepted by the council without demur) left several officials of the government – especially Peter Stewart and Thomas Desbrisay – dissatisfied with their acquisitions, while it did not really remove the likelihood of protest in Britain by those proprietors whose lots had already been sold. If Patterson equated delinquency with lack of proprietorial interest in preserving their properties, he was sadly mistaken. To his local critics, it appeared that Patterson, while preventing others from acquiring land and obtaining what he wanted, continued to seek to block others from their fair share. All of the governor's subsequent defences were vitiated by two indisputable facts. The first was that he had been the principal beneficiary of the 1781 sales. The second, perhaps still more damning, was that he did not bother to inform the British government of any of his proceedings until after the proprietors had registered their protests in London.

If any on the Island had hoped to keep news of land sales from reaching London in time for protest, there was to be disappointment. Captain John MacDonald, mistakenly convinced that he had lost both his own lot 36 and his coveted lot 35 in the auction, departed from New York for England at the close of 1781 "to get these matters if possible, restored to their former footing." To his sister he explained that given the British disaster at Yorktown, he recognized that "the Ministry would foolishly give up America" and concluded that "our Property on St. John's was the best thing for us to hold by."[27] It would take some time for MacDonald to rally the proprietors, obtain authentic information on the proceedings on the Island, and find a ministry stable enough to petition for redress. The official silence from London may have misled those on the Island. In any event, the political situation on St John became increasingly complex. Governor Patterson pressed ahead as though there would be no protests over the land sales, and over the next few years he would both complicate the land situation and bring into existence an organized faction unalterably opposed to his administration.

In his regular report to the colonial secretary after the land sales, Patterson studiously ignored the entire matter. Instead he noted proudly that he had constructed a special boat to be manned by "Frenchmen" that would attempt "at our expence" to maintain connections with the outside world over the winter months. The bulk of his letter was concerned with the problems of keeping a provost marshal – the official responsible for land sales – in office. According to the governor, the military garrison led to much lawlessness in Charlottetown. "There is no having an Animal fit to hold, nor a Garden near the Town," he claimed. When, in November 1781, a soldier was found guilty of breaking into Surveyor Wright's office, none could be found to carry out the sentence of execution for fear of reprisals from the military. The acting provost marshal resigned on the morning fixed for the execution, and when Patterson even accompanied his replacement, James Curtis, to the site to assist him in carrying out his duty, Curtis had resigned as well. Patterson finally had to pardon the culprit, he reported, although he had confessed while in gaol and incriminated others.[28] This discussion of the problems of the provost marshal's office may help explain the delays in holding the land auctions, although the sales may have also contributed to the turnover of officials.

As for the council, its concerns in the months after the land sales were with the question of renaming the Island, and in retroactively dividing some of the townships sold as half lots during the auction. The last session of the House of Assembly in 1780 had agreed to petition the Crown for a change of name of the colony from St John's to New Ireland. Given the fact that few of the existing settlers were Irish – most being either Acadian French or Highland Scots – the name is at first glance a bit surprising. But in fairness to the legislators, Nova Scotia had already appropriated the name "New Scotland," and the present name of the colony did lead to continual confusion with other places called St John in the Gulf of St Lawrence region. "New Ireland" doubtless reflected the origins of the Island's leading officials rather than its settlers. But the government was informed late in 1781 by the British authorities that New Ireland was already taken, although further petitions for a change of name would be entertained.[29]

The legislature in 1780 had also passed a law permitting the division of townships held by more than one proprietor and providing a mechanism for so doing despite the absence of the owners.[30] The Crown had accepted the legislation, apparently not appreciating that the pressing need for such divisions would come mainly in the context of the distraint and sale of proprietorial holdings. The purchaser of a partial lot would need to know what land he had acquired if he were to improve the property. The first lots divided under the legislation were lots 17, 25, and 65, half of each having been purchased by the governor late in 1781. In accordance with the law, the surveyor was instructed to prepare large-scale maps and to indicate divisions, while Attorney-General Callbeck was appointed agent for the absentees. The divisions were drawn by ballot before a full council in February 1782.[31] No evidence of resistance to these actions within the council exists, suggesting that the opposition to Patterson had not yet fully crystallized. The divisions also indicated that Patterson was anxious to improve these lots, undoubtedly aware that settlement and development would make their acquisition more difficult to overturn.

Over the spring and summer of 1782, the Island continued to be relatively quiet and its political life uneventful. The council agreed with Patterson that there was no need to summon an assembly because of lack of specific business to transact, and it made routine appointments, divided the Island into militia districts (thus providing military commands for most of the councillors). and devoted much energy to seeking the court martial of a former officer of the garrison.[32] But this tranquillity was deceptive, the lull before the storm. Captain John MacDonald was in London organizing a protest against the land sales, and in a series of events on the Island over the autumn and winter of 1782/3, the Stewart family and its allies were further and permanently alienated from the governor. Over some of these developments, Governor Patterson had little control, but he bore full responsibility for his involvement with Sarah Stewart, the wife of the chief justice.

Like most newly settled communities, the Island of St John was lacking in eligible females, and the shortage was felt acutely by the colony's elite. The wife of David Higgins left him in 1781 for "the bed" of Walter Berry, an agent of Robert Clark and an incipient merchant, and the ensuing scandal had contributed to Higgin's demise from excessive drinking.[33] In autumn 1782, Chief Justice Stewart was incapacitated with rheumatism, and was flattered and grateful for the assiduous attention shown him by Governor Patterson, who provided him with medications and constant company.[34] Patterson was living as a bachelor at the time, his wife and family in

England. Whether he began spending so much time with Stewart because of the attractions of Mrs Stewart or whether he discovered Sarah in the course of his ministrations is not clear. Nor is it entirely clear what Patterson and Mrs Stewart had done, although the chief justice was certain his wife had been seduced by the governor. What is known is that Stewart confronted his wife with charges of misbehaviour, and that Patterson subsequently assisted Sarah and several of her children to leave her husband and the Island for Quebec. Even the governor's supporters were dismayed by the development. David Lawson, who reported Mrs Stewart's departure to the chief justice, was brought to exclaim that Patterson was "a damned Villain, for taking away another Man's wife, and his Bairns, without saying anything to him about it."[35] Stewart's family rallied round him, and his elder sons by a previous marriage joined the remainder of the Island in blaming Patterson for the marital breakdown. The governor would subsequently insist that Stewart's older boys had always disliked their stepmother and were pleased of an opportunity to vilify both her and her erstwhile protector.[36]

Into this highly charged atmosphere came a letter from the Lords of Trade condemning the Charlottetown land transactions of 1780, suggesting dismissal for Thomas Desbrisay and censure for the others involved, although allowing the culprits to keep those lots granted to family members. Patterson read portions of the letter to his council of 2 January 1783. Although everyone at the meeting was well aware that the governor was holding a full 170,000 acres purchased at the 1781 auctions, Patterson self-righteously insisted on the return of the lots, and pointedly entered the surrenders on the records of both Supreme Court and council as he had been directed.[37] Those involved might well wonder about the selectivity of Patterson's insistence on total compliance with British instructions.

Between January and April 1783, the council received the surrenders of Charlottetown lots from its councillors in dribbles and drabs. No simple business, the lots had passed out of the hands of council members in some cases, and in most instances the original grants were unavailable. Chief Justice Stewart felt particularly aggrieved, claiming that twelve of his lots had been procured for Walter Berry, at the time speaker of the assembly, for the erection of a sawmill. Stewart was forced to return lots granted to family members to make up his total.[38] Thomas Wright insisted he had no lots but those granted to his family and others bought over the years from legitimate grantees, and he was not pressed about them.[39] Timothy Hierlihy was now in Nova Scotia and not only failed to return his lots but put them on the open market in defiance of the governor.[40]

Noting the complications of the surrenders, Governor Patterson ultimately suggested to the Lords of Trade that both the grants and the registers of them should be destroyed, and the surrenders not entered in the court records, "so there shall appear no traces of there ever having been any such Grants given." Were this policy pursued, Patterson continued, new registry books would be required, and "all Grants, Deeds, and matter whatever from the Commencement of the Gov't shall be fairly copied from the old Books into the new, only leaving out the above Grants, after which, and having undergone a Strict Examination before the Council, the old Books are to be burned."[41] While such a program might deal with the Charlottetown confusion, it obviously offered numerous other opportunities for chicanery. It would not be Patterson's only attempt to rewrite the legal records of his administration.

While the Charlottetown land transactions were before the council on the Island, Captain John MacDonald was after bigger game before the Privy Council in London. Since neither the British government nor the proprietors had ever received formal information on the quitrent proceedings, it was literally necessary to establish that the sales had occurred before any remedial action could taken. Not until April 1783 was a semi-authentic list available of the lots actually auctioned, and it did not contain the names of purchasers.[42] MacDonald's initial protest had been on behalf of proprietors like himself who were off the Island serving in the military during the war, but the proprietors soon broadened his arguments, insisting that the American war had interrupted normal development, that they had not been properly notified, and that in any case the quitrents they failed to pay were excessive.[43] An act was drawn up by the Crown attorneys providing for new quitrent proceedings and the return of the auctioned lots. Lord North, the new secretary of state for the colonies, forwarded the bill to Patterson with instructions to place it before the Island's assembly and to "recommend in the strongest manner ... to them ... the passing of the same."[44] Under normal circumstances these instructions should have ended the matter.

Lord North's draft bill was quite reasonable, and acceptance of its provisions would have both assured a viable procedure sanctioned by Britain for future actions against delinquent proprietors, while allowing the 1781 purchasers to retain most of their land. The bill repealed earlier legislation, provided for future quitrent payments either in London or on the Island, and exempted proprietors who paid their full arrears to 1783 from further payments for six years. Since the proprietors were strongly opposed to paying any arrearages at original rates, this proposal was a considerable victory for the

Island. Moreover, the auctioned lots would be returned only if the former holder paid within one month of final acceptance of the legislation the 1781 purchase price to the new owner, as well as interest and compensation for all improvements.[45] Few proprietors whose lots had been sold were likely to comply with these conditions. Only lot 35, purchased by Phillips Callbeck, was likely to be removed from possession of the 1781 purchaser, since its potential value was widely accepted.

The proposed legislation was in no way punitive. At this point the proprietors assumed that all legal forms had been observed in 1781, and they were unaware that Walter Patterson was the principal purchaser. The local action, although mysteriously unreported to the British authorities by the governor, was treated as a legitimate conflict of interest between the Island and its landholders in which the latter had been treated unfairly but without malice or illegality. In Britain, the entire process of restoration seemed quite as straightforward as the surrender of the Charlottetown lots. Only Captain John MacDonald had his doubts. Despite Lord North's view that the sales were "very objectionable & that it was never intended they should be gone about at that time & manner," wrote MacDonald to his sister on the Island, he was curious

how the Gentlemen will receive this order of the Council & how they will Act in consequence of the Same, that is to say whether they will restore the Lots without any more Ado, or whether they will struggle by a remonstrance against restoring them at all, or endeavour to elude and disappoint any part of the order – In these latter cases a Contest would ensue in which I firmly believe they & the Government of the Island will undoubtedly be over Set.

He added his personal suspicion that the officers would "be so Obstinate, & short-sighted as to make all the Struggle they can."[46]

In such an event, Captain John predicted their strategy:

their first Step will be to send home a Remonstrance against restoring the Lots, affecting to show that the Council here has been misinformed, or has misconceived the Case; and therefore praying that the Council will alter the order: they will also probably vour to show an impossibility to comply with the order on the Score of Expences laid out on the Lots since the Sales or of houses built on them, or of part of the Lots being Sett, since that time to settlers.

MacDonald was not at all persuaded that the Privy Council's actions would end the matter, and he planned to remain in London until news was received from the Island. He enclosed to his sister a detailed list of questions about Island affairs that wanted answering, since "most cursed noise I will make if I am obliged to do it."

Captain John's suspicions that the Patterson administration would not willingly comply with the directions from the Privy Council were quite accurate. The governor acknowledged receipt of Lord North's dispatch in November of 1783, noting that he had stopped proceedings after one sale and that most of the distrained lots had not been sold for want of bidders. He spent most of the letter of acknowledgment complaining about the failure of the British authorities to confirm his appointments, maintaining this attitude "tends to make such a shadow of me, in the Eyes of the People."[47] Significantly, he did not promise swift compliance with the instructions. In letters to colony agent John Stuart, Patterson defended the sales, comparing the scrupulousness of the Island toward its proprietors with Nova Scotia's actions, where millions of acres had been summarily escheated on a few weeks' notice. It would be hard to get the legislation through the assembly, he added, for it would be ex post facto and a dangerous precedent. What the Island needed, the governor insisted, were laws requiring that proprietors be resident or at least maintain resident attorneys and distinguishing between active and inactive proprietors.[48]

At the same time, Patterson made no effort to convey to his council the instructions of Lord North or to consult them on policy. Instead, he led the Island into a new round of land granting, this time to the Loyalists and disbanded soldiers of the late war. The governor told none on the Island, with the possible exception of Phillips Callbeck, of the existence of North's instructions before calling an assembly election and attempting to meet the assembly early in 1784. As Captain John MacDonald had predicted, Patterson worked to make return of the auctioned lots as difficult as possible. He did so in the midst of growing political opposition to his administration, even without the added knowledge of his disregard of the royal will. When the opposition came to comprehend what he had done, it would reach crescendo proportions.

CHAPTER SIX

Welcoming the Loyalists, 1783–1784

While the principal source of settlers for the Island of St John before 1775 had been Great Britain, most new arrivals in the 1780s were refugees from the American civil war, which had finally concluded in 1783. Like other jurisdictions in the loyal colonies of British North America, the Island experienced an influx of Loyalist exiles and soldiers disbanded from provincial army units that had fought in the war. Because the numbers were small by comparison with the thousands arriving in Nova Scotia and Quebec – the names of approximately 550 refugees and soldiers appear in surviving records – the Island has never figured prominently in historical accounts of the Loyalist diaspora.[1] But although precise totals can never be calculated, when the dependents of the Loyalists are included, the new arrivals substantially increased the population of the Island and potentially represented a major factor in its early development. As was true everywhere in British North America, this movement of population occurred within a context of considerable local conflict.

In the case of the Island, the familiar confrontations between the newcomers and the established residents became inevitably intertwined with the complex politics of the land question. Moreover, several distinctive features of the Island's dealings with the Loyalist refugees, including the fact that many of the disbanded soldiers had links to the Island and the fact that most of the newcomers did not receive their land grants directly from the Crown, further muddied the situation. As is so often the case in dealing with the early history of the Island, unusual local conditions produced results not always easy to integrate into larger historical patterns. But as is also so often the case, the Island's isolation and small size have prevented its peculiarities, however complex, from becoming generally known even as exceptions to the general picture.

From almost the outset of open hostilities between Britain and her American colonies, some on the Island had expected to benefit from the dislocation of loyal Americans, who had begun exile even before the first shots of war were fired at Lexington and Concord. Walter Patterson and the proprietors had emphasized the advantages of the Island for Loyalist settlement as early as 1776, and these arguments were among the most persuasive the Island had at the time for the continued British support it enjoyed. Nevertheless, the proprietors did not follow up on these insights and were exceedingly slow to formulate a policy for Loyalist settlement, while failing utterly to co-ordinate their efforts with those of the government. Major questions of principle and practice were left unanswered. Walter Patterson attempted to turn the Loyalist influx to his own advantage, but he was able to do so because of the policy vacuum. Part of the problem was general lack of organization among the proprietors, but the failure was further complicated by the defensive position of the proprietors after 1781, as they sought to protect their property instead of improving it.[2]

While the British government attempted after 1781 to extricate itself from a lost cause by negotiating a peace treaty with the United States, Loyalists were drawn to New York, the major centre of British authority and military power on the eastern seaboard. The prospective exiles waited anxiously for word about the outcome of the peace negotiations and about British policy toward those who had supported the mother country. Agents fanned out across the remaining American empire, investigating land and political conditions. Not all eyes were turned north to the colonies of Quebec and Nova Scotia, but certainly many agents were active in the Gulf of St Lawrence region over the summer of 1782.[3] Walter Patterson and the government of the Island took no initiatives regarding these preliminary investigations. The isolation of the Island combined with its unsavoury reputation on the mainland meant that few initially showed any serious interest in settlement there. Perhaps equally important, Patterson was too remote from the centres of power to have any genuine feel for the direction of British policy, and he had in any case very little Crown land at his disposal.

The governor may have encouraged the one initiative that originated on the Island regarding the newcomers, a broadside dated 30 November 1782 "To the Loyal Refugees, who either have already left, or who hereafter may leave their Respective Countries in search of other Habitations."[4] This advertisement appeared under the names of the officers of the King's Rangers stationed on the Island, headed by Captain Samuel Hayden, who had been appointed to the council months earlier. It emphasized that the subscribers were New Jersey men who had found the Island congenial and much maligned. The soil was good, while fevers and agues were virtually unknown. Taxes were light and raised solely for the purposes of the inhabitants. The Island had room for thousands of settlers, said the broadside, concluding with the observation that its subscribers had been told "the worst things possible" about the Island, including tales of starving settlers. Such reports should be ignored, it insisted. Significantly, this advertisement did not offer specific terms to prospective settlers, but merely advised them not to overlook the Island. A similar invitation was issued about the same time from New York by Captain John MacDonald of the 84th Regiment, the proprietor of lot 36.[5]

By autumn 1782, Sir Guy Carleton in New York had arranged with a large body of Loyalists for emigration to Nova Scotia, where Governor John Parr had been warned to reserve as much land as possible for their settlement. On 22 September of that year, Carleton sketched out a policy for Loyalist relocation, emphasizing that land grants were to be "considered as well founded Claims of Justice rather than of mere Favor," to be made without fees or quitrents. Carleton expected that families would receive 600 acres and single men 300 acres, and promised tools from the New York stores. Nova Scotia would be required to make available additional assistance.[6] Two points are worth stressing here. One is that policy for the Loyalist relocation was being developed very much on an ad hoc basis. At this stage, Carleton had neither firm commitments from Nova Scotia nor the British government for specific terms. Second, his primary concern was to accommodate the Loyalist civilian refugees in New York, rather than the soldiers in the various provincial regiments recruited in America to fight the rebels. This oversight was pointed out to Carleton in a memorial from regimental officers early in 1783. They observed that those British Americans who from "purest principles of Loyalty, and attachment to the British-Government, their Sovereign, and British Nation" had fought for the Crown would be unable to return to their homes, whatever the conditions of peace. "The personal animosities that arose from civil dissension," the memorialists argued, "have been so heightened by the Blood that has been shed in the Contest, that the Parties can never be reconciled."[7] The regiments wanted land grants and assistance parallel to that extended the Loyalist civilians. The acceptance of soldier claims meant further complications for settlement policy.[8]

Loyalists began arriving in large numbers in Nova Scotia in October 1782. The first official recognition of the possibility that this movement from the south might affect the Island occurred in the council meeting of 21 May 1783, when new elections were recommended for the assembly, "to give an opportunity to some of the New Settlers who are expected, if they chuse to become members."⁹ This same meeting also voted to request the British military to disband on the Island those soldiers stationed there. It suggested no policy of land grants or other forms of assistance, however. Indeed, the council could not very well articulate a policy when the only land readily available for distribution by the Crown was in the royalties. The distrained lots not auctioned in 1781 were not considered at this point. But the government obviously needed more land for the Loyalists, and Governor Patterson had already begun working behind the scenes to find some.

On 29 June 1783, a group of eighteen Island proprietors claiming possession of 426,000 acres of land submitted in London a petition to the Crown offering gratis one-quarter of this land to "loyal Emigrants" after surveying, division by the surveyor into parcels of at least 1,000 acres, and balloting before the governor and council.¹⁰ The petition echoed earlier arguments that such land allocation would "greatly advance the prosperity of the infant colony," which "from its natural and vital situation, is peculiarly adapted to becoming a permanent and valuable possession of Great Britain." The petition concluded by suggesting that Guy Carleton in New York "furnish such Loyalists as prefer a settlement in St. John's, with provisions and transport to convey them to Charlottetown." By this time, unfortunately, New York had been almost totally evacuated, and the offer, even if accepted, was unlikely to bring Loyalists directly from the United States to the Island.

While the eighteen signatories included several original proprietors, notably Laurence Sulivan, James Montgomery, and Lord Townshend, conspicuous by his presence was Walter Patterson's brother John, formerly a customs official in Philadelphia, both on his own behalf and as attorney for the governor and three other purchasers of distrained lots in the 1781 auction. The petition listed amounts of land held by the subscribers, but did not specify lot numbers, probably a wise precaution in view of the fact that Lord North had only a month earlier instructed Patterson to reverse the 1781 sales. This initiative was clearly set under way by the Patterson interests, and the failure of more proprietors to join in the offer reflects less their reluctance to accommodate the Loyalists than their uncertainty over the state of their holdings. It was hardly in the best interests of any proprietor to deny the refugees, for quite apart from the machinations of the Pattersons and the political goodwill a generous gesture could generate in Whitehall, encouraging settlement was good business. As any land speculator knew, population spawned more population. The remaining land on lots partially settled by Loyalists would increase in value and become far more desirable property. At least one of the subscribers would subsequently complain bitterly that his offer of land in 1783 had not seriously been taken up.[11]

Making land available for Loyalist resettlement was a problem in many places, notwithstanding the enormous amounts of unsettled land in existence. Nova Scotia, for example, was forced between 1783 and 1788 to escheat nearly two-and-one-half million acres of land previously granted, which it did through a provincial court of escheat and forfeitures. While this process produced many problems and much discontent, in Nova Scotia and New Brunswick the land was returned directly to the Crown, which could reassign it to incoming Loyalists and other settlers.[12]. The Island of St John, however, had another mechanism sanctioned by provincial law for dealing with the repossession of its undeveloped land, at least until altered by new legislation. Distraint and subsequent resale did not return land to the Crown, but merely shifted its ownership. The new owners, such as Walter Patterson, were uniquely placed to employ the political system to maintain their possession and to benefit themselves. Patterson's subsequent machinations in all quarters, as well as the Island record regarding Loyalists, are all but incomprehensible if his vested interests are not clearly understood.

Despite the enormous influx of new settlers into Nova Scotia over the spring and summer of 1783, the Island made little effort to attract them. The council did agree in August of that year to make distrained land available to the refugees, but such a policy was never seriously pursued, undoubtedly because of the arrival of word of the proprietorial offer.[13] The council also granted lot 66, a small township reserved in 1767 as Crown demesne, to Gilbert Totten of New York as a "Loyal Refugee and a real and much injured American sufferer."[14] But this lot would be regranted several times over the ensuing years and was never actively settled. As late as 1816 it had "No Inhabitants – but Bears and Foxes."[15] In September of 1783 council memorialized the commander-in-chief to extend the king's bounty for refugees and disbanded troops to include the Island, noting that only Nova Scotia had hitherto been mentioned in general orders.[16] Such desultory moves hardly added up to a concerted or vigorous policy. The situation altered dramatically in October 1783, when the colony's London agent forwarded a copy of the proprietors' petition to the governor and informed him that "all was entirely acquiesced in, and approved by, Lord North."[17] At least, so Walter Patterson informed his council. North of course had done nothing of the sort, partly because the British government was still working out its Loyalist policy and partly because of the confused state of land ownership on the Island. North was waiting to hear that the 1781 sales had been reversed and the new legislation passed by the assembly.

In any event, Patterson not only assumed (erroneously or wilfully) that the proprietorial offer had been accepted, but also that the same terms for Loyalists that were being offered in Nova Scotia were to be extended to the Island. As a result, on 14 October 1783 he and his council issued a proclamation to be circulated throughout North America:

Whereas a number of the Proprietors of this Island have very generously given up a considerable portion of their estates to be distributed among such of the Refugees, Provincial Troops or other American Emigrants, as are desirous to become its inhabitants, the lands to be granted by the Governor and Council in the same proportion and on the same terms as are offered in Nova Scotia, and to be given out of the different townships by Lot: in the fairest and most equitable manner, according to the quantity assigned for by each proprietor. And Whereas, His Majesty has been graciously pleased to extend his Royal Bountys and Gratuities, to all persons of the above description in every respect, and in the manner as to those who settle in Nova Scotia. I do therefore, by and with the advice of His Majesty's Council, issue this Proclamation hereby giving notice to all such of the Refugees, as wish to become settlers in this colony, that in a few days after their arrival at Charlottetown, they shall be put in possession of such lands, as they shall be entitled to, free of every expense. That they may depend upon the lands being good, neither mountainous, rocky nor swampy, continuous to naviga-ble harbours, many ports convenient for the fishery, and in every respect preferable to any lands unoccupied throughout His Majesty's American Dominion, and as to further encouragement, they will meet with a Government very warmly inclined to give them every assistance and protection in their power, and with loyal fellow subjects, from whom they will receive a most cordial and hearty welcome.[18]

That same day Patterson wrote Lord North that he awaited further instructions for dealing with the new arrivals.[19] Whatever informa-tion Patterson had received from agent John Stuart in October of 1783, it had undoubtedly arrived at the same time as Lord North's draft bill and instructions for undoing the 1781 sales. Throughout his subsequent dealings with the British authorities, Patterson consistent-ly attempted to separate his Loyalist policy from the land question, seldom mentioning both matters in the same dispatch and never in conjunction with one another. But his refusal to inform his council of North's bill and his failure to act upon his instructions regarding the land were both clearly related to the Loyalist business. As Captain John had suspected, Patterson wanted to settle the newcomers, not coincidentally upon lands purchased by himself in 1781, before he had to deal publicly with the land question. He might have been able to get away with excessive zeal for the Loyalists, but that zeal was always suspect.

Apart from its announcement of a policy for which authorization was dubious, the governor's proclamation was interesting in several other respects. In the first place, it distinguished not merely the usual two categories of land recipients – refugees and soldiers – but added a third in the phrase "other American emigrants." The term "refugee" became the common one on the Island to refer to those civilians exiled for reasons of loyalty from the American states. While the term "provincial troops" in the proclamation was plain enough, "other American emigrants" was far more ambiguous. It apparently was intended to refer to those who chose for non-political reasons to move to the Island. "American" in the nomenclature of the time was not solely associated with the United States: Nova Scotians, New-foundlanders, and other British Americans would be included in the category. Finally, Patterson emphasized that the welcoming population also was loyal. Any effort to view receipt of "Loyalist" land on the Island of St John as evidence of a particular political ideology must take account of the inclusiveness of the policy, and the nebulousness of at least one of its categories.[20] Moreover, more than one disbanded soldier chose to apply for land as a refugee, an understandable decision given the fact that grants to refugees were substantially more generous than those to soldiers.

When Patterson extended to emigrants the same terms and bounties as in Nova Scotia, he had no clear notion of what these entailed, and he would make little effort to sort out the details for some months. At the time of the proclamation, therefore, the government of the Island did not know what land quantities would be made available or what would be included in the other assistance. Patterson would report to his council in November 1783, for example, that he had no word from Britain regarding provisions, hardly surprising given the government's attitude toward the Island.[21] The council applied available stores to the Loyalists. The exceeding of authority quickly cumulated. Despite the uncertainties, the council began quickly to receive applications for land and to arrange the preliminaries of allocation. Two weeks after the proclamation, it ordered the Island's surveyor to divide each lot and partial lot surrendered by the proprietors for the Loyalists. The portion to be given to the newcomers would be drawn by ballot when the divisions were completed on the maps.[23] This procedure was somewhat at variance with the offer, although it did preserve the principle of random selection. The spirit of the proprietors' offer would receive considerably more alteration in subsequent actions.

The first applicants for land under Patterson's proclamation were not civilian refugees, but soldiers of the King's Rangers garrisoned on the Island and recently disbanded there. Seventy non-commissioned officers and privates of the First Battalion of the King's Rangers, headed by Captain Samuel Hayden, requested land on 28 October 1783.[24] There would be subsequent controversy over the validity of this list, Patterson maintaining that Hayden had forged signatures on it, but the King's Rangers would represent the largest single group of disbanded soldiers given land on the Island, ultimately totalling 100 recipients.[25] The Rangers had been organized in 1780 by Colonel Robert Rogers and his brother James, the latter based in Quebec. The First Battalion had been sent to the Island in spring 1782 to replace Major Timothy Hierlihy's Independent Provincial Companies from New York, and it would remain on duty at Charlottetown until disbanded early in the autumn of 1783.[26] The pressure to accommodate the King's Rangers doubtless contributed to the speed with which events moved on the Island after the publication of the governor's proclamation. The need to act was pressing, if the local disbandment of the First Battalion were to have any positive effect on settlement. The men would have to be assured land and support to prevent them from leaving the Island for other opportunities.

Immediately behind Captain Hayden was Captain Phillips Callbeck on behalf of the St John's Volunteers, the independent militia company raised by the acting governor during the war.[27] The St John's Volunteers had never served in battle on or off the Island, and their loyalty had been tested mainly through general conditions on the Island during the war. The muster roll was composed entirely of individuals already resident on the Island.[28] A few weeks later, the King's Rangers and the St John's Volunteers were joined in the land sweepstakes by the Royal Nova Scotia Volunteers. Charles Stewart, recently a lieutenant in that brigade and son of Island Chief Justice Peter Stewart, prayed for land on behalf of a number of his former corps.[29] Despite its name, the Royal Nova Scotia Volunteer Regiment was in part the direct successor to Timothy Hierlihy's provincial companies, which had served on the Island from 1778 to 1782. Upon their transfer to Halifax, they had been incorporated into the Nova Scotia Volunteers, and disbanded as part of that regiment on 20 October 1783.[30]

The First Battalion of King's Rangers, the St John's Volunteers, and the Nova Scotia Volunteers would ultimately provide 170 of the total of 279 individuals who can be identified as authorized to receive land as disbanded soldiers on the Island. If the 14 men of the 84th Regiment (Royal Highland Emigrants), mainly recruited on the Island by Captain John MacDonald and his brother, are added to the 170 from the three other units, 184 (or 66 per cent) of the soldiers granted land had some previous link to the Island, either as soldiers garrisoned there or as residents recruited into some form of military service during the war. Many of the Island's disbanded soldiers were obviously not strangers to it, and some, particularly among the St John's Volunteers, already had improved land. Whether or not the Island was typical in this regard among loyal British colonies receiving disbanded provincial troops is not clear, but it seems worth emphasizing that not all "Loyalists" were political refugees from the United States or strangers to their newly chosen homes.

At a council meeting on 1 November 1783, Phillips Callbeck pointed out to his colleagues that while balloting for land was valuable in principle, his men were "in general fishermen and propose again following the same line of life," thus rendering land "of no use to them" unless contiguous to a harbour so that "their farming and fishing may be carried on together."[31] Captain Hayden supported Callbeck, adding that transporting "bagage, Provisions, and farming Utensils" to inaccessible land would be difficult, and land near Charlottetown had the additional advantage of an available market. The council agreed on the importance of keeping the soldiers "satisfied and happy," and allowed Callbeck and Hayden to "chuse such situation as they like best for their respective Corps" without prejudice to further applications. Despite the caveat, this decision established the practice of permitting the specification of locations in applications that persisted throughout the Loyalist granting period. Prospective grantees, especially if acting as a group, could expect to have their preferences on approved lots fulfilled. Naturally, most chose land along the harbours and rivers. The original terms of the proprietorial offer were, in the process, materially altered.

In February 1784, the Island surveyor produced plans of a number of lots divided into four equal shares, and the council witnessed the drawing of the "Refugee Share" of these townships at that time.[32] The lots thus divided were 5, 24, 31, 32, 49, 50, 54, 57, and 58. Of these townships, lots 24, 31, 32, 49, and 57 had all been purchased by Walter Patterson and his associates in November 1781; lot 5 belonged to Edward Lewis, but was in the remote, unsettled, and less desirable west end of the Island; lot 50 had been partially owned by Patterson from 1769, and lot 54 was in Patterson's hands by 1780.[33] Therefore, of the first nine lots formally subdivided for Loyalist resettlement, seven were entirely or partially owned by Patterson or his friends, and five of these townships had been ordered restored to their previous owners in the legislation sent Patterson by Lord North in 1783. The lots involved in this division, as was true for those subsequently added, were not chosen in terms of their potential utility for settlement, although Patterson's strategy for land accumulation had been to concentrate on acquiring land around Charlottetown and around Bedeque Bay. Nevertheless, the thread uniting the Loyalist townships was principally Walter Patterson's relationship to them.[34] Over the next few months in 1784, the council heard additional requests for land from other groups of disbanded soldiers. It added lot 65, also partially owned by the governor in 1780, to those from which land was allocated, and shares were drawn for 16 (owned by Edward Boehm in 1780), as well as 17, 18, and 19 (all purchased in whole or part by Patterson and friends in 1781). By the spring of 1784, therefore, fourteen townships were opened for Loyalist settlement, and eleven of these were under Patterson's control, most the subject of potential disputed ownership.

By the end of the winter of 1783/4, new settlement on the Island had made the desirability of new elections to the assembly as apparent as the necessity for its meeting, an event the governor had avoided since 1780. An election was duly called, and to his surprise, the "father of the province" (as Patterson liked to be styled) met fierce opposition to his policies on the hustings and at the poll, even though the critics did not yet know about the instructions from Lord North. In the "campaigning" that preceded the actual day of polling, young Jack Stewart, the eldest son of the chief justice – "a very intemperate young Man," commented the governor – toured the countryside "infusing the people" with rumours of new government taxation.[35] At this point Stewart does not appear to have introduced any particular criticism of Patterson's past performance, although such charges would eventually be added to a growing list of complaints. Nor were the Loyalists in any way an issue. Instead, Stewart focused on prospective new policy, which he described as including a general tax of £400 per annum to be levied on all inhabitants, an impost duty on produce, and the potential seizure of cattle and crops by force if settlers refused to pay. In a colony where most rural inhabitants lived at the margin of subsistence and where cash was in short supply, new taxation was a serious business. Stewart got an attentive audience for his visitations.

Although he used rhetorical slogans such as "tyranny and oppression" loosely and openly in his travels, there was a hard core of constitutional concern behind Stewart's accusations. According to one hostile witness, Stewart attempted to persuade the public that Patterson "by his own Authority intended to raise a Tax of four hundred pounds to be paid annually and that all the produce of the Country such as Cattle corn and Roots of all sorts were to pay a proportion to the Tax."[36] The operative phrase here was "by his own Authority." Another Patterson supporter reported that Stewart had much influenced the minds of "the lower class of People amongst whom the majority of the Electors were" with statements "that Slavery was hanging over their heads – and beware of themselves."[37] Stewart was apparently arguing that the Patterson administration increasingly represented government by executive fiat and decree, in which the elected representatives of the people were being bypassed. He was able to fit such an interpretation into the larger Whig ideology of the eighteenth century, with its conviction that the power of the executive was despotic, and it is no accident that the opposition he was attempting to organize to the "Court Party" on the Island was labelled "The Country Party."[38] While the importation of external labels onto the Island was in some ways pretentious, while the factions were clearly riddled with personal animosities that went well beyond (or perhaps below) political ideology or constitutional questions, such matters were not totally irrelevant in 1784.[39]

A good deal of detailed evidence survives for the events of the actual day of election in March 1784, thanks to Patterson's subsequent efforts to use Chief Justice Peter Stewart's behaviour on that day as grounds for suspending him from office. Most of the leading participants testified at length before the council on the matter, as part of the process of gathering evidence on the suspension question.[40] Thus we can gain a rather complete picture of electoral proceedings on the Island at this point, a critical juncture that marked the first appearance of organized political parties in any jurisdiction which would become part of Canada.

There was still only one polling place for the entire Island in the 1784 election, and the voters assembled in Charlottetown, probably in the house of schoolmaster Alexander Richardson, for what would prove a tempestuous gathering. As the first arrivals began gathering and the room was being prepared for the poll, Jack Stewart opened a litany of complaints about the procedures. His first objection was that the returning officer, councillor John Russell Spence, was not impartial but was a supporter of the governor. Stewart next protested the presence of other members of the council at the poll, many of whom were known to be partial to the governor, since they would influence the result and hence impinge upon the independence of the assembly. There was also considerable disagreement over the tendering of oaths to disputed voters, either because they were suspected of not holding property or because they were Catholics. Attorney-General Phillips Callbeck, apparently by this point seated at the polling table along with Stewart and Spence, attempted to answer the objections with constitutional and legal arguments, and the younger man responded by demanding another opinion – from his father, the only other legal officer on the Island, who was not present. A "general murmur" from the crowd led to the summoning of the chief justice; the "whole cry of the people was send for him send for him," reported one witness.[41]

While the group awaited the appearance of the elder Stewart, whose residence was some blocks away, Jack Stewart and Phillips Callbeck began another argument over the question of taxation, which was in full flight as the chief justice entered the room. Callbeck, obviously acting as spokesman for the executive, complained that the opposition had been accusing the governor and council of planning to levy a tax. Chief Justice Stewart, making his entrance at this point, observed that Callbeck was well aware that the council had discussed the matter of taxation, to which the attorney-general responded that the governor and the upper house had it within their power to tax. The question of who had introduced the subject of taxation publicly was the one that subsequently came under scrutiny, although the weight of the evidence appears to be that the chief justice, while he certainly had confirmed the fact that the subject had been agitated in council, had not – as the governor would maintain – raised the matter publicly in support of his son's general charges. Lost in the fuss over whether Stewart had taken the intitive in raising the taxation issue was the larger constitutional one of whether the governor and council has the right to entertain such a discussion apart from the assembly. Such legal niceties doubtless made little impression on the elctorate on this day, however.

The problem of the prerogative over money matters merged almost naturally into the question of the presence of members of the council at the poll, not merely as observers but as managers and in at least the case of Callbeck as a candidate as well. Both Callbeck and Jack Stewart had prepared lists or slates of candidates for all eighteen seats, a "governor's list" and a "country list." Voters could either submit the prepared list as it stood or amend it to suit their own preferences; many signed lists from voters not present were ready to be submitted. Chief Justice Stewart told the attorney-general that in his opinion members of the council should neither be present at the poll or vote in it. He pointed out that the upper House had never previously been involved in assembly elections, adding that Callbeck as a member of one house certainly had no right to be a candidate in the other. Callbeck answered that he had resigned from the council. But not in writing, responded the chief justice. The attorney-general hastily "wrote a few lines which I conceiv'd to be a resignation," recalled one later witness. Amidst a scene of much "confusion – and much noise," Callbeck and the chief justice exchanged further words, and Stewart retired, saying he wanted no part of the proceedings. In addition to Spence, who as returning officer was obliged to be present, councillors Callbeck, Wright, Nisbett, and Burns – supporting the "governor's list" – remained in the room until the poll closed. Witnesses agreed there were a number of lists circulating amidst a good deal of confusion. Spence rejected one list signed by a number of West River inhabitants who were not actually in attendance at the poll.

Despite the efforts of the pro-Patterson supporters, the election resulted in a victory for the "country party." Patterson would have to face the British authorities not with the support of a sympathetic popular assembly but with the criticisms of a hostile one. Fortunately for the governor, the assembly that met in the wake of the 1784 election was not well prepared to engage in political combat with his administration. Jack Stewart had been forced to recruit hastily the members of his party among political "outs" within the ranks of the elite and among relative newcomers and untested people in the settlements. Moreover, neither Stewart nor those elected on his list had any background or experience in opposing an entrenched executive. Not all the members of the new assembly were committed to Stewart, and there was no Island tradition of assembly independence or many outside models upon which to rely, especially in terms of political organization. The concept of party was anathema in both Britain and America at this time. Stewart's people were united in their fear of taxation more than in their opposition to Walter Patterson, and it was difficult to oppose financial measures that were never actually brought before the legislature. Stewart was forced to look for other clubs with which the administration could be beaten, and not all members of the assembly were as unremittingly hostile to Patterson as he. While Patterson had not withheld Lord North's instructions because he feared a hostile assembly, his decision must have appeared sensible given the results of the 1784 poll. The assembly began its deliberations without the one piece of information that might have solidified the opposition.

The 1784 assembly began its session on 6 March. From the outset it was clear that many legislators were critical of Patterson but were unable to focus their hostility. Not surprisingly, Jack Stewart was easily elected speaker of the house, but he would later come under severe criticism for his management. Duncan McEwan would later testify that Stewart had argued that "he knew our Education did not entitle us to know so much about the Law as what he did and whatever side he went to when the House was divided, to go to the same side, and we might depend on it we would be right."[42] Much would be made by the governor and his supporters of the low quality of the members of this assembly. Patterson informed Lord North that half of its members had been selected from "the lowest and most ignorant of inhabitants."[43] But evidence before the council later in 1784 made quite clear that the members of the 1784 assembly were not better or worse than previous ones so far as education or social standing was concerned. What was important was not the "ignorance" of the legislators but their sense of independence. Duncan McEwan answered Stewart's condescension by stating emphatically that he would be guided by his own conscience, and obviously nursed a grievance against Stewart for his attitude.

If members of his own "party" were prepared to vote with their consciences, Jack Stewart needed issues that would offend those sensibilities. He raised the question of the tax that had so distressed people in 1780, but its repeal provoked no confrontations. A series of initiatives intended to annoy Patterson and the majority of the council were undertaken. A motion was introduced, for example, to increase the salaries of the chief justice and the lieutenant-governor, in the course of which Peter Stewart and Thomas Desbrisay were pointedly praised. While this resolution was taken by the Patterson people as evidence of the key role Stewart and Desbrisay were taking behind the scenes in leading the opposition, it seems equally likely that they were being employed as symbols to aggravate the governor. A few days later, the assembly turned to an earlier act giving the governor permission to lease the Charlottetown Common rent free for ten years. The House also asked questions about the £3,000 parliamentary grant for buildings and requires, enquiring how it had been spent and by whose authority. About the same time, the legislators began discussing the governor's address to both houses transmitted at the opening of the session. In its response, the assembly accepted without comment Patterson's remarks about the "Patriotic, Expanded and Benevolent Conduct" of the proprietors towards the Loyalists. It concentrated instead on a draft phrase of its own which thanked the governor for the "very early, active expensive and fatiguing part" he had played in the early development of the colony, omitting after much debate the terms "expensive and fatiguing." Such a debate was not likely to galvanize an opposition.

On 19 March, Patterson responded to the queries about the parliamentary grant by denying the assembly's competence on the matter, since it was a vote of the British Parliament. The legislators found this response unsatisfactory and might have been on the trail of something damaging to Patterson. By this time, however, the number of members in attendance was constantly diminishing, as the rural legislators began returning to their communities and those annoyed by the obvious partisanship of the majority ceased to appear. The session drifted on aimlessly until 24 March, when it adjourned for two weeks. It would never again achieve a quorum, and Patterson was able to declare its subsequent attempts at meeting as illegal, disbanding it on 13 April upon advice of the council. A rump house unanimously branded the governor's action as "unconstitutional," designed to invalidate complaints against him as a "public Defaulter."[44] Charges against Patterson were also posted by the rump assembly publicly in Charlottetown. These accusations are useful, since they indicate how far the assembly had gotten in uncovering Patterson's behaviour. He was accused of appropriating money to his own use, granting land to his friends, permitting the 1781 land auction to be conducted arbitrarily, and "by conversation and example spreading the principles of infidelity and irreligion thro' the Colony, to the ruin of the most respectable families and the destruction of the peace and harmony of the Colony."[45] This last accusation was obviously critical, referring obliquely to the governor's philandering. But such a litany of wrongdoing was a tired one, collecting old grievances and petty personal ones. The assembly, in April 1784, was really not cognizant of Patterson's more recent manipulations.

That Jack Stewart was not being closely advised by his father and the lieutenant-governor is suggested by the fact that the assembly did not in the spring of 1784 raise the matter of new quitrent legislation, although Patterson had finally laid this material before the council on 13 March.[46] Debate in the council, fully attended, occurred over the question a week later, while the assembly was still searching for issues.[47] There would over the years be much dispute about this meeting, especially regarding the position of the councillors. Peter Stewart and Thomas Desbrisay would persistently maintain that they and two other members had opposed the final decision not to lay Lord North's bill before the assembly, and subsequent events substantiated this insistence, particularly for Stewart.[48] According to the council minutes, which the minority insisted had been doctored, the meeting agreed that the complaints of the proprietors were "about totally groundless." The only real hardship to proprietors resulting from the Island's quitrent legislation was the imputation that quitrents had to be paid in cash on the Island, but in practice "there has never been One shilling of Quit Rent received upon the Island." The lots auctioned were in arrears, their quitrents unpaid anywhere, and not one lot had been auctioned upon which a penny had been spent in improvements. In contrast, the lots sold in 1781 had been improved, with merchants and others investing in them. More significantly, much of the contested land had been given up for refugees and provincial troops. Overturning the grants would cause great hardship.[49] Captain John MacDonald's predictions were coming true.

Had Peter Stewart been the real leader of the country party, as Governor Patterson always maintained, some word of this discussion ought to have been leaked to the assembly and some response from it ought to have taken place. As matters stood, however, the insistence of Jack Stewart that "I conduct my Life in my own Opinion" seems quite legitimate.[50] The controversies between the governor and Peter Stewart may have contributed to Jack's enmity, but such an analysis is not quite the same as viewing the chief justice as the power behind the scenes. Nevertheless, the council began hearings in May of 1784 regarding Peter Stewart's political activities, and by June he would write to the British authorities, "I have every reason to believe an attempt is now to be made of depriving me of my place as Chief Justice, which I have held since 1775, and of turning me and my numerous family of eleven children out of our only subsistence."[52] Stewart's concerns, as he would ultimately discover, were not ill founded.

While Patterson defended to the British government his actions in dismissing the 1784 assembly and wrote desperate letters to Governor Parr to ascertain Nova Scotia policy regarding Loyalists, another son of Peter Stewart entered the scene.[53] Charles Stewart had obtained on the mainland an appointment as Deputy Muster Master of the Refugees and Disbanded Troops for Nova Scotia and the Island of St John.[54] Arriving on the Island on 3 June 1784, Stewart almost immediately reported to his superiors in Nova Scotia difficulties in executing his orders to muster the disbanded troops and refugees. The men had been scattered across the Island, he complained, continuing:

From the information I have as yet received there has been not a single Warrant of Survey Executed to any discharged or disbanded Man on this

Island and that the greatest number of the Men have sold the provisions they received for the past six months and are now dispersed over the face of the Country besides some who have gone a fishing and others run off the Island intirely, in short that the intentions of Government have not in any instance been cqmplied with by the disbanded troops on the Island.[55]

Despite the difficulties, Stewart proceeded with his task, insisting that he was "scrupulously exact" in his execution.[56]

In a subsequent report from Charlottetown, Stewart elaborated on his earlier impressions, noting "the Success of the Settlements within this Province is at present very doubtful notwithstanding the many natural advantages with which it is blessed."[56] The principal difficulty was the scattering of the new settlers, for which Stewart assigned three causes. The first was lack of co-operation from Governor Patterson, who "chooses not to have any partial Concern in it, since he has not the whole." Stewart insisted that Patterson seemed most concerned that orders and directives were coming from outside his government rather than with the welfare of the settlers or the Island. Secondly, Stewart complained that many soldiers were being seduced "from their officers through the schemes and contrivance of a Mr. McMillan lately dismissed His Majesty's Service at Halifax by the sentence of a General Court Martial, but now encouraged supported and abetted by the Governor in such practices." As a result, the officers' plans for orderly settlement were being thwarted. This charge receives some substantiation from the council records, where Alexander McMillan's name heads lists of several groups of disbanded soldiers petitioning for land on lots possessed by Walter Patterson; McMillan was appointed by Patterson as agent for refugees as $2 per diem.[57]

Finally, Stewart noted:

Another cause of delay arises from the frequent practice of the soldiers had, before my appointment fallen into of selling their provisions for very inadequate considerations, but tho: they should obtain their full value it removes the very possibility of settling, as without provisions nothing can be done. The Effect of this is that the men are now scattered about the Country in dissipation and idleness, the generality of them having previously drank out the amount of what they got for their provisions.

Stewart had called such practices to the council's attention in an effort to stop them, but "was not a little astonished" to receive a reply from the governor "that the men had an undoubted right to dispose of their provisions as they thought fit." For his part, Patterson complained that Stewart mustered many disqualified individuals who set bad examples by "their idle and disorderly conduct."[58]

Stewart's report must be read in the general context of the political struggle under way between Patterson and his enemies, headed by the clan Stewart. The deputy muster master turned all his complaints – which were legitimate enough – into direct accusations against Walter Patterson, a personalization of the problem that was not entirely fair. The confused and overlapping lines of authority regarding Loyalists was not entirely the governor's fault, and it was certainly not his responsibility that many of the troops were improvident enough to trade their provisions for drink. Such short-sightedness was characteristic of many soldiers, particularly those who had no other training and no family responsibilities. Alexander McMillan's interference may have been a problem, but the heart of the difficulty resided in the way Loyalist lots had been selected in the first place. The selection process owed much to Patterson's self-interest, but Stewart did not comment on this point. Charles Stewart did address the major drawbacks to the program of soldier settlement on the Island, however, particularly the absence of co-ordination and planning. This problem remained beyond Patterson's control, although he was prepared to manoeuvre in the gray areas.

By summer 1784, refugee Loyalists had been added to the disbanded soldiers seeking resettlement on the Island. Most drifted across from the mainland as single families or in small parties, although six vessels with refugees had arrived by September 1784, leaving Walter Patterson with a bill for transport that he could not find anyone willing to pay.[59] The Island received few refugees who had made it their first choice. More commonly, those who found their grants unsatisfactory in Nova Scotia, particularly around the Shelburne area, packed up again in hopes of better opportunities on the Island. Patterson continued to write about the impending arrival of "Vast numbers of useful Inhabitants," but his optimism was not borne out by events.[60] If the Island wanted more refugees, it should have been recruiting them in New York much earlier. Nevertheless, there were more settlers than official records indicated.

Charles Stewart continued to operate as muster master for refugees as well as for disbanded soldiers, reporting to Nova Scotia rather than Charlottetown. He had set his first muster date in mid June 1784, at which time he reported 202 adult males, 60 adult females, 27 children over ten, 65 under ten, and 26 servants (most probably blacks), for a total of 380 settlers.[62] These numbers represented almost entirely disbanded soldiers. Stewart mustered other groups over the summer as they arrived, and completed his task with another series of musters in September, adding 118 adult males, 27 adult females, 20 children over ten, and 18 children under ten, or 183 new settlers. In total, Stewart formally mustered 320 adult males, 87 adult females, 47 children over ten, 83 children under ten, and 26 servants, for a grand sum of 563 Loyalists. Broken down into refugees and disbanded soldiers, there were 97 in the refugee category (50 adult males, 18 adult females, 16 children over ten and 13 under ten) and 466 in the soldier category (270 adult males, 69 adult females, 31 children over ten, 70 children under ten, and 26 servants). Stewart himself acknowledged his difficulty in assembling all those applying for land, and his musters were completed by early autumn 1784. Another 225 adult males, mainly refugees, can be identified from other sources, and thus Stewart's muster rolls, while providing more detail about the Island Loyalist arrivals than other records, can hardly be regarded as definitive.

In addition to Stewart's musters, a number of other sources for identifying Loyalist exiles on the Island must be taken into account. The most inclusive is also the most exasperating. In 1841, the Prince Edward Island legislative Assembly included as appendix J in its printed journal a "List of Claimants appearing in the Journals of the Council as Loyalists and Disbanded Soldiers, so far as the Committee has been able to ascertain."[62] The list of names, 342 in total, was printed without further detail. It is possible to obtain further information from other sources for most of those listed in 1841, although fifty names appear here and nowhere else in the records, perhaps because records were available in 1841 which no longer survive, perhaps because the list was compiled by people who had trouble accurately transcribing the names. The surviving council records do contain many lists of names, often duplicated from one list to another, and there is also an annotated voting list for 1785 that includes some names and details available nowhere else.[63] Family genealogies compiled and recently printed by the Abegweit Branch of the United Empire Loyalist Association provide additional information.[64] From these sources it has been possible to compile a master list of 545 names, for 495 of which varying amounts of detailed biographical information are available.

Were analysis confined to Charles Stewart's muster rolls, it would appear that 270 of 320 adult male Loyalist arrivals (or 84.4 per cent) were disbanded soldiers. The larger master list adds the names of only 14 new soldiers, but an additional 130 civilian refugees, for totals of 180 refugees and 284 disbanded soldiers. In percentage terms, 38.8 per cent of those for whom status is known were refugees, including some who came later than 1784, and 61.2 per cent were soldiers. While this proportion is considerably more evenly distributed than that contained in Stewart's records, it does suggest the importance of the disbanded soldiers for the Island. Although there is no readily comparable data for Nova Scotia (including New Brunswick) or Quebec (including Upper Canada), some figures suggest that elsewhere the proportions of refugees and disbanded soldiers were more nearly equal. The provision musters of Thomas Knox for New Brunswick in 1784, for example, show 1847 provincials (not including 199 soldiers from British regiments and 89 from black companies) and 1966 Loyal Refugees.[65] The Island percentage of 38.8 in the refugee category, it must be added, is somewhat inflated by later arrivals and by the fact that refugees received more land than common soldiers, thus tempting stray arrivals to claim civilian rather than military status. The question of amounts of land is important, for according to Island policy (reflecting that in Nova Scotia), married refugees received 500 acres and single refugees received 300 acres, while officers received 500 acres, non-commissioned soldiers received 200 acres, and those in private rank (including drummers and volunteers) received 100 acres. Of the 266 disbanded soldiers for whom rank is known, only 65 (or 24.4 per cent) were above the rank of private. Thus at least 201 Loyalist settlers on the Island should have received grants of only 100 acres, hardly a substantial holding given the extensive agricultural practices of the eighteenth century.

Other information regarding the soldier settlers can also be gleaned from the available evidence. Of the sixty-five above the rank of private, for example, there were thirty-four officers and thirty-one non-commissioned soldiers, broken down as follows:

Officers		Non-commissioned ranks	
Major	4	Sergeant	14
Adjutant	1	Corporal	15
Captain	10	Unspecified	1
Lieutenant	13		
Cornet	1		
Ensign	4		

Twelve of these field officers (35 per cent) and ten of the non-coms (32.2 per cent) brought dependants, while within the ranks of the private soldiers, only twenty-four (11.9 per cent) brought dependants. In total, 46 of the 266 soldiers (17.3 per cent) for whom rank is known came with dependants, and the likelihood of dependants was three times as great above the rank of private soldier. The typical disbanded soldier, especially in the private ranks, was single and footloose. He was not, however, a youngster.

The twentieth century normally conceives military service to involve predominantly the young, but the situation was different in the eighteenth century. Of those for whom age is known in the St John's Volunteers and the Nova Scotia Volunteers, for example, the average age at the time of disbandment was 33 years and 32 years respectively, and the average age for 109 soldiers from other regiments was also 32. Less than 3 per cent of the soldiers were under the age of 20, and a full 20 per cent were over the age of 40. To some extent, these ages reflect the length of the war, but they also indicate that in the American Revolution few colonials on the British side had enlisted as teenagers. This fact suggests that military service for Loyalists probably occurred more frequently among those for whom success in life had not been marked, or who had little future ahead. In any case, the Island's disbanded soldiers were not, in 1784, young men with their lives ahead of them, but older men who had missed normality in the critical years from age 20 to age 30 in their life cycle, when most colonial Americans married, established families, and built farms and vocations.[66] The typical disbanded soldier on the Island was unattached and approaching middle age. He was a recipient of rations that he sold for drink, and 100 acres of unimproved land. Not surprisingly, such men were not inclined to stability and permanent settlement, particularly given the chronic shortage of women on the Island.

Over the spring and summer of 1784, the council heard many petitions from incoming civilian refugees and allocated land to them, often combining grants to refugees and to disbanded soldiers on the same lot.[67] For the most part, the lands were on the fourteen lots already noted, although three new ones – lot 26 (partially purchased for Patterson in 1781), lot 56 (owned by Lord Townshend), and lot 67 (purchased by Patterson in 1781) – were added. By autumn 1784, the bulk of the land allocations had been made. While refugees continued to trickle onto the Island over the next few years, most did not receive any promises or commitments of land. They and their descendants would constitute the bulk of the disgruntled Loyalists who would continually surface to complain of their maltreatment. Subsequent political events may have contributed to the problems of these late arrivals, but there exists little evidence to suggest that those who had been awarded or promised land in 1784 were unable to get titles if they remained legitimately resident upon it after a legislative enactment of 1790 cut through the legal morass of the 1780s and authorized the granting of titles.[68]

Because a large percentage of the civilian refugees escaped formal mustering, detailed information on them is somewhat less complete than for the soldiers. Nevertheless, it is possible to venture some generalizations. For seventy-three names among the refugees, ages can be determined. The average age of these refugees in 1784 was 35.6 years, thus making the refugees an even older population than the soldiers. Forty-three of the 180 known refugees can be positively identified as bringing wives or dependants, a percentage of 23.8 in contrast to 17.3 per cent among all disbanded soldiers and 11.9 per cent in private ranks. This figure of 23.8 per cent is probably low, since it does not include refugees who were awarded the 500 acres that went to those married, but for whom there is no other evidence of a spouse. The problem here is that it is not at all clear whether the Island government insisted that spouses or dependants actually be on the Island in order to claim the married allowance, and there is some evidence that the government was not at all careful in this regard. In any event, like the disbanded soldier, the typical Island refugee Loyalist was single and approaching middle age. The surviving evidence of geographical origin is too scanty to quantify, although there were few New Englanders and a high proportion of individuals from the Middle Colonies of New York, New Jersey, and Pennsylvania. The evidence of the genealogies, again impressionistic rather than quantifiable, is that a substantial number of the refugees had been born in Europe rather than in the American colonies. The tendency of the record keepers (and perhaps even the Loyalists) to anglicize names makes any generalizations about ethnic origin difficult, but there would appear to be a substantial number of non-English surnames among the new arrivals, and a number of Quakers. Such impressions confirm the commonly accepted notion that pacifist religious beliefs and recent arrival in America were important factors in producing Loyalist refugees.[69]

The settlement of the Loyalist refugees and soldiers, mainly on land obtained by Walter Patterson and his friends at the auction of 1781, was executed under considerable pressure of time quite apart from the obvious immediate needs of the newcomers. Settlement had to be completed before knowledge of the British government's attitude to the 1781 sales was known. Early in 1784 an agent of proprietor Robert Clark had appeared in Charlottetown on a fact-finding mission. Naturally John Cambridge discovered a good deal, returning to London with a new perspective on the situation.[70] A new petition to the Board of Trade was prepared by some of the proprietors, far less defensive and guarded than previous efforts, providing evidence that the governor had not placed Lord North's draft bill before the assembly and that he and the council were planning to oppose restitution. Even before this petition was heard, the government had hinted its lack of enthusiasm for Patterson. The decision taken in spring 1784 to reduce the status of the Island to a lieutenant-governorship responsible to Nova Scotia was part of a general reorganization of the Maritime colonies in the wake of the Loyalist influx and the creation of New Brunswick as a separate colony. It was not directed at Walter Patterson. But the letter to him announcing the action did not encourage him to remain at the helm. Instead it spoke of allowing Patterson to decide whether he could accept the demotion, and obviously hoped he could not.[71]

Upon hearing the Clark petition in August 1784, the Lords of Trade were understandably upset that Patterson and his council should take upon themselves to "disobey a positive injunction of His Majesty," and surprised that they had not shown a "greater degree of impatience to justify their proceedings to His Majesty on a point of so much weight."[72] Patterson had written in April criticizing the bill and defending his actions, but as Captain John MacDonald reported to his sister, "Government here is tired with your St. John's Government."[73] Indeed, a very nearly apopleptic Lord Fawkener, noting the absence of any official communication from the Island, successfully applied for a special naval vessel to sail immediately for the sole purpose of collecting "the papers and Evidence that the Governor and Council must naturally be so anxious to submit to the Lords of the Committee."[74] Never were the Island's communications with Britain better than upon this occasion. The sloop of war arrived at Charlottetown in early December of 1784. The entire Island soon knew of its mission. Partisan lines for and against Walter Patterson would finally crystallize.

CHAPTER SEVEN

Loyalists versus Proprietors, 1784–1786

The eighteen-month period from December 1784, when the British sloop arrived in Charlottetown, to June 1786, when Walter Patterson was recalled to England, was one of the most confused in the Island's history, as Loyalist refugees and proprietors were brought into active although indirect opposition to one another over the land question. The lieutenant-governor succeeded in reasserting his dominance over Island politics, chiefly by enlisting the Loyalist newcomers in support of his land policies. This alliance gave a certain outward appearance of stability to Patterson's administration in these months, at the same time that his position was constantly eroding in London, as increasing evidence became available of the machinations involved in and resulting from the land sales of 1781. The proprietors began their assault with caution, and both they and the British authorities gave Patterson every opportunity to alter his course. Instead, Patterson responded to his critics by enlarging his policy of entrenching the 1781 proceedings so deeply in the Island's system as to make reversal virtually impossible. Gradually it became clear that the lieutenant-governor, backed by the legislature and probably by a majority of the electorate, was prepared to defy openly the Board of Trade, even the Privy Council and the king. While these proceedings unfolded, of course, the orderly settlement and development of the Island of St John were yet again placed on hold. Perhaps even more significantly, instead of an unsatisfactory land system being on trial, it was Walter Patterson and his administration that provided the focus of attention.

Even before the arrival of the British sloop sent the Island's leaders scurrying about to protect their own positions, Patterson had finally set his own defence in motion. He had initially hoped to quiet criticism with a letter to Lord North of 10 April 1784, which had reported that the quitrent legislation had been laid before the council but not the assembly.[1] At the very least, this dispatch was designed to buy time. In it Patterson explained the delays in a variety of ways. Communications were slow, and as he would point out a few days later, the current meeting of the assembly was an awkward one. More significantly, however, he insisted that the draft bill was based upon "misrepresentations" and "unjust reflections" and therefore "appeared to require very mature consideration." Patterson maintained that at the time of the auction in 1781, the land involved was without value because of rumours of the Island's cession to France. Conceding that he himself had made purchases, he insisted all those officers who had done so were owed back salary, and would "much rather have had the Money than the Land." None of the lots had been improved, after all, and only altered circumstances since 1781 occasioned complaint; "had the War continued twenty years, your Lordship would not during that time have heard a word on the subject." He had offered by proclamation a fourth part of the lots sold in 1781 to incoming Loyalists, and complained that there was no money in the quitrent fund to reimburse officers for their fees in handling Loyalist land transactions.

Unfortunately, while Patterson's explanations of delay were probably sufficiently credible to keep everyone out of trouble had they been accompanied by information that the draft legislation would soon be adopted, they were hardly enough to force the British authorities to change their minds about the propriety of the legislation itself, or to acquit Patterson and the council of disobedience. Patterson seemed to take for granted that once the "facts" were fairly represented, the Board of Trade would withdraw its efforts to reverse the 1781 sales. But under no circumstances was he prepared to undo those proceedings. He must have realized himself that the April letter did not justify continued disobedience, but he made no further effort to explain his conduct to the British authorities – beyond his report dealing with the 1784 assembly – until November 1784, when he produced a lengthy statement on the Loyalists.[2] Apparently Patterson wrote a series of explanatory letters to colony agent John Stuart, but there is no evidence that Stuart presented them to the authorities in London before 1785. In his account of the Loyalist settlement, Patterson assumed an air of the beleaguered administrator, attempting desperately to do the right thing but frustrated by failures of communication, co-operation from fellow governors, and lack of government support at home.

He began by noting the receipt of the letter from Stuart informing him of government assurances that the same terms for Loyalists would apply to the Island as in Nova Scotia. This approach in effect turned the responsibility back to Stuart if anything had been misunderstood. Only in September 1784, Patterson observed, had he learned that passage money to the Island would be authorized only for those who had not yet accepted land grants in Nova Scotia. By this time he had drawn on London for passage money. Not only was there a shortage of direction from Britain but also an absence of information from Governor Parr in Nova Scotia. He was thus forced to act without formal instructions and "guided intirely by my own Reason," always on the assumption that government intended to treat Island Loyalists as in the neighbouring colonies. From his perspective, the governor argued, he was in a particularly "delicate situation," bound to obey the ministry but constantly watched by a "jealous and interested Proprietary" eager to misconstrue his conduct. How, for example, could he defray the expenses of granting land to Loyalists without fees when he was unable to enforce the collection of quitrents and hence had no revenue? He complained of the "degrading distinction" of not having the same confidence from the British authorities he felt had been extended to other governors, and insisted that he was continuing to expend in the Loyalist business his own private fortune, much as he had done in earlier settlements. He did not mean to give advice, Patterson gratuitously concluded, for "His Majesty's Councils are replete with Wisdom, and greatly equal to every Emergency of State."

The governor returned to martyred self-justification in another letter dated 2 December 1784, immediately after the arrival of the British sloop. He had acknowledged the arrival of the dispatches requesting information a day earlier, noting "I shall very humbly offer all I have to say in my justification, and in so doing, I shall, as in all occasions, adhere rigidly to the truth; after which I shall hope my errors, if any, will not be found to be those of the Heart."[3] In elaboration of his sincerity, Patterson employed the occasion of the receipt of his new appointment as lieutenant-governor of the Island, an action he chose to interpret "as a Gracious mark of His Majesty's Approbation of my past Conduct."[4] He had taken advantage of the restructuring of the colony's government to appoint a new council, replacing Thomas Desbrisay with Collector of Customs William Townshend. The loss of rank was not a matter of consequence, Patterson insisted, since he was only "ambitious of a good name." Revealingly, he continued, "I was vain of this Country. It is my Child. I have fostered it, at the expence of my Fortune and a great part of the prime of my Life." This sense of identification with the colony undoubtedly contributed to his inability to recognize the force of the criticisms mounting against him. He then moved on to attack Nova Scotia as an enemy of the Island and to rehearse the early problems of settlement, partly to argue his own contribution and partly to criticize Robert Clark's colonization activities. Turning to the Loyalists, he maintained that several thousand would have abandoned Shelburne for the Island had not Governor Parr been so hostile. Parr, he added, "thinks this Country as bad as Churchill's picture of Scotland," and was no friend to the Island. While his assessment of Parr's attitude may have been accurate, there were obviously more pressing factors explaining the lack of Loyalist migration from Nova Scotia.

Establishing a posture as a well-meaning and sincere administrator frustrated by a lack of support from proprietors, British authorities, and fellow officials was not Walter Patterson's only initiative in the autumn of 1784. He had also resumed hearings in the council regarding the political behaviour of Chief Justice Peter Stewart, a process begun in May and abruptly halted at the end of June. What Patterson hoped to accomplish either by the delay or the resumption of proceedings is not at all clear. Stewart himself would claim that the governor offered to end them in June if the chief justice and his wife would settle their differences and become reconciled, the only explanation any of the participants would ever offer for the interruption.[5] But there were obviously political as well as personal issues involved. If Patterson hoped to menace or silence the opposition by attacking Stewart, his tactics were doomed to failure, particularly after the news arrived that the British government was energetically pursuing its investigations of the Island's administration. Patterson might intimidate on the Island, but he could not prevent the criticisms of the Stewart clan from reaching the ears of the government in Whitehall.

The fresh round of examinations in the Stewart case, which began on 27 November 1784, started routinely enough, with testimony from a number of witnesses mainly sympathetic to the governor about the political opposition led by Jack Stewart and allegedly supported by his father. The hearings took their first dramatic turn on 30 November, when Annabella Stewart, the spinster daughter of the chief justice, introduced the adultery business into the situation.[6] She testified that one of the previous witnesses, David Lawson of Stanhope and a supporter of the governor, had been responsible for bringing the family the news that the governor was assisting Sarah Stewart and her children to depart from the Island. Testimony resumed routinely to 4 December, when Charles Stewart arrived to insist that he be allowed to attend the hearing on behalf of his father, with the privilege of cross-examining witnesses. This move by the Stewarts was undoubtedly related to the arrival of the government sloop, which had suddenly transformed the hearings from a local squabble into ones to which the British government was likely to pay close and immediate attention. Simultaneously a subtle change of tone in the testimony could be detected, with witnesses far more conscious that it was Walter Patterson as well as Peter Stewart whose activities were under scrutiny. The Stewarts complained that they were allowed to cross-examine witnesses only if they gave in questions in writing, and insisted that the whole proceedings constituted trial in a court "which legally has no Cognizance in such matters."[7]

The chief justice managed to introduce evidence regarding his stance on the draft bill, and Patterson was forced to write an exculpatory letter to Lord Sydney that labelled the Stewart accusations of adultery a "vile, false Story, contrived by the Chief Justices Children, by a former Wife, on purpose to get rid of a step Mother." Peter Stewart, the governor admitted, had acted "under the influence of a passion of the most gauling nature," but he was mistaken in his conclusions. Patterson further attempted to limit the damage to his reputation by shifting attention to the political arena, where he accused the chief Justice of heading a "party of Men, some of very indifferent Characters, mostly of desperate Fortunes; all my Enemies, because I dislike them too much to have them at my Table."[8] That same day, which saw the drafting of the letter to Sydney, also produced charges against Stewart, for abetting his son and others "in opposition to the known wishes of the Governor" in electing a discreditable assembly. The chief justice was also accused of divulging a secret discussion of council at the hustings, making it impossible for the governor to raise a revenue, and advising disobedience to the governor's authority.[9] The charges were, at best, arguable.

While Patterson concentrated on Peter Stewart, the Island's officialdom prepared affidavits defending their own actions in 1780 and 1781, as well as those in the wake of the arrival of the draft legislation. Attorney-General Callbeck, for example, acknowledged that he and Peter Stewart had been asked by the council in spring 1784 to prepare papers on the land business, but illness and confinement for seven months had prevented him from completing the work; he attached a surgeon's certificate.[10] Stewart for his part swore that he was "ever ready to attend to any public business on the shortest notice," and blamed delay on Callbeck.[11] In a separate statement, the chief justice supplied a certification that all the Supreme Court proceedings on the forfeited lots "were conducted with the utmost Attention upon the part of all the Members of that Court, and with all the Lenity possible towards the said Proprietors."[12] The terms of the 1774 act had been fully observed, he maintained. All other officers involved in the 1780–1 proceedings produced affidavits exempting themselves from any culpability. James Curtis, who conducted the auction, insisted it had been executed quite properly.[13] William Nisbett, receiver-general of quitrents, was certain that "so far as Deponent's Duty required," the 1781 business had been legally done.[14] Surveyor Thomas Wright swore that there had been no improvements carried out on any of the auctioned lots except for a small dwelling house built by William Allanby on lot 18.[15] James Campbell, John Russell Spence, and Alexander Acheson testified that the sales had been fairly conducted before all possible purchasers.[16] Thomas Wright also attested that most of the lots purchased in 1781 had been partially surrendered by their new owners for the use of the Loyalists.[17] Walter Berry of Grand Rustico swore that he and James MacNutt had improved lot 24 under lease from Isaac Todd of Montreal, who had purchased it in 1781.[18] Should Todd be dispossessed, he added, they and many fishermen would be "considerable loosers." The air around Charlottetown positively reeked with protestations of innocence and assiduous attention to the public interest during December 1784.

While the Island's officialdom was convinced that it had done nothing worthy of blame, the rump assembly – undoubtedly in the person of Jack Stewart – was equally certain it knew who was responsible for the Island's problems. It submitted a long memorial to Lord Sydney that indicted Walter Patterson for a long series of abuses of his authority. Pointing to the attacks on Chief Justice Stewart in the council as an example of the governor's style, the memorial naturally insisted that the assembly was in no way responsible for the difficulties in which the Island found itself.[19] The assembly's charges, eleven in all, accused Patterson of misappropriation of funds and conversion of property to his own use, as well as of purchasing distrained lots at an illegal auction. The governor was labelled an instrument of "infidelity and Irreligion" who sought to ruin "some of the most Respectable families" on the Island. Moreover, he had infringed on the "most valuable right of British subjects" to free elections by employing councillors to influence them. An accompanying "Summary of Facts" elaborated on Patterson's relations with his assembly, claiming that he had failed to obtain a house "Obsequious to his Will," refused to work with the one elected solely because of its insistence on its legitimate rights.[20] The net result, the assembly's statement concluded, was to drive away settlers and hamper the proper development of the Island.

The Patterson forces attempted to lessen the impact of the assembly's charges by submitting affidavits from Thomas Wright and James Curtis demonstrating that Jack Stewart was a troublemaker with a violent temper. According to Wright, Stewart's unhappiness with proceedings in the Supreme Court in autumn 1784 had led him to unprovoked attacks in the street against Wright and those who came to his assistance. In the resulting melee, Curtis had been struck and kicked by an angry Stewart, who used much abusive language. Brother Charles had made excuses for Jack, claiming the ill temper was caused by the sickness of his wife.[21] This evidence was neither the first nor the last demonstrating that Stewart, commonly known on the Island as "Hellfire Jack," could behave violently in public. Stewart could hardly have answered that he was a man of peace, but he might well have queried whether his temper had any bearing upon the criticisms of Patterson, beyond demonstrating that harmony did not always prevail in Charlottetown.

Perhaps more significant than evidence of Jack Stewart's hot-headedness was the fact that his virulent extremism hindered his cause, even among his erstwhile supporters. Indeed, several who had opposed the governor in the assembly testified before the council that they had changed their minds about Patterson, despite Stewart's continued insistence that the governor was "a Gone Man." While many had wished the governor removed in previous times, comment-ed William Craig, they now feared a worse one and were most unhappy with the public political divisions on the Island. Since Craig, who had been clerk of the 1784 assembly, was a key member of the Country Party, his evidence is suggestive. In any event, despite the criticisms of the assembly, the council voted unanimously on 16 December 1784 that the colony's agent should defend Walter Patterson before any hearings at the Board of Trade, with expenses to be defrayed out of the quitrent revenue.[22] The battle would have to be fought on two fronts. While the evidence brought back to the Board of Trade was obviously contradictory and confusing, it did demonstrate a substantial polarization of political opinion and conflict on the Island of St John that made it difficult for Walter Patterson to govern it. Moreover, nothing in the extensive documen-tation was likely to change the mind of the Board of Trade about the need to provide relief for the proprietors, who if not quite innocent victims in the controversy had been more sinned against than sinners. To defend himself properly in London, Patterson had not only to answer the proprietors. He had also to gain political control of the Island.

By December 1784, Patterson had unquestionably reasserted his dominance over the council. In the previous months Captain Samuel Hayden had been forced to resign, Thomas Desbrisay had been dropped under excuse of reorganization, and Chief Justice Stewart had now been formally charged with misbehaviour. The unanimity of support Patterson received from the council for his prospective hearing before the Board of Trade demonstrated that he had silenced his critics in the upper House. Could he also bring the popularly elected House of Assembly under his sway? Obviously the first step was to call for a new election, done on 8 February 1785. The council subsequently decided that the election would be held on the day assigned, although bad weather (including six feet of accumulated snow on the ground) had prevented the requisite proclamation from reaching distant settlements; the decision was not a precedent, it noted. When the specified day arrived, a request from candidates for an extension was accepted, and the poll was held open for two extra day.[23] The result pleased Patterson, who labelled the assembly which began meeting on 19 March 1785, "the most respectable, and best intentioned House of Representatives, which have ever met on this Island."[24]

As might have been expected, not everyone on the Island was as satisfied with the results of the hotly contested 1785 elections as Walter Patterson. The losing candidates complained that the governor had packed the poll with refugees and disbanded soldiers, having used emissaries to tour the Island for votes and to "pre-engage the Electors," adding this was "the first Instance ... we suppose, of the Representatives of Majesty so openly interesting himself in such an occasion."[25] Patterson might well have responded that he was only following the example set in 1784 by Jack Stewart. In the days before responsible government, governors who sought to avoid continual conflict with their assemblies had little choice but to become party leaders.[26] Patterson's actions were not so much unusual as blatant. The voters were bought with liquor and kept in a state of intoxication in Charlottetown, marching the streets headed by members of the council with "Drum beating & Colours flying."[27] The losers noted that heavy snow meant that many remote settlers had received no notification of the election, while those only recently arrived on the Island were brought to the capital expecting to revel in "Riot & Dissipation" as a reward for supporting the Patterson list.[28] They also insisted that not only were propertied voters effectually denied the vote, but the sheriff refused to accept protests against voters "who have formed no Settlements herein, nor are in possession of Houses, Land, or other property whatever and many of them menial servants." As a result, the "Old Inhabitants" had been denied a fair election. The protest was accompanied by references to Locke and Blackstone on the dangers of executive vote-mongering.

While complaints about the quality of one's opponents were common fare in the early political rhetoric of the Island, the critique of the 1785 assembly was particularly virulent. The defeated party claimed that of the members elected, only three or four possessed any Island property beyond unimproved lots. Many were "Low, Ignorant & Illiterate." The speaker of the House, James Curtis, was a former servant to Phillips Callbeck whose allegiance to Patterson had been bought with the office of "Storekeeper and Distributor of the Working Utensils given by the Crown to the Loyalists and disbanded Troops" at five shillings per day.[29] A later pamphlet published in England provided even more lurid details, describing one member of the assembly as having had "in the preceding stage of life ... a complete course of parliamentary education in the galley of a ship of war.[30] The critics were not much kinder to the electorate. Of the 130 voters polled in 1785, claimed *Remarks on the Conduct of the Governor and Council of the Island,* six were councillors, three were menial servants, one was a visiting ship's captain, thirty-three were refugee Loyalists, and fifty-three were disbanded soldiers, leaving only thirty-three independent voters.[31] An annotated copy of the poll list forwarded to England by the opposition provided some substantiation of this analysis on a name-by-name basis.[32]

Although too much attention should not be given to the bitter invective addressed by the losing party of 1785 against the winners, two points do stand out. The first is that the personnel of the 1785 assembly did not contain many established landholders on the Island. The second and perhaps more important point was that this 1785 assembly unquestionably owed its election to the so-called "Loyalist" vote. While some of the Loyalist electorate may well have been bought with liquor, many were undoubtedly equally influenced by that unstated issue of 1785, the land question. The party that claimed to represent the "old inhabitants" clearly opposed Walter Patterson and his policies, including his failure to execute the Board of Trade's instructions to reverse the land auction of 1781. It was a group, it should be emphasized, not so much well disposed to the proprietors as opposed to Walter Patterson. Nevertheless, most of the newcomers, even if they had not yet improved their land and put down roots, by this time realized that they had been located on disputed property. As the governor had anticipated, his policy of placing Loyalists on land purchased in 1781 had provided a complicating factor in Island politics. Patterson now not only had an assembly that would support him and lend credence to any arguments of popular support on the Island, he also had an assembly elected to office by voters whose interests could in no way be served by accepting the Board of Trade's direction to pass new legislation undoing the 1781 sales. The Loyalists had been conscripted on behalf of the Patterson interests. Like the proprietors, they had become virtual pawns in the complex local struggle for control of the Island.

Given the total rout of the "old party" in the assembly elections – curiously, Patterson's opponents did not use the label "country party" in 1785 – and the governor's intimidation of critics in the council, it is not surprising that the resultant meeting of the legislature took place without any serious clash of factions. Indeed, the legislature congratulated itself on elimination of faction. Patterson addressed the joint houses on 22 March 1785, observing that his efforts for the "suffering Loyalists" had been previously obstructed by the "malicious machinations of some noisy and pretended patriots."[33] Only Chief Justice Peter Stewart dissented in council from the fulsome acceptance of the governor's remarks, which trusted "that the late discountenance shewn to Faction and Party by honest and worthy Members of Society will effectually crush that Hydra of Dissention, and that the Grand Criterion Truth, will resume her Seat of Empire."[34] The assembly's deliberations were without incident until 2 April, when the council called to its attention the "mutilated" copy of the journal of the previous house, which omitted most of Patterson's response to the address regarding the £3,000 parliamentary grant.[35] Witnesses were called who testified that Jack Stewart held the originals and that the copies made had been tampered with. The copies had themselves been rescued from the house of the chief justice just before the assembly's convocation. The only contentious debate occurred in the council over a draft bill from Attorney-General Callbeck on divorce, incest, and polygamy, which was dropped because of the disagreement.[36]

Although Patterson's critics labelled this session as a "do-nothing" one, it passed considerable legislation, including an act allowing Quakers to make an affirmation rather than take an oath and two bills regulating land-granting procedures in the colony that were both later disallowed by the British government.[37] This assembly also voted a grant of £161.2.11 for support of his majesty's government, the first time local funds, however miniscule, were voted for this purpose.[38] Governor Patterson undoubtedly hoped this evidence that the Island was beginning to assume financial responsibility would redound to his benefit in Whitehall. Perhaps significantly, this assembly session was not asked to deal directly with the land question, although it did so indirectly through acts reorganizing the land records of the Island and repealing the 1776 fee schedule.

In London, both the proprietors and the Patterson forces prepared for the critical hearings before the Board of Trade, which began on 25 April 1785, just as the Island legislature was concluding its 1785 session. Both Patterson and the proprietors found it advisable to be represented by legal counsel, and all the available evidence was considered before a considerable audience of interested parties. The board concluded that Patterson "ought to have convened the Assembly and laid before them the draft of the Bill sent from England in 1783, with all convenient speed after it came into his hands, and that the facts and reasons assigned for not having done so, did not justify the neglect."[39] The minutes of the Island's council were themselves conclusive evidence, wrote Captain John MacDonald to his sisters, of the illegality of the 1781 sales. He observed:

I never thought but ther was more knowledge of Law on the Island that these Sales imply – the Affidavits and Certificates in favor of the Sales did not appear to be thought worth the paper on which they were wrote – the Lord President of the Council said that if, instead of a simple application for restitution of the Lots, we had brought a crimination, the Council must have proceeded immediately to punishment: but moderation was our view.[40]

In a separate letter MacDonald noted that it was a pity the governor and council had not simply passed the draft bill, for "It would have Made Government well pleased with them."[41] But MacDonald and his fellow proprietors would come to regret their failure to deliver the finishing blow to Walter Patterson in 1785. A petition from a number of proprietors to replace Patterson with Captain Henry Mowat was not pursued seriously, and while still in office the governor and his friends had room to manoeuvre – both on and off the Island.[42]

A few days after the Board of Trade hearing, the British Cabinet ordered Walter Patterson to lay a new draft bill before his assembly.[43] But there was a delay in preparing the new legislation, initially while lawyers for the contending parties argued over the implications of the British decision. The lawyer for Patterson had initiated discussions before the cabinet action, offering "to meet you upon terms of Accommodation" in hopes that "if the former Act with such Alterations as all parties could approve of is sent out, that all grounds of Complaint on every Side might be removed & that no more is necessary to attain so desirable an end, but to point out what such alterations might be."[44] The attorney for the proprietors responded immediately after the Cabinet order, arguing that the Privy Council had in effect recommended "to the Parties (meaning the Governor & the Counsel in the Island, the Purchasers of the Sales) to propose such terms of Accomodation as would meet the Justice of the Case, and not put the Proprietors of the sold Lots to pursue their remedy at Law." Noting "there seem'd but one opinion, not only as to the Illegality but also to the Misconduct of the Governor and Counsel in withholding the Bill from the Assembly on groundless pretences, and it was lamented that the Charges had not come in a more Criminating Light," William Birch demanded "such propositions on behalf of the Delinquents as shall Manifest their Sence of the Wrong they have done, and their readiness to attone for it." Otherwise, he threatened legal action on the Island both to recover not only the lands but damages, as well as the bringing of "Articles of Charge against the Governor and Counsel." Since he had hitherto sought merely redress rather than crimination, Birch concluded, "I would gladly Listen to any means of Obtaining the former without having recourse to the latter."[45]

In the end, these discussions apparently were unsuccessful, perhaps because each side insisted that the other make the first suggestions for alteration. The proprietors were forced to insist on the delay of the transmission of the bill in order to remove clauses forcing them to pay for improvements on their lots since the sales. According to John MacDonald, these clauses had been placed in the 1783 draft legislation when it was supposed the sales had been conducted legally, but they were now to be altered to make the purchasers liable to damages for having kept the proprietors out of possession for a critical period when "the best Opportunities for settling have been lost."[45]

Walter Patterson learned privately from John Stuart of the proceedings at the Board of Trade and the Privy Council, correctly inferring that while the results had been critical of him they were not conclusive. His immediate response was to put the Island's Supreme Court, which had been in limbo since the suspension of Chief Justice Stewart, in commission to three of his most dependable supporters, Thomas Wright, George Burns, and Alexander Fletcher. None of these "assistant judges" had either legal training or judicial experience, but it was unlikely that the proprietors would attempt to recover their lands or damages from such a court. With the legal system at least temporarily under control, the council continued to allocate land on the disputed lots to Loyalist, principally refugee, applicants.[47] Eventually Peter Stewart was force to step down from the council upon being informed that it would formally consider the charges against him. Thomas Wright entered into the council minutes a denial that he had ever suggested to Stewart that the charges against him would be dropped if the chief justice and his wife became reconciled.[48] For his part, Stewart continued to maintain that his marital situation was responsible for the attacks against him, and in a letter to Patterson declared his refusal to "take back my Wife and live with her as such a Woman who had so long and with so little reserve

continued in a criminal intercourse with you."[49] Whatever the origins
of the charges, Stewart failed to appreciate that there were now larger
political reasons for keeping him off the bench.

Although the British authorities continued to delay forwarding
new draft legislation to Patterson, he ought not to have assumed that
the hiatus implied any residual sympathy for him. In July 1785, the
Lords of the Committee of the Privy Council had reaffirmed the
earlier order in council, rejecting arguments from John Stuart and
others friendly to the governor.[50] Moreover, by autumn 1785,
Captain John MacDonald had decided that "moderation" would no
longer suffice in dealing with the Island's government, and he began
pressing for the removal from office of Walter Patterson and his
council. In a paper on the conduct of Patterson dated 26 October,
MacDonald observed that the Privy Council had "condemned and
reprobated" Patterson's actions, finding them aggravated by disobedience to a direct instruction. Other complaints had been brought
from the Island, he added.[51] MacDonald elaborated his case in a
subsequent submission labelled "Considerations for removing the
respective Officers and Council of St. John's Island," dated 5
November.[52] Here he pointed out that the officials in 1781 had
known that "the Civil War, which had thrown all America into
confusion, and reduced the infant Settlement of that Island to a
peculiar Situation," would soon end, and had therefore ordered the
lots sold at a time when only local officers could purchase them.
Rehearsing the various contraventions of the 1774 legislation,
MacDonald noted that Patterson and his council had attempted to
control the assembly to defend their position, with the result that the
assembly "is become Contemptible and pernicious, as it is not treated
Constitutionally." If the assembly remained as the passive tool of the
upper House, he added, the older settlers would be forced to leave.
"The Affairs of St. John's Island have become the ridicule of the
Neighbouring Provinces," MacDonald concluded, "and your very
Plague here."

At a meeting of the Lords of Trade in mid January of 1786, two acts
of the 1785 assembly dealing with land matters were pre-emptorily
disallowed at the behest of Lord Sydney, indicating that Captain John
MacDonald's arguments had struck home. The act that had abolished
the 1776 fee schedule had not substituted a new table of fees, Sydney
observed, and appeared to be designed to evade instructions to grant
land to Loyalists at reduced fees.[53] The legislation to recopy existing
land grants and deeds while destroying the unbound documents did
not have a suspending clause, and the committee found the authorization of the destruction of existing material "highly Exceptiona-

ble."[54] The government was obviously highly suspicious of any legislation involving land transactions on the Island of St John, not a healthy sign for Walter Patterson.

While preparing for his next move in what was rapidly becoming a desperate chess game played against the British authorities, Walter Patterson continued to correspond with Lord Sydney as if all were quite normal. He complained bitterly about the Loyalist situation. In early January 1786, the governor reported that far fewer Loyalists had arrived on the Island in the previous year than had been anticipated, perhaps only a total of 200 people.[55] Those who came were in considerable distress, partly because of their inability to harvest crops given the lateness of the season, partly because funds from the mainland had not arrived. He did note the appearance of some very "respectable people" from Rhode Island who were unhappy with developments in the United States. These "late Loyalists" would subsequently become the centre of considerable controversy. Having had no word to the contrary, Patterson concluded, he had continued to pay the passage money of refugees to the Island. A few days later, Patterson registered a protest about the deadlines of the Loyalist Claims Commission, which would hold hearings in Halifax for claimants resident on the Island.[56] Because of winter ice, he asserted, no claimants from his government would be able to get to Halifax by 1 May 1786 and hence would be excluded from legitimate compensation. Once again, Patterson implied, the Island was being treated as a second-class colony.

Patterson's major response to the unfavourable news from London was to involve the legislature directly in the land question, something he had up to this point avoided. He undoubtedly hoped to demonstrate the strength of popular feeling and support for his policies to the British, thus confirming his insistence over the years that reversal of the 1781 sales was a political impossibility. Moreover, a legislative entrenchment of Patterson's land policy would create a constitutional problem for the British authorities, since they would have to grapple with the popular will as expressed by the assembly. The governor quite legitimately suspected that those who administered the second British Empire might well back away from such a confrontation, reminiscent of those that had produced the American rebellion. While to some extent his analysis of the reluctance of the British government to oppose openly a colonial assembly was accurate, Patterson failed to appreciate that there was somehow a difference between the Massachusetts or Virginia assemblies, representing as they did thousands of colonials, and the assembly of the Island of St John, chosen as it was, in an election involving 130 voters. He did understand, however, that in the process of confrontation he might well lose his position. Nevertheless, he was sufficiently desperate to take the gamble.

In a crowded council chamber on 15 March 1786, Walter Patterson addressed a joint session of the reconvened legislature of the Island. Because the proprietors had not vested Island authorities with the power to grant deeds to land allocated to Loyalists, he explained, all land assigned to the Loyalists would have to be temporarily vested in the Crown so deeds could be properly granted. In order to execute this manoeuvre, of course, it would be necessary to confirm the titles to the land in question.[57] Before it did anything on the land question, the assembly debated and passed a bill "for Quieting the Minds of, and establishing certain priviledges to His Majesty's Subjects professing the Popish Religion," which was quickly put through the required three readings by both houses.[58] This legislation extended freedom of worship and the right to hold property to Catholics, not only appealing to a large constituency on the Island but, in effect, seeking to co-opt them into the land question as well.

With the Catholics "quieted," the assembly turned to the more important business. James Curtis, seconded by David Lawson, moved that a suspending clause (required in the governor's instructions for any extraordinary legislation) would retard Island settlement. The assembly agreed unanimously. Curtis and Lawson were appointed a committee to consult with the governor on the matter, and went armed with a letter calling for immediate execution of the bill. Patterson was able to respond by pointing out the necessity for a suspending clause. In the House, Curtis and Lawson then moved that because of rumours of measures in Britain to set aside the 1781 sales, Patterson be asked to furnish the assembly with all papers on the matter. The assembly so addressed Patterson, observing that "Loyalists, and other Emigrants now settled or who wish to become Settlers upon those Lands are naturally alarmed as to the legality of their titles." Patterson responded with "all the authentic papers I have received on the Subject of the Sales of Lots," adding that he had reason to believe that the colony's agent and the proprietors' lawyer had been successful in negotiating a compromise bill to invalidate the sales. Otherwise, he noted, he would have had to withhold the papers.[59] Although he did not say so, the governor clearly left the impression that the success of the negotiations spelled trouble for the Island unless something were quickly done about the sales.

Not surprisingly, the assembly decided to proceed with its own investigation into the propriety and legality of the 1781 sales, prior to legislating on the subject. Advertisements were posted in Charlottetown inviting agents and trustees of the original proprietors of the disputed lots, along with other witnesses, to be heard by the House.[60] The only response to the advertisements was from John Cambridge, who wrote that he was acting for Robert Clark and was the only agent on the Island.[61] This latter point was the one the House wished to emphasize. Cambridge advised against hasty proceedings, and asked to see the available material.[62] He subsequently labelled the assembly's draft bill an attempt to confirm illegal proceedings, but he agreed to testify.[63] The assembly passed detailed resolutions setting down rules for examining the evidence, including a motion that "according to the ancient Privileges inherent in the British House of Commons, and Houses of Representatives in His Majesty's Colonies," any member had a right to examine and cross-examine all witnesses. It also rejected the contention of Cambridge's legal counsel, Daniel Grandin, that all witnesses should be sworn, refusing to allow this step for its own members.[64] With its "privileges" secured, the House of Assembly turned to its investigations.

Testimony regarding the 1781 proceedings before the assembly began on 7 April and continued until 17 April. During the ten days of hearings, witnesses from all ranks on the Island, including tenants of Captain John MacDonald, examined in Gaelic through an interpreter, were heard. As well as seeking details on the actual conduct of the sales, the assembly seemed particularly interested in ascertaining whether it would have been possible to observe those terms of the quitrent legislation that called for seizure and sale of property on the distrained lots and whether substantial improvements had been made on any of them before or after the sales.[65] While the Island's officials maintained that property seizures (chiefly of livestock) would, as James Curtis asserted, have ended "in rebellion," the owners of the livestock (mainly Highland Catholic tenants of Captain John) refused to commit themselves so categorically. As Ronald MacDonald put it, he was "sure the People could not help themselves if the Law of the place required it."[66]

If the evidence seemed inconclusive on the seizure issue, it was far more definite on the improvement one. Little had been done by their owners on any of the disputed lots either before or after the auction, although it was allowed that Robert Clark had invested considerable sums of money in other townships. Alexander McMillan furnished a return of Loyalists settled on the lots, by implication the bulk of the population on them.[67] The testimony did not really deal with most of the complaints of the proprietors about the legality of the sales, particularly the failure to provide them with due warning. The assembly concluded that Walter Patterson had acted properly. It therefore not only unanimously passed an act "to render good and valid all and every of the proceedings in the Years 1780 and 1781 ... any want of legal form, or other irregularity whatever in such proceedings notwithstanding," but it pressed the governor to assent to the bill without a suspending clause, in order to ensure there would be no local lawsuits by the proprietors to attempt to recover the land.[68] On 22 April, Patterson assented to all legislation passed by the two houses, including the land acts, and again addressed the houses jointly. After thanking them for their efforts, he observed that he had asked for permission to retire and anticipated that this meeting would be their last together.[69]

With his legislation blocking local attempts to recover the land as evidence of popular support for his actions, Walter Patterson again sat down to defend himself to Lord Sydney. He began by discussing the acts recently passed by the legislature, attempting to distinguish the reinvestment act – intended solely to provide land titles to Loyalists, he claimed – from the confirmation act, although he admitted that many Loyalists on the disputed lots were concerned they would lose their lands.[70] Disingenuously, he added that since he had received no further word on the 1783 draft legislation, he assumed "His Majesty's Ministers in their wisdom had seen fit to let the matter drop." Again Patterson reiterated that no land had been sold that had been improved by its proprietor or upon which any quitrents had been paid. Captain John MacDonald had lost nothing in 1781 except access to a lot belonging to General Maitland where his tenantry pastured their cattle and cut hay. Such people "understand no part of Husbandry but that of raising stock," he observed, "which they may do pretty well, as long as they are suffered to take Hay and pasture for nothing." Patterson devoted much time to a proclamation dated 20 March 1781 forbidding anyone from cutting timber and hay or occupying the distrained lots. He did not understand how Captain MacDonald had gained access to the proclamation, for "it never had the desired Effect," and "neither it or any of the minutes taken on that occasion were ever transcribed in the Copies which have been transmitted" to the British government. This astounding admission, that the council minutes forwarded to Whitehall had been edited, could only raise rather than resolve questions.

Turning to the improvement of the lots, Patterson insisted that any settlement on them had been without the knowledge and expense of the proprietors. Not one proprietor whose lot had been sold, he added, "ever so much as wrote a Line to any one here to look after their Lands in any one Respect," and the neglect of the settlers on them had given the Island "so bad a name as has stopped emigration ever since." Finally, Patterson pointed out that, contrary to the memorials written by Captain John MacDonald, none of the proprietors whose lots had been sold were active in military service and most had offered nothing for the Loyalists. In many ways this lengthy letter was Patterson's most credible and persuasive defence. As an indictment of the behaviour of many of the Island's first proprietors, particularly those whose lots had been sold in 1781, it was quite devastating. Patterson proved conclusively that the proprietorial system had not worked. What he could not do, of course, was to explain why his government had cut so many corners in 1780 and 1781, especially since the chief beneficiary of the policy had been Walter Patterson himself. Moreover, Patterson admitted openly that records transmitted to London had been altered, and in effect, challenged the British government to assert its authority over that of the Island. Curiously enough, despite his earlier statements to the legislature, Patterson made no mention of stepping down.

Although Captain John MacDonald was convinced that Lord Sydney was a minister "without consideration & Bowels," who dithered interminably over the question of Walter Patterson, not even Sydney could tolerate the audacity of the governor's latest performance. John Patterson argued desperately that to call his brother home was an unwarranted presumption of censure, but Sydney took the step.[72] On 30 June 1786, he informed Walter Patterson that "so many representations had been made of improper proceedings on your part in the exerccise of your power as governor that you must repair to England as soon as possible to give an account of your conduct." With what Sydney undoubtedly regarded as British fair play – and John MacDonald would have interpreted as typical pusillanimity – Sydney merely appointed Edmund Fanning of Nova Scotia to replace Patterson "during his absence," although Patterson was instructed to leave the Island in charge of its senior officer if Fanning did not appear and ordered to deliver up "the papers and documents necessary to carry on the public service of the Island."[73]

While most men would have bowed to the inevitable at this juncture, Walter Patterson was not most men. He had not been dismissed, but merely replaced during his absence. And so Patterson, quite simply, refused to be absent. The result, as might have been expected, was further chaos.

CHAPTER EIGHT

Fanning Fights for Control, 1786–1789

Few colonial governors ever experienced so inauspicious a beginning to their term of office as did Edmund Fanning on the Island of St John – or ultimately enjoyed so long a tenure. Perhaps his earlier tumultuous experiences in North Carolina helped prepare Fanning for his problems on the Island. Born in New York in 1739, Fanning had attended Yale College before moving to the frontier of Hillsborough (Orange) County, North Carolina.[1] Reputedly the "best educated man in the province," he became a protege of Governor William Tryon and the target of public opposition as a carpet-bagging plural office holder in satirized in verse:

> When Fanning first to Orange came
> He looked both pale and wan,
> An old patched coat upon his back,
> An old mare he rode on.

> Both man and mare wa'nt worth five pounds
> As I've often been told;
> But by his civil robberies
> He's laced his coat with gold.[2]

The major symbol of "exploiter" for a back-country uprising known as the "Regulator" movement, Fanning was also its chief recipient of violence. His house was set afire and he was publicly dragged through the streets in 1770 by a mob. Not surprisingly, he followed Tryon to New York in 1771, and during the American rebellion he received permission to raise and lead a Loyalist force, the "Associated Refugees" or "King's American Regiment," notorious for its ferocity in battle.[3]

Immortalized in American mythology as an oppressive tyrant,

much of Fanning's reputation was undeserved, for he was made a scapegoat of public opinion.[4] But his brushes with public hostility in North Carolina had made him chary of ostentatious leadership of the sort in which Walter Patterson revelled, and more than the circumstances in which he operated on the Island explain his compulsion for courting popular favour and working behind the scenes through the agency of others. Edmund Fanning had learned the need to disguise his real opinion about anything potentially controversial. He was not confrontationist, but was rather a wily survivor. His seventeen years in office were hardly uneventful, but he was the Island's only early governor who retired of his own volition under no immediate threat of dismissal.

To a considerable extent Fanning allowed the Island to drift its own way, although he took great care to manoeuvre it between the Scylla of the absentee proprietors and the Charybdis of local ambitions. His manipulative politics helped him remain in office, but his lengthy term represented another period in which the Island's critical problems, particularly the land question, remained unresolved. Walter Patterson's behaviour had turned the governor, rather than the land system, into the chief issue of controversy on the Island and in Whitehall. Fanning did not expose the governor's position if he could avoid it, which meant that he essayed no frontal assaults on anything, including the proprietorial system. Patterson's mistake had been to be too obvious about his activities, especially in the land sales of 1781. Edmund Fanning also managed to accumulate large amounts of Island land (ironically enough, chiefly lots earlier purchased by Patterson) without bringing his government down in the process, and another round of attacks against the proprietors would be mounted inconclusively during his years in office.

In 1782 Fanning had abandoned New York, and he ended up in 1783 as lieutenant-governor of Nova Scotia under John Parr. In that appointment he kept a low profile, and was an obvious choice to take over from Walter Patterson when the latter was called home in the summer of 1786. Fanning reluctantly gave up his comfortable life in Halifax in November of that year for a "small, unfinished, comfortless, rented cottage" on the Island, viewing the move as a temporary one.[5] His first months on the Island must have led him many times to doubt the wisdom of his decision. Receiving word of his new posting in mid October, Fanning had arrived on the Island on 4 November. In Charlottetown he was met by Walter Patterson, who refused to summon the council to receive the dispatches ordering the changeover.[6] Patterson declared that he would remain at the helm until there were clearer instructions from home. To Lord Sydney, Patterson wrote of insurmountable difficulties which made it impossible for him to answer the summons immediately. He requested time until spring to clear up his private business and collect the evidence necessary to defend himself. Fanning might winter on the Island, but his appointment was conditional on Patterson's absence.[7] Patterson informed Fanning that he would not hand over the seals until he was ready to leave the Island or clearly directed to do.[8] Whether Fanning acquiesced in this arrangement is uncertain, although Patterson would later claim that he did.[9]

The immediate factor behind Walter Patterson's astonishing behaviour was undoubtedly his surprise at Fanning's prompt appearance just as the Island's assembly was about to reconvene to consider the new draft of the quitrent legislation, finally received from London. Patterson obviously did not expect the bill to prove acceptable to the assembly, and apparently intended to provide alternative legislation that might satisfy the British authorities while keeping alive the changes of ownership of 1781. Patterson, moreover, was also engaged in some deep business involving a new group of settlers, mainly merchants from Rhode Island and Nantucket, Massachusetts.

Two days after his letter to Sydney pleading for more time, Patterson penned a longer one dealing with these new arrivals. They deserved encouragement, he argued, and "this has induced me to continue to treat them still in some respects as Loyalist – which in fact they are not – not by subjecting the Crown to any expense on their Accounts, but by granting them Indulgences," especially the right to vest the property they would import in whatever suited the Island market, principally rum, molasses, and tobacco, normally prohibited articles of trade.[10] These people had vessels and trading connections, and their arrival would greatly benefit the Island, particularly the fishery, Patterson insisted.

At the same time, there is the evidence of the local customs department. Customs Collector William Townshend complained in 1786 to the Board of Trade that Patterson had, in 1785, ordered him to land American goods from two sloops that Thomas Haszard and his sons from Rhode Island had brought to the Island. Patterson, he insisted, had purchased and sold these goods. The governor had also admitted two more American vessels in 1786 and allowed them to be registered on the Island.[11] Critics of Patterson would later claim that this activity was designed to open the "door to American peddling and smuggling."[12] But Patterson was associating himself with commercial activity and development of the Island, a position that obviously appealed to many residents.

Edmund Fanning was probably not, in November 1786, fully cognizant of the widening circles of Pattersonian business, but he could hardly miss the bustle of the legislative proceedings in the tiny capital of Charlottetown. Shortly after his arrival, he received an address from a number of inhabitants assuring him that they were "good subjects."[13] The signatories included the leading members of the Stewart and Desbrisay families and their supporters, in effect the candidates defeated in the 1785 election. Thereafter, Fanning was undoubtedly kept in touch with events by the Stewart party, although he received no formal information from Patterson. As for Patterson, he carried on as if nothing were amiss. On 8 November, he addressed a joint session of the legislature, laying before them the draft bill. Claiming he had delayed submitting the bill because of injurious and ill-founded reflections in it against himself and his council, he insisted "I have received permission to leave those reflections out." He had hoped that the bill had been dropped in London, but if it were to be passed, a clause securing Loyalist lands should be added.[14]

As Patterson anticipated, a committee of the whole house of Assembly voted unanimously on 10 November that the bill was "highly detrimental to the settlement of the Colony," especially the retention of the clause distraining the tenantry for proprietorial debts before selling the land.[15] The earlier testimony about such distraint had obviously made an impact upon the legislators.[16] A few days later, James Curtis brought in a private bill to set aside the 1781 proceedings and to repeal the earlier act confirming the sales. It passed unanimously, and after a few minor amendments in council, was accepted on 17 November.[17] A bill granting £354.16.3 for the support of the government was tabled by the council, because it disagreed with the assembly over fees allowed to James Curtis.[18] Responding to questions, Patterson informed the assembly that he had sold the tools and supplies sent for the Loyalists to an American, but he did not indicate what had become of the money. In his closing address to the joint houses on 18 November, the governor observed that his ambition to retire was delayed by his enemies. He was now "called upon to answer representations of misconduct to the very nature of which I am a total stranger," but he hoped to return to the Island in a private station. Fanning was commended as "fortunately unconnected upon the Island," but Patterson made no statement about a change of administration.[19]

Fanning wrote Sydney on 17 November, the day the quitrent bill was passed, that the new legislation was for "sinister and interested" purposes, but he had not interfered in the legislature's proceedings.[20] He would subsequently label the legislation "not as a Remedial Law in favor of the original Claimants, but as a beneficial Act in behalf of the late Purchasers manifestly calculated in its Operation to cure the Defects of a bad Title."[21] The bill set aside the sales of 1781, except for half of lot 18, lot 33, and lot 35, in effect dealing solely with Patterson's purchases. The proprietors had to apply within twelve months for repossession by memorial to the governor and council. Within one month of their application, they were required to repay the purchase price with interest and reimbursement for improvements. Any timber cut from the lots "for repairs" was excluded from consideration. The Supreme Court of the Island would settle all disputes, and any deeds and grants made by the purchasers after 1781 remained good and binding.[22] This legislation was modelled on the original draft bill of 1783, produced by the Board of Trade before the hearings of 1785 had established the illegality of the sales, with the addition of a clause protecting the Loyalists. Ironically enough, of course, Patterson and his supporters in 1783 could have gotten away with such legislation, which most proprietors would have found made recovery of their lands too troublesome and cumbersome, but not in 1786. Patterson forwarded the legislation immediately to London, noting the failure of the new draft bill to gain support in the assembly.[23]

The presence of two chief executive officers on the Island inevitably produced much confusion. Edmund Fanning received a series of memorials over the next few months pledging support from an ever-widening circle of Islanders.[24] As for Walter Patterson, as early as December 1786 he was complaining, "Self-preservation is inevitable; for being it seems heavily laden with my own misconduct, I am unable at present to bear any addition of other People's." He was unable to get documents properly executed, he protested, and his requests were "either treated with Ridicule or inattention."[25] A few days later, Fanning reported to Evan Nepean that the population of the Island was uneasy, many arguing that Patterson would hold out as long as possible, however much he was bringing the government into disrepute.

Attempting to secure his position at home, Fanning asked Nepean to serve as the Island's agent in London.[26] By February 1787, Fanning was writing anxiously to Sydney that he found Patterson's delaying tactics increasingly irksome, and he felt his situation "a very singular one."[27] Attempts to gain access to the Island's records through its clerk Thomas Desbrisay failed dismally. The old man had earlier put his post in the hands of a deputy who was a supporter of Patterson and who refused to deliver up the papers.[28] Protests got nowhere and Desbrisay informed Fanning darkly that he suspected "some Foul

Play is intended."[29] Long-time clerk and coroner John Budd, for years a Stewart man, found himself out of office, replaced by a "menial servant" of Walter Patterson.[30]

Edmund Fanning's growing irritation with developments – and the lack of them – was matched by increasing pressure from Patterson's opponents to do something to end the "Anarchy and Confusion."[31] Finally Fanning acted. Upon advice from Halifax, he informed Lord Sydney, he had on 10 April 1787 published his commission. Patterson had responded by posting a public advertisement reiterating his position that Fanning was only to serve in the lieutenant-governor's absence, and that there were no instructions dismissing the lieutenant-governor.[32] The Patterson proclamation also identified a real problem for Fanning, the fact that only one member of the council supported him. A subsequent public notice from Patterson forbade Islanders to obey Fanning.[33] It was pulled down by Jack Stewart, who with John Cambridge was assaulted and abused by Patterson's servant.[34] Although Fanning dissolved the assembly on 3 May, Patterson merely prorogued it two days later. According to Fanning there was no excuse for Patterson's delaying tactics. Transportation was not a problem. Patterson could have left the Island on the schooner that brought Fanning, and even if that departure were impossible, at least two schooners had sailed for Halifax in the spring.[35] The erstwhile governor struggled to assemble a council, reporting in May that while he had no word from Britain, the council was still struggling against the "Enormity" of their behaviour with deception, misrepresentation, bribery, and promises.[36]

On 2 June 1787, Walter Patterson finally departed from the Island on board His Majesty's Frigate *Thisbe*, headed to Quebec for "consultations" with Lord Dorchester, the governor-general. Fanning at this point noted that three councillors (George Burns, Phillips Callbeck, and Thomas Wright) had refused to obey his orders and another had resigned. Captain Dalrymple of the garrison had refused to obey Fanning as well.[37] Patterson obviously received little support in Quebec, for Dorchester wrote to Fanning of his surprise at disobedience from the garrison, ordering the commander removed immediately. The governor-general emphasized his abhorrence at "caballing," and recommended that Fanning immediately suspend the entire council and all inferior civil officers.[38] Whether or not Fanning went so far is unclear, but in June and July of 1787, he did manage to reconstruct his council. An old Loyalist colleague, Colonel Robert Gray, was brought in from Nova Scotia as Fanning's private secretary, and received a seat at the council. The Desbrisays –

Thomas and Theophilus – both resumed their attendance, as did William Townshend (Peter Stewart's son-in-law) and John Budd.[39]

Like Patterson before him, Fanning ultimately had more trouble with the assembly than with the council. The elections in July 1787 were for the first time held outside Charlottetown as well as in the capital, with polls at Princetown and Saint Peters. Given the recent history of elections on the Island, it was not surprising that there were two competing lists of candidates. One was headed by Captain Alexander Fletcher, whose "friends" supported Walter Patterson. The other was organized by Jack Stewart as the "Richmond Bay" list, and backed Edmund Fanning. The Stewart party did well in the outlying districts, collecting 45 votes to 15 for Fletcher's people at Princetown and 72 votes to 45 at Saint Peters. The most heavily contested and attended poll was at Charlottetown, where the returning officer was Samuel Hayden, no friend to Walter Patterson. There, only 113 voted for Richmond Bay, and 182 for Captain Fletcher, giving the overall victory to the Patterson forces by 242 to 230 votes.[40] Obviously the 1785 single poll during bad weather had greatly misrepresented the size of the electorate, for this election in high summer 1787 more than tripled the total number of votes cast. Captain Hayden in Charlottetown complained of much confusion and disorder by the Fletcher people, including "military interference & violence" to the returning officer; he refused to certify the return, thus rendering the entire election invalid.[41]

Fanning found the matter "of such a new and Extraordinary Nature, and Involving in it Questions of such Constitutional and legal Importance," that he referred it to Phillips Callbeck and Peter Stewart for legal opinions. Stewart called for new elections, citing Blackstone on the need for free voting, while Callbeck argued that if there were violence, the poll should have been closed instead of remaining open until the vote was counted.[42] Once that count had been made, the attorney-general opined, only the house itself could decide. The council, on 18 July, unanimously decided on new writs, on the grounds that election of all eighteen members on one writ for the entire Island (with no geographical representation) was "unprecedented in any of His Majesty's Governments in America."[43] It was impossible for any house to decide disputes without overturning an entire election under existing procedures. In future, the council declared, representatives should be elected by towns, counties, and districts. It recommended four members for each of the three counties (King's, Queen's, and Prince), and two each for Georgetown, Princetown, and Charlottetown. There would thus be six writs issued instead of one. The council reiterated that voters must be Protestants, and in possession of a freehold estate located on a single lot. Perhaps significantly, the new clerk at this council meeting was Charles Stewart.[44]

While the council was doubtless accurate in its assertion that "at large" assembly elections were uncommon American practice, and equally correct that such a procedure made it difficult to challenge results, the reform of the electoral system on the Island owed much less to such considerations than to the fact that Fanning's supporters had lost under the old system, and Fanning controlled the council. Characteristically, Fanning moved to a decentralized arrangement that would minimize the opportunities for political organization, especially for opponents of the government. He also reduced the political importance of Charlottetown and Queen's County in the new apportionment of seats, probably reflecting his assessment of the location of his popular support in 1787. The British authorities would subsequently support the new arrangements.[45] The victorious candidates in the July elections subsequently protested against this series of decisions, claiming that the council had acted with "despotic power of absolutely deciding *ex parte*" without bothering to hear the evidence. They also complained that Fanning's people were already actively canvassing for votes against them, and demanded a recall of the new election writs.[46] Fanning responded that there was no precedent for recalling writs, and he refused to do so. A petition against the writs by 113 residents was dismissed by the governor as coming from the "lowest order and class of inhabitants, more than thirty of whom being either servants, Roman Catholics, or minors ... are not entitled to vote."[47] Little more was done by the opposition about the electoral reforms beyond these protests, although the complaints would later reappear in 1791 in charges levelled against Fanning and his officers.

For the moment, Fanning's chief concerns were not with electoral grievances, real or contrived. He continued to strengthen his hold on the council, adding another ex-Nova Scotia Loyalist, Joseph Aplin, to it. He also used the council to relieve James Curtis of his post as storekeeper of Loyalist donations, when Curtis claimed he had reported on his accounts to Patterson's council and then destroyed his vouchers.[48] But Fanning's more pressing concerns were the sorting out of the complex strands of the land question, both to allow settlement to resume and to satisfy those recently arrived, chiefly the Loyalists. The same council meeting that heard the protests of Captain Fletcher's candidates also adopted a new policy for settlement, albeit as an interim measure. The new approach had been worked out in consultation with Robert Clark, acting as agent for the proprietors, who were becoming very concerned with claims of persons residing on land without proprietorial permission. Licences of occupation would be granted by the council to those improving the land of absentee proprietors, the licences to run until the landlord appeared on the Island to confirm or reject them. The licensee was to pay his fair share of the quitrents owing on the land and a "reasonable rent" to the proprietor, and no licence was to exceed 200 acres per tenant.[49]

This policy represented the first attempt to deal with the problem of squatting, a common occurrence on an Island where so much land was held by proprietors who had no local agents to reach agreements with prospective tenants. It was plainly intended to pressure absentee and inactive proprietors to appoint local agents. If they did not, land would be allocated without their consent. The policy was also clearly designed as an interim measure, for it made no provision in the event of continued failure to act on the part of the proprietor. Licences may have provided some security of tenure for settlers on unimproved lots by turning the government into a de facto agent for delinquent proprietors, but at best they dealt with the settler as a tenant and not as a potential freeholder. Acadians were the first to take advantage of the new arrangement.[50] Licensing nevertheless marked a critical shift in the Island's relationship with the proprietors. During the Patterson years, the principal complaint about the proprietors was that they were not paying their quitrents. Under Fanning, quitrent revenue would become far less important than development.

In a series of letters written early in October 1787 to the British authorities, Fanning turned to the related issues of the 1781 sales and the subsequent grants to Loyalists. Regarding the sales, he noted to Lord Sydney, he had received no instructions from the government.[51] Indeed, the only correspondence from London Fanning had received he would not dare mention to Sydney, since Evan Nepean had privately informed Fanning that it was his opinion the acting lieutenant-governor had been wrong to issue any proclamation while Patterson still controlled the government.[52] Fanning ignored this rebuke and carried on, in the hopes – eventually realized – that the British would overlook his zealousness in their general annoyance with Patterson's behaviour. Fortunately he had inadvertently waited until two days after Sydney in London had written the formal letter of dismissal.

To Sydney, Fanning merely reported that the Supreme Court had no records dealing with the sales, which were not conducted on the day advertised and were executed by the governor and council rather than by the court. All court records were in the hands of Phillips Callbeck. Fanning opined that one court suit by a proprietor in the

Island's Supreme Court – and Robert Clark was on the Island representing the proprietors – would undoubtedly resolve the matter. A day later Fanning dealt with the Loyalists, thus perpetuating Patterson's distinction between the sales and the subsequent settlement program.[53] He needed instructions, he informed Sydney, for dealing with the grants to Loyalists of one-quarter of proprietorial lots subscribed in 1783. He had assumed that the grants were to be made by the governor and council, but the proprietors (here he undoubtedly referred to a Board of Resident Proprietors recently established by the Patterson forces) maintained "the Loyalist is to have the Land, or not, as he [the proprietor] pleases, and what quantity he pleases; that the Loyalist must hold of him and not under the Crown." The proprietors also maintained that the Loyalist was obliged to pay quitrents, that grants were to be signed by the proprietor, and that if lands were not properly applied for they would revert to the proprietor. Fanning emphasized the need for conditions of Loyalist land-granting similar to those in Nova Scotia, observing that Loyalists were accustomed to holding land directly from the Crown.

A letter to Evan Nepean dated the same day as the formal one to Lord Sydney provided further details on the Loyalist situation, including some hint of the political implications of the latest moves by Walter Patterson, who was back on the Island. By this time Patterson must have received the dispatch from Lord Sydney, dated 5 April 1787, informing him that "his Majesty has no further occasion for your services as Lieutenant Governor of the Island of St. John," and summoning him home to answer complaints.[54] In early June, Fanning reported, he and a party of men had departed Charlottetown in a six-oared open boat to travel down the Hillsborough River. On the land adjacent to the water, they had discovered virtually no settlement, although most of the river lots had been ostensibly allocated to Loyalists. As a result of his survey, Fanning concluded there were no more than 500 families resident on the Island, including French and Highlanders. Given the lack of instructions from the absentee proprietors regarding Loyalist lands, Fanning was particularly distressed by the activities of the "Board of resident proprietors and agents." He suspected ill from the resident board, he noted, unless "some liberal plan should be adopted by the *non-resident proprietors.*"

The formation of the Board of Resident Proprietors and Agents was formally announced in an early issue of *The Royal American Gazette and Weekly Intelligencer of the Island of Saint John,* the Island's first newspaper. According to the public advertisement, dated 20 September 1787, the board had been established to facilitate "the speedy Settlement of this Colony" by opening a correspondence between proprietors and agents resident on the Island and those in Britain, to inform the latter of "the general state of the Colony" and "the particular State of their Lands." It called for a "regular System" and a "faithful adherence to Certain Conditions of Settlement to be adjusted to the actual and increasing value of their lands," in order to encourage settlers and prevent "unfair Advantages being taken of the exertions of the most active." The goals were a "fair and just return for their Trouble and Expense" and the prevention of depreciation of land by competition for tenants. Concerted effort was called for among proprietors on and off the Island to regulate "by such united Authority, the several Rates at which Lands will, from Time to Time, be rented or sold." The signatories – John Patterson, Walter Patterson, Alexander Fletcher, Thomas Wright, Phillips Callbeck, George Burns, and David Lawson – claimed to be "Proprietors of 302,550 Acres and Agents for 427,200 Acres, which together, include more than Half the Lands contained in this Island." The board was obviously the "Patterson gang," consisting almost entirely of the Patterson brothers and those members of council who supported Walter Patterson. Its operation has not often been noted by previous chroniclers of the Patterson regime.[55]

While the board's assertions of amounts of land owned and controlled were somewhat dubious – much of the 302,500 acres were in disputed lots purchased in 1781 and nearly half of the land in agency was held by proprietor James Montgomery, who was actively attempting to replace David Lawson as his agent – the board does demonstrate the extent to which the Patterson forces represented resident interests.[56] Not all inhabitants were pleased with the appearance of the board, however. Edward Allen reported in October 1787 that many settlers were determined to leave the Island. "The Board of Agents & Proprietors," he insisted, "have ruin'd all prospects of their ever getting settlers on the terms propos'd."[57] Allen maintained that farmers should organize to fix prices they would pay for land, adding, "its necessary to make some little stir against monopolisers." Edmund Fanning wrote to Evan Nepean in expansion of his earlier comments that the board had offered to lease lands to Loyalists and disbanded soldiers on lot 47, but without titles.[58] Terms of the leases, offered by John Patterson as agent for Isaac Panchaud, were – according to an accompanying document – free rent for the first two years and then progressive rises to two shillings per acre after twenty years.[59] These rents were high by anyone's standards, and again illustrated that the

Patterson people were no friends to the ordinary inhabitant. On 19 November 1787, James Curtis on behalf of the board advertised in the *Royal American Gazette* that it was prepared to perfect deeds for all lands held by its members, except for lots 50 and 56. Only those actually settled, obviously mainly Loyalists and disbanded soldiers, should apply. Since much of the land involved was in dispute as part of the 1781 sales, this offer was worth far less than one from the Crown would have been.

Despite the flurry of activity and reform on the part of the council, obviously dominated by Fanning, the governor continued to be concerned about the forthcoming assembly elections and the strong possibility that the Patterson forces would again emerge triumphant. Moreover, his experiences in North Carolina and general knowledge of British North America doubtless suggested to Fanning that chief executive officers who attempted to govern colonies which were in a constant state of political turmoil did not long hold their appointments. Sooner or later, the British authorities would tire of the stream of complaints from the contending factions and replace the governor. He therefore attempted to exploit his momentary advantages to come to terms with the Patterson faction. Negotiations were carried on in early October 1787 between Fanning and John Patterson, recently arrived on the Island. The resulting arrangements were complex. Phillips Callbeck, Thomas Wright, and George Burns were to be restored and John Budd and Theophilus Desbrisay removed from the council. After several discussions, it was agreed that Thomas Desbrisay would remain as president of the council while Lord Dorchester's opinion was sought as to whether Callbeck should be restored as president.

Remaining issues "to satisfy the Gentlemen for whom Mr Patterson acted" were the restoration to office of James Curtis and the question of Callbeck's seniority. But Fanning assured Patterson that Curtis would "be no looser," and Callbeck dropped his seniority demands. Governor Patterson's friends thereupon agreed to declare their support of Fanning, who informed Lord Sydney on 1 November 1787 that Callbeck, Wright, and Burns had been restored to the council and Wright to his office as surveyor general.[60] According to council minutes John Patterson was also restored to his former seat.[61] This understanding would later backfire on Fanning. It was a dangerous move, which suggests that Fanning felt his fundamental position to be weak. The governor obviously hoped that it would have wider implications than mere acceptance of his authority as chief executive officer, but he was doomed to disappointment. Part of the problem was that he was prepared to conciliate the Patterson faction, but not surrender to them. His appointment on 26 November of close friend Robert Gray as resident receiver of quitrents upset the Pattersons.[62]

Any hopes for a conclusion to party strife were dashed in the new assembly elections held late in 1787. The Fletcher group emerged victorious, despite the electoral reforms, although both John and Charles Stewart did obtain seats. When the assembly met in January 1788, it chose Phillips Callbeck as speaker and proceeded to engage in debate that Fanning found "filled with the spirit of former party animosity and dissension."[63] There were the usual disputes over elections, and members kept leaving in disgust for their homes. Attempts by the Stewarts to investigate the disposition of the Loyalist stores and reinstate their father as chief justice failed. Perhaps more significantly, Walter Patterson refused to give the house details of his dealings with the Rhode Islanders, arguing he was answerable only to Britain for his conduct as governor.[64] These battles had not been encouraged by Fanning and he found them repugnant, raking up the past rather than looking to the future. He clearly had not yet mastered the Stewarts, much less their old opponents.

Only one piece of minor legislation was passed in the course of a four-week sitting, and Fanning ultimately prorogued the session, telling its members that since he had not "been furnished by the House after sitting for upwards of four weeks with a sight of a single page of the Journals of their proceedings contrary to what has been the invariable practice in all of His Majesty's British North American colonies ... I am unable to bear testimony to that public approbation you very probably might have merited."[65] The governor continued to fret about the continuation of faction. He would a few months later admit to Evan Nepean that it was impossible to conceive "of the rancour and acrimony with which those parties have hitherto aspersed and opposed each other."[66] Certainly he was over-sanguine in asserting that "unanimity is almost wholly restored among all except a *very few* who most probably never will or can be reconciled." The old issues refused to go away, and the "very few" were ingenious in their continued practices.

One of the ongoing problems of the past surfaced again in spring 1788, both publicly and in private dispatches to Fanning. The public manifestation, not surprisingly, involved the Loyalists. On 6 March, *The Royal American Gazette* published a new advertisement calling for a meeting of a Board of Resident Loyal Refugees, Officers, and Disbanded Soldiers.[67] The advertisement noted that the board had petitioned the House of Assembly for action on Loyalist grants but had been informed that the matter was outside its jurisdiction. By implication, only the governor could resolve the problem. The chairman of this board was Thomas Haszard, the Rhode Islander whose property had been admitted to the Island by Walter Patterson over the objections of the customs agents and who even Patterson had allowed was not properly speaking a Loyalist. Board secretary was Walter Berry, whose Loyalist claims were equally dubious. Fanning may have had legitimate reasons for doubting the disinterested motives of the moving spirits behind the board, but he recognized the importance of the popular sentiments they could stir. He wrote pleadingly to Lord Sydney in April about the Loyalists, observing pointedly that he had only recently received the official instructions of 1783 regarding Loyalist settlement. Could Sydney recommend to the proprietors that they authorize the lieutenant-governor to execute deeds and instruct their agents to obey him?[68]

As if to emphasize the tangled nature of the Loyalist problem, Fanning had received from Lord Sydney a dispatch "entirely" disapproving of the interference by Walter Patterson with the customs collection in a series of cases, including that of Thomas Haszard. Not surprisingly, when John Dowley arrived from New York in early summer 1788 with twenty-nine people (including six shipwrights, two millwrights, two coopers, and two house carpenters) and what he claimed were six months provisions for them, Fanning refused to interfere in the customs officers' seizure of the vessel. In a report to his superiors, Customs Collector William Townshend explained that the vessel had imported directly from New York to the Island, with its bulk broken at Walter Patterson's farm, where the seizure had occurred. The venture had been financed by the Pattersons and the Livington family of New York, whose daughter was married to John Patterson.[69] The incident was one that would be used by the Pattersons to demonstrate that Fanning and his officials were opposed to commercial development of the Island; the Fanning forces retorted that Patterson was illicitly trading under cover of development.

The Pattersons had not given up easily. The entire family – Walter, John, and William – had been involved in commercial activity since 1785, and they were probably the leading merchants on the Island. Since the end of the American war, a number of men had undertaken commercial operations on the Island with varying degrees of success. An attempt to restart operations at Three Rivers, financed grudgingly by James Montgomery, had done badly, although Walter Berry was supplying fishermen more profitably from lot 18.[70] James Curtis ran a store at Stanhope, his critics alleging much of the trade goods there were part of the supplies intended for the Loyalists. But the Patterson operation was more ambitious, and through John Patterson connected with American capital. It proved sufficiently promising to encourage others, principally John Cambridge, John Hill, and William Bowley, to form a partnership for another major trading operation.

John Patterson asked the council in September 1788 for a proclamation permitting the importation of American goods on an emergency basis, but the Island's farmers were not enthusiastic.[71] Patterson was, in addition, collecting agencies for absentee proprietors, claiming in the autumn of 1788 to be representing the owner of half of lot 20 and the heir of Laurence Sulivan, who held lots 9, 22, and 61.[72] By this point the Island was sufficiently settled to be producing an agricultural surplus, and sufficiently populated to provide at least a limited market for imported goods. Most of the Island's exports probably went to Newfoundland, and it was no accident that John Hill was a major fish merchant there. Nevertheless, those who became involved in Island trade insisted that they required the support of the government and special concessions, and they continued to complain of customs-house harassment that was politically inspired.

Not all members of the Patterson group could hold on indefinitely. David Lawson of Stanhope, one of Walter Patterson's staunchest supporters, was in 1788 stripped of his agency by proprietor James Montgomery, who had been attempting for years to acquire an accounting of Lawson's stewardship on the Island. Montgomery had received no reports from Lawson since the beginning of the American war, and he was understandably unhappy. He wanted an evaluation of his Island assets and a careful statement of all transactions to show "what I have lost or gained, without putting any value upon the lands originally."[73] Unfortunately, Lawson claimed he had kept no accounts. As he wrote plaintively in 1788, "to state Every day's labour for 18 year back with Every thing purchased ... and Every thing sold ... to this day and to whom sold, it will be the longest Account Ever on the Island."[74] While this observation might have been true, it was equally clear that Lawson had been infected by the Island disease of assuming that the proprietors were powerless to control those in residence.

Considerable evidence cumulated that Lawson had assumed de facto ownership of Montgomery's holdings after 1775, but the proprietor was unable to act because of the confusion caused first by the war and then by the political turmoil of the Patterson period.[75] Bringing Lawson to account was less a result of Patterson's removal than the fortuitous posting of the proprietor's son to the Maritime region. Operating under a severe time constraint, William Montgomery decided on draconian measures when Lawson continued to temporize. He appeared in late October 1788 at Stanhope Farm

– the centre of Lawson's operations – with three assessors, who proceeded to take an inventory of its improvements, stock, and crops. The assessment demonstrated that the value of the farm did not begin to approach the advances to Lawson from Montgomery.[76] Lawson was summarily evicted, and the farm re-rented to a family of Loyalists named Bovyer.

James Montgomery's experiences illustrate the difficulties that even active – especially active – proprietors had in finding reliable associates on the spot. Absentee proprietorship did not work. In his dealings after 1788, Montgomery was unusually fortunate. Pleased with the assistance of one of the Lawson assessors, Comptroller of Customs James Douglas, William Montgomery recommended to his father that Douglas be appointed agent for the Montgomery interests on the Island. Understandably cautious about local agents, Montgomery hedged his bets in appointing Douglas, putting him in charge of lots 30, 34, 12, and 7, while merchant David Irving (virtually the only known tenant at Three Rivers) was to run lots 51 and 59.[77] Both men were to be under the general superintendency of Edmund Fanning.

In James Douglas, Montgomery had fallen upon that *rara avis* in colonial North America, a scrupulously honest man. A younger brother of an Edinburgh lawyer, James had emigrated to the Canadian frontier and clerked for a firm of Indian traders working the territory between Niagara and Detroit. In 1781, he had complained to Governor Haldimand of Quebec of a huge fraud over Indian presents being practised by the Niagara merchants who employed him, and he assisted Haldimand in a successful prosecution of the offenders.[78] Thereafter Douglas found himself harassed by the sullen resentment of most of the merchants of the region, and with Haldimand's assistance he petitioned the British government for relief. Instead of a pecuniary reward, Douglas found himself appointed Comptroller of Customs on the Island of St John at £40 per annum, and he moved to the Island in 1787 to take up his post. James Douglas brought with him the finest traditions of eighteenth-century Scottish estate management: loyalty, integrity, tenacity, and attention to detail. Had he been followed by others of his ilk, the Island might have developed quite differently. He managed to remain out of politics until the mid 1790s, when he would become one of the principal critics of Edmund Fanning. His appointment should have symbolized a new era for the Island, when absentee proprietors would have dependable agents on the scene and could attempt seriously to improve their holdings. Instead, Douglas remained a unique specimen.

As for Walter Patterson himself, the winter of 1788/9 saw him back in London, attempting to organize his proprietorial supporters in defence of his policies and on behalf of a new commercial relationship with the United States. A hostile pamphlet dated 13 February 1789 noted that Patterson had called several meetings of a group labelled "A Select Meeting of the Proprietors of the Island of St. John's, in the Gulph of St. Lawrence, under the Auspices of Walter Patterson, Esq. the late Lieutenant Governor."[79] This group consisted mainly of those involved in the 1781 sales, and the pamphlet alleged, it had proposed a petition to government for remission of quitrents and a suspension of trade acts to allow American settlers to come to the Island with their property. The pamphlet warned against illusions of quick profits, observing that if the proprietors "would enhance the value of their lots in *St. John's Island*, they will have to beware of all desperate Quackery, and to employ a competent share of Capital, of which they have been so sparing in the past time, to bring Settlers."[80] This sensible advice was never heeded, by Patterson or anyone else.

A few days later Patterson forwarded a draft petition to Evan Nepean, subsequently printed.[81] It argued that the Island could supply foodstuffs for the West Indies and adjacent British settlements, if it were properly settled and developed. One obstacle to settlement was the British Navigation Acts, which "press with too much Severity upon this Colony, in its present State."[82] The recent legislation that prevented Americans from trading with the British colonies precluded American settlers – who were the most useful prospective inhabitants of the Island – from immigrating with anything but cash. The Americans were accustomed to American goods and required many items unobtainable from Britain. Several thousand Quakers from Pennsylvania and people from the Hudson Valley in New York were eager to come to St John if encouraged. The petition in effect wanted a special policy for "late Loyalists."

Legislation was requested allowing American settlers to bring to the Island on British vessels "their Wearing Apparel, Household Effects, Tools, and Farming Utensils; and the Remainder of their Property in any Kind of Grain, Flour, Bread, Salted Provisions, Cattle, Poultry, Bees, Honey, Fruit, Fruit Trees, Cyder, Perry, Methlin, Flax, Flax Seed, Hemp, Hemp Seed, and unwrought Iron," provided such goods were trans-shipped from the Island only to Great Britain or Ireland.[83] This list of goods probably offers an accurate picture of what was – or could be – in short supply on the Island at the end of the 1780s. The problem was how to ensure that the newcomers were not importing for local commercial purposes. While the question of American settlers and their effects was a real one for British North

America, requests from Walter Patterson were not likely to be viewed with enthusiasm by the British authorities in 1789.

According to John MacDonald, "Mr. Patterson has tried several of the Saint John's tricks, as well as his very few friends; but he finds this to be a different place from St. John's."[84] MacDonald continued, "the old tricks are become rather Stale & threadbare, and the great Men & the public offices are very dry to him, considering themselves as Affronted by his Conduct." Patterson published in the newspapers that he was in England consulting with the ministry, reported Captain John, having left behind "an amazing pitch of Prosperity" and the "unanimous blessing of the Inhabitants, who wish anxiously for his return." These accounts were answered by "Some Assassin or party man" who reduced the ex-governor to an object of ridicule, and he was forced to live "within the verge of the Court, where none can be touched for debt."[85]

Patterson was obviously in serious trouble, and events were marching inexorably toward their conclusion. A petition from a large group of proprietors in April 1787 had asked the king in Council for permission to prefer charges against Patterson and the members of his council. Originally submitted as a result of the failure of the negotiations between the proprietors and Patterson's attorney over the revised draft bill, it was intended chiefly to force the restoration of Chief Justice Stewart so that legal action would again be possible on the Island.[56] But its acceptance in May 1787 in the wake of reports from Edmund Fanning and Patterson's dismissal from office meant that a criminating complaint hung over the head of Patterson, and his emergence in London in 1789 made action inevitable. The illness of George III over the winter of 1788/9 caused some delays, but the Lords of the Committee of the Privy Council were finally prepared to hear the case in July 1789. However deserved a condemnation of Walter Patterson and his associates may have been, whether such action would benefit the Island of St John was another matter entirely.

Governors Attacked and Highlanders Arrived, 1789–1792

The year 1789 saw Walter Patterson, his associates, and their land policy totally rebuked by the British government. The year 1792 found Edmund Fanning and his friends completely vindicated by the government in Whitehall from charges levied against them by a small group of pro-Patterson merchant-proprietors. In between these two imperial developments in London, Island politics continued to be characterized by conflict between the Fanning administration and the Patterson forces. Not until 1792 was Edmund Fanning able to regard himself as being comfortably in control, and the land question continued to provoke the suspicion of absentee proprietors against resident officials of the Island. Perhaps the major development of these years, one almost beyond the control of those running the Island, was the arrival of a new wave of immigration from the Highlands of Scotland, confirming the Island as a principal destination for Highlanders, especially those of Roman Catholic religious persuasion. The appearance of new settlers was virtually lost in the ongoing political controversies, however, and the immigration finished before anyone was able to generate any concerted program of settlement to employ it to best advantage.

Walter Patterson was summoned before the Lords of Committee of the Privy Council in July 1789. According to Captain John MacDonald, who assisted in the prosecution, Patterson cut a "wretched" figure at the hearings.[1] The ex-governor had hoped to curry favour with the lord president of the council by appointing that worthy's nephew as his advocate – "thinking that all the world are equally to be bought & sold," commented Captain John acerbically – but the lord president merely reprimanded his nephew for requesting more time to study the evidence. Patterson continued his practice of delaying answers, some of which ought to have been prepared years ago, until the last minute, "in order that we might be confused." But, maintained the doughty Scot, his cause was good and "every thing would bear the test of the strongest light & deepest examination," while the opposition's was bad, with "every syllable furnished ... in apology ... falsehood itself"; the prosecution had no serious problems. Its case was assisted by much "authentic Information" from Jack Stewart, in London on a variety of business.

John MacDonald described the scene of 10 July 1789 to his sisters in graphic detail:

On that day the council chamber was an aweful sight. Imagine to yourself a room fourty feet long & twenty five feet high. The cabinet ministers sitting on red velvet covered chairs around a green covered long table railed in with mahogany rails. The clerks having a place aside for themselves & the lawyers another. The rest of it was full of spectators, for curiosity excited many to be present, & every one here from Nova Scotia & Canada was there: those of Nova Scotia dislike their Governor as much as we did ours & were very solicitous for our success, saying that the example would shew themselves how to act, and also terrify their officers to behave well, while it would also open the Eyes of Government. I never saw Mr. Patterson look so ill; but he owed it entirely to himself – we had no wish originally to hurt him or any of them – nor, if possible, to bring it so far.[2]

After the charges were read, which took fifteen minutes, the lord president observed that since Patterson was already dismissed it would not be necessary to discuss his part in the affair, although he could be heard "in defence of his own character & conduct." Patterson and his counsel refused to rise to the bait, greatly disappointing the audience and humiliating the ex-governor, who had "carried matters higher than any King in Europe would have done, in St. John's," but before this august tribunal was in the position of "not choosing, nay not daring, to say a word in support of a character so interestingly attacked." Among the councillors only Thomas Wright was present, and he was given three days to make his response.

The complainants were pleased that Wright chose to answer, since his activities were inseparable from those of Patterson, who had gotten off so lightly. Patterson's lawyers were overheard advising the ex-governor to remain silent, since any defence would only "make bad worse." Wright was easily "parboiled & roasted," the lord president particularly reprimanding him for supporting Patterson after Fanning's arrival, noting "that tho Col. Fanning forgave it, they were not bound to forgive it – indeed he found great fault with Gov. Fanning for forgiving it." But Wright's office as surveyor-general was not stripped from him, because of his "great family." In the end, the accused were found guilty of everything alleged against them. Captain John MacDonald admitted that this great victory did not change much, although he hoped "that there never will be officers there, who will so completely endeavour to enslave the Island, & to turn every thing to their own private advantage, as they did – Nor any whose parts, cunning & audacity will be so dangerous and well calculated to succeed in enslaving & bringing every thing into their own clutches."[3] Even in these limited hopes he may once again have been too sanguine.

Admitting he found the decision "a most mortifying circumstance to me," Walter Patterson requested a suspension of judgment and drafted letters of explanation of his conduct, particularly his refusal to give the administration of the Island over to Fanning. These missives demonstrated his lawyers to be correct in maintaining silence at the hearings, since they were hardly convincing. He had not expected the recall until the very moment of Fanning's arrival, Patterson argued, and had "near one hundred persons depending on me for their Winters subsistence."[4] Four days was not enough time to prepare for their provisioning, and besides, he had answered the old charges adequately and "it could not therefore be those that I was summoned to answer." New charges would require new evidence, collectable only on the Island. His council had advised him to remain in office, but when an impatient Fanning "contrary to his Agreement" assumed the government, Patterson caused no further trouble and had even departed for Quebec. He would have been "insane to have entertained any such Idea" of disobeying the king, he insisted. He continued to maintain he had never "acted intentionally wrong."[5]

Despite his efforts, Patterson could not arrest the inexorable process of condemnation. The final act was played out at Weymouth, where the court was in summer residence. On 8 August 1789, George III in council met on the criminating complaint against Patterson, Phillips Callbeck, Thomas Wright, William Nisbett, William Townshend, Captain George Burns, and John Russell Spence.[6] The charges were that they had illegally and arbitrarily seized and sold land, and had subsequently led an assembly to pass legislation supporting their illegal proceedings. The council heard a report from its committee, which rehearsed the entire history of the land auction of 1781. The committee emphasized that it would have recommended the removal of Walter Patterson if that had not already been done. It also noted that the memorialists agreed to exempt William Townshend from their complaint. It pointed out the slowness with which Patterson and his council had answered the charges, pronounced them fully proven, and recommended that all councillors as well as the attorney-general and receiver-general of quitrents should be dismissed. The king concurred and issued the order.

The final valedictory on Walter Patterson was pronounced, fittingly enough, by his most earnest opponent, Captain John MacDonald, who wrote to his sisters of the ex-governor:

Indeed his conduct was that of a man who looked on all mankind, excepting himself, to be fools. It was also in every shape the management of a downright fool. He has an amazing cleverness, but I am sure it is mixed with an equal proportion of folly and madness. He rose from nothing, & would have done extremely well, had he known where to stop, but the being too successful had led him constantly to goe too far – indeed he could not possibly have succeeded in going so far, but in such a place as St. John's.[7]

Patterson would spend his last years in penury and debt, no longer a moving force in Island affairs.[8] But his legacies, including the bitterness of his many supporters, long remained.

The proprietors immediately publicized the success of their attempts to remove from office those involved in the 1781 sales, printing a pamphlet entitled *The Criminating Complaint of the Proprietors of the Island of St. John ... With the Report of the Honourable the Lords of the Committee of Council ... And His Majesty's Order Thereupon.* This pamphlet produced in turn a printed response sympathetic to Patterson, which quickly shifted into an attack upon the government and policies of his successor.[9] Patterson had spent nineteen years on the Island caring for settlers, the pamphlet maintained, and the cost of getting the Island onto the civil list had exhausted his fortune and loaded him with debt. He was beloved by the populace, and opposed only by troublemakers, headed by Chief Justice Peter Stewart, who was first criticized and later quoted as stating in 1785, "Where there is no security for property no man of common prudence will ever risk his fortune or reduce himself to such a situation as may expose him to the dangers of being ousted of his all." The pamphlet, of course, viewed overturning the 1781 sales as the crucial attack upon property.[10]

Patterson's defenders went on to expose the "duplicity and treachery" of Edmund Fanning, hinting he had issued his April 1787 proclamation taking over the government mainly to find appointments for his friends. Among those dismissed had been Thomas Wright, who had nine children "depending on bread" from his office. The new officers and councillors, the pamphlet continued, had no property interests in the Island, and some of the new magistrates were papists and non-jurors. Three Loyalist associates of Fanning were singled out. One was a lawyer "notorious for public caning in Nova Scotia and dextrous at managing both sides of a dispute," obviously Joseph Aplin. Another, a former captain in Fanning's regiment (Robert Gray), was now a member of council, assistant Judge, provincial treasurer, deputy secretary and register, deputy surveyor-general, surrogate private secretary, and a major of militia. A third, Mr Robinson the printer, was accused of drawing a salary for not printing the journals of an assembly which did not meet.[11] The friends of Walter Patterson were plainly not prepared to end the conflict.

The humiliating condemnation of Walter Patterson and dismissal of his councillors did not really resolve many problems for Edmund Fanning, and indeed succeeded in raising some Fanning would rather have buried. Fanning, after all, had come to terms with the culprits, restoring to his council men now personally dismissed by the king himself. Perhaps more seriously, the success of the criminating complaint did absolutely nothing about the land sales of 1781, the Loyalist claims, or the proprietorial system in general. These issues, not official malfeasance, were the really critical ones of 1789. The proprietors who had lost property in 1781 had not yet recovered it, and many never would do so. The Loyalists still lacked secure titles. Moreover, the question of future development remained most uncertain. What was really required was some master stroke by the British government, cutting through the past and starting afresh on the basis of the situation as it presently existed on the Island. Even if the British authorities were unwilling to scrap the proprietorial system, it needed extensive overhauling. The failure to do so merely encouraged Island politicans and officials to continue to manipulate the system to their own advantage.

Local litigation by the proprietors against the purchasers of 1781 was made possible by the restoration of Chief Justice Peter Stewart to the Island's Supreme Court in June 1789. The test case was Samuel Hayden on demise of Robert Clark v. Patterson in action of ejectment on lot 49. Heard on 7 July 1789, the case was immediately appealed to the council upon the decision in favour of the plaintiff. Not surprisingly, the appeal was denied.[12] At least legally, the door was now open for all proprietors who had lost land in 1781 to take action. With the Patterson affair closed, Captain John MacDonald announced his plans to return to the Island in 1790 to resume his residence there, and he offered to act as agent for those seeking to undertake suits. Following on the test case, the proprietors expected to be awarded their improvements, their expenses, and any quitrent arrears caused by the protracted struggle.

In a circular letter to the proprietors, MacDonald advocated prosecution of the ex-governor and council for damages, writing it "will be a capital stroke, and it will give us a whip to hold over their heads for years."[13] He also sought to recover his out-of-pocket expenses for the last seven years – nearly £350 – from his fellow proprietors. Relatively unsuccessful in the latter effort, MacDonald did better in the former, reporting to his sisters, "I may have as many Powers of Attorney, as I choose to take, as the Proprietors have every confidence in me."[14] He further observed: "It is now in the power of the injured Proprietors, if they choose, not to leave a farthing in the world to Gov'r Patterson, to Callbeck, to Capt. Fletcher, Curtis, Campbell, Craig, Higgins, the Lawsons, & Webster, and over & above to bring them in as much more debt. The doing this does not depend on an assembly."[15] But MacDonald also added, "I believe the Proprietors will now see the necessity of doing something each in order to get the Island settled, or to quit, for otherwise they will not be able – indeed it will not be worth while – to hold their Lots."[16] In this analysis MacDonald failed to reckon with the growing inertia of most of the proprietors, who continued only to attempt to hold on to their property without expense.

The political complications on the Island resulting from the continued opposition of the Patterson forces and the dismissal from the council of those associated with the 1781 land sales made Edmund Fanning increasingly dependent upon the Stewart/Desbrisay faction. Peter Stewart, Thomas Desbrisay, and Theophilus Desbrisay were all restored to the council, where they joined William Townshend, Peter Stewart's son-in-law. Charles Stewart was the council clerk and general man of business. Fanning attempted to leaven this family influence with Loyalist associates such as Robert Gray and Joseph Aplin, but the Stewart/Desbrisay interests were obviously dominant and increasingly self-confident, particularly given their parallel control of the Island's legal system. The governor continued to have difficulties with old animosities. When merchant John Hill arrived in Charlottetown in July 1789, he took an instant dislike to Fanning and his chief officials, largely – Fanning later insisted – because of preconceptions given him by Walter Patterson and Thomas Wright.[17] This hostility turned only to rage when the customs officials adopted an unyielding attitude toward trade goods being imported by Hill's associates John Cambridge and William Bowley.

The key event was the seizure of the schooner *Adventurer* by the customs folk in October 1789. Arriving on the Island from New York, the *Adventurer* was carrying American goods allowable as imports under recent parliamentary legislation (29 George III, c. 16), but it also had illegal goods on board. John Cambridge acknowledged the presence of the contraband, but denied any attempt at fraud. Fanning attempted unsuccessfully to persuade his officials that no deliberate transgression had been attempted, but he did not otherwise interfere. The governor did write to the British customs commissioners that Cambridge had been "of greater service to the Trade of this Colony and its Fisheries, than any person if not all the persons, that ever attempted to do Business on this Island."[18] He observed that Cambridge had erected over £2,000 worth of buildings at Charlottetown, as well as constructing three vessels and purchasing an additional three. Moreover, he had built a large sawmill and other facilities at Murray Harbour, and with his friends had formed a company to bring settlers to the Island on land they had acquired. This sort of development was obviously to be encouraged, but the Cambridge partners were quickly turned into political enemies by what they regarded as official obstructionism and venality, particularly after further vessels – the *Elizabeth* and the *Industry* – were also seized.

Although Fanning's supporters emerged triumphant in the 1790 elections, the struggle was hard fought. The Cambridge interests joined the remnants of the Patterson forces, led by William Patterson, who attempted to rally support in the name of his disgraced brother and that of the recently deceased Phillips Callbeck. To one correspondent William wrote, "it is very material to his [Callbeck's] Children that their friends carry their election – it is indeed very material to this Island to every man who intends to live in it."[19] James Curtis would assist in campaigning in Princetown, Patterson added, and "Mr. Cambridge who from a full conviction of its necessity is our friend on this election ... will have some liquor and etc. for our friends." One of the candidates from Queen's County was none other than Walter Patterson, still resident in London. It was subsequently charged that the Stewart faction had campaigned on the platform that "the Proprietors had forfeited their Lands ... and that if their own Friends and those of the Governor were elected" there would be escheat and redistribution "as soon as his Interest was established."[20]

The selection of Colonel Joseph Robinson, a recently arrived Loyalist and friend of Edmund Fanning, as speaker of the 1790 House of Assembly signalled that Fanning's supporters were in control of the house. As one of its first items of business, the house examined the qualifications of Walter Patterson to sit in it. A division over the question of hearing counsel on the issue indicated the strength of the respective factions. Only five legislators – William Bowley, Walter Berry, Donald McFarlane, John Clark, and William

Lawson – supported the ex-governor, while eight – Thomas Haszard, Charles Stewart, Sr, Benjamin Darby, Bartholomew McKie, John Montgomery, Samuel Hayden, Joseph Robinson, and Charles Stewart, Jr – voted against him. The House then moved that Patterson was disqualified from sitting by virtue of non-residence, declaring Loyalist Joseph Beers elected in his place.[21] Of the five Patterson supporters, only McFarlane could be regarded as a Loyalist, while Haszard, Darby, McKie, Hayden, and Robinson all had Loyalist connections. Fanning had obviously won over the Loyalists to his side. He was sufficiently satisfied with this assembly to keep it for twelve years.

When the assembly turned to the important business of the session, the reasons for Fanning's success among the Loyalists became clear. The first major item was a bill to empower the governor to make grants to Loyalists and disbanded soldiers by virtue of previous locations. It passed easily in both the House of Assembly and the council.[22] The Loyalists came up once again later in the session, as the house heard a petition from his majesty's "suffering American Loyalists and disbanded troops" seeking recovery of the proceeds from the sale of tools and other articles sent by the king for Loyalist use. These goods had been sold by Walter Patterson, who had never turned the money over to the settlers. The House neither acted on this petition nor on another one calling for measures to recover the £3,000 that Parliament had granted for buildings on the Island and which the petitioners insisted Patterson had converted "to his own private use." Such petitions were merely a way of keeping Patterson's delinquencies alive. The assembly also failed to act upon a bill introduced by Walter Berry to admit Roman Catholics to voting privileges, Berry withdrawing the bill to enable members to canvass public opinion in their districts.[23] Catholics would have to wait forty years for enfranchisement on the Island. The house did pass an act "to oblige the respective Proprietors of Lots or Townships ... and who have contributed nothing towards the Settlement or Improvement of this Island, and whose Lands lie in a waste and uncultivated State," to pay their fair share of highway construction.[24]

With the passage of the act on Loyalist grants, accepted in 1793 by the Crown, Fanning's administration slowly moved toward some resolution of the vexing issue of the Loyalists. The legislation simply ignored the question of ownership and accepted the allocations of Patterson and his council during the period of settlement. It was probably the only sensible way to proceed. In addition, the act on highway construction suggested the new direction of thinking of Fanning and his advisers, chiefly the Stewarts, on the equally vexing issue of the proprietors. Instead of concentrating solely on the arrearages of quitrents, it emphasized instead what a petition from Prince County would subsequently describe as "the Failure of the Proprietors in Settling their Lands, by which Means the greatest part of the Island is kept in a waste and unpeopled state."[25] One of the major themes of the 1790s would be the mounting criticism on the Island of the proprietors for their neglect of settlement and development, a tactic that undoubtedly carried more weight than concentrating upon the quitrents.

As for the quitrents, they were increasingly viewed only with cynicism by the Island's leading officials, an attitude symbolized by the story in common circulation about the deal made over the office of receiver-general of quitrents. According to the gossip, Colonel Robert Gray had been sent by Fanning to London in 1790 to lobby for new initiatives by the proprietors, and also to obtain confirmation of his appointment as receiver-general. In England, Gray discovered that Jack Stewart was also on the scene attempting to acquire the office. As the tale was told,

Mr. Stewart declared to a Proprietor that he had offered Mr. Gray £80 a year to withdraw his Application. Upon being asked how Mr. Gray could give up his half pay of £86 a year as Captain for a Salary of £50 a Year or how he could afford to execute a troublesome Office attended with some expence for £8 a Year the difference between the Salary and his Lieutenants Half pay of £42 pr. Annum, and how he could besides give Mr. Gray £80 yearly, he [Stewart] answered that the Treasury never called the Receivers of American Quit Rents to Account and he would pocket what he received. That he would sue the Lots of several of the proprietors to a Sale, and keep the proceeds and that Mr. Patterson's fault was having forfeited the Lots in an illegal manner; but he would go legally to work.[26]

Whatever the truth of the story, Jack Stewart did receive the appointment as receiver-general, and he did not report all his receipts.

The year 1790 marked what seemed to be a return to orderly development for the Island after the turmoil of the Patterson period. The future in many respects appeared bright. A number of the older absentee proprietors had begun to appoint local agents for their lands, and at least one – James Douglas acting for James Montgomery – had started to regularize his administration, producing the first accurate tenant lists for the property under his control, and for any land on the Island.[27] There were also new entrepreneurs moving into both Island landholding and commerce. Loyalists John Brecken and

Robert Hodgson opened a large store in Charlottetown, and John Cambridge was actively developing lots 63 and 64 (around Murray Harbour) on lease, building facilities and vessels in association with a number of English partners. Cambridge sought to exploit the timber possibilities of the Island in conjunction with fishing and sealing, exporting those commodities to Europe and the West Indies (as well as Newfoundland) in his own vessels and importing finished goods for the Island market. His critics pointed out that he had imported more goods than the Island could afford to purchase – at least for cash – and that his building activities were conducted in a economy that featured high costs for wages and materials.[28] Cambridge was hardly the first entrepreneur to attempt such an ambitious enterprise – David Higgins had engaged in a similar business in the same district before the American war – and he would run into the usual problems when those supplying the capital demanded some immediate return on their investment. But his activities did momentarily provide further evidence of renewed confidence in the Island's possibilities.

Perhaps even more important than the fresh surge of investment interest in the Island, however, was the return in 1790 of settlers from across the Atlantic, chiefly from the Highlands of Scotland. As early as 1785, Captain John MacDonald had been importuned by discontented Highlanders to "take them by the hand," but he had resisted. To his sisters he observed that he dared not show his face in the north of Scotland because of "the people perhaps for fifty miles round flicking about me." He added, "I doubt not but many hundreds of useful hands might be got among them for the Island; And it is very possible if the Sale of the Lots had not happened at the unseasonable time, I would have fallen on means to shew the way to the Island to some choice persons, but as matters stood I would much sooner have dissuaded them."[29] Despite MacDonald's indifference the pressures for emigration in the north of Scotland continued to grow, especially in the Catholic districts of the western Highlands and Islands. By 1786, Captain John's brother, the priest Augustin MacDonald, was attempting to organize an emigration from his district of Moydart, and Augustin was undoubtedly connected with the departure in 1790 of three vessels from Drimindarach and Duchames for British North America.[30] Two of these vessels, the *Jane* and the *Lucy*, contained 328 passengers, mainly Roman Catholics from the Clanranald estates, bound for the Island of St John. Passenger lists survive for this sailing, affording an opportunity to examine in some detail the pattern of Highland immigration to the Island in this period.

There were fifty-three heads of families on board the *Jane*, and thirty-four heads of families on board the *Lucy*. Of these, only seventeen on the *Jane* and five on the *Lucy* travelled unaccompanied, meaning that thirty-six heads of families on the former vessel and twenty-nine the latter, or 75 per cent of the total heads of families, emigrated with some sort of family grouping. There were 129 children under twelve on the two vessels, and the average family size for those coming to the Island with families was 4.69 for the *Jane* and 4.72 for the *Lucy*. These figures were fairly typical for parties of Highland emigrants, but of course are in marked distinction to the Loyalist movement of a few years earlier, which was essentially one of single men.[32] Not all heads of families are assigned an occupation, but of those that are, twenty-six are listed as tenant, four as resident, and six given craft or merchant employment. The term "resident" is not at all clear, but the term "tenant" meant that the individual so designated held land and livestock, which in Highland terms placed him or her in the middling ranks of society. Reflecting Highland economic structure, the number with non-agrarian skills was small.

Whatever the occupation, those emigrating had sufficient capital to pay for their passages, which probably averaged around £3 per adult passenger. James Montgomery later wrote to his agent James Douglas that many of the emigrating Highlanders "had some little money of their own."[33] While the small number of surnames among the immigrants makes it impossible to trace them precisely after their arrival on the Island, most appear to have settled on lots 36, 37, and 38 along the Hillsborough River. Lot 36 was Captain John MacDonald's estate, suggesting some connection between the MacDonald family and the immigrants, even if not a sponsoring relationship. Lot 37 was being developed by Jack Stewart, and was adjacent to MacDonald land, while lot 38 was controlled by George Burns. Both Stewart and Burns were in Britain at this time, and may have made some contact or arrangements with the leaders of the new arrivals.

In any case, the newcomers observed the common Highlander practices of joining their compatriots already settled in North America and of congregating together in contiguous communities, probably of kin groups. These people were both Gaelic speaking and Roman Catholic, and the districts they settled along the Hillsborough long remained the centres of Highland Catholicism on the Island, particularly after the settlement of Father Angus MacEachern who accompanied the emigrants, on lot 38 at Savage Harbour.[34] While it is uncertain how much capital and skills beyond livestock raising the newcomers brought with them, and while as Gaelic-speaking Roman Catholics from the British Isles they neither fulfilled the original terms of the grants regarding eligible settlers nor could assume a full place in the political life of the Island, these Highlanders were in many respects a people better suited to permanent settlement than were the Loyalists and disbanded soldiers who had preceded them.

The *Jane* and the *Lucy* were followed by other vessels from Scotland. In 1791, the *Molly* (or *Mally*) brought 174 passengers and the *Queen* carried 240. Both these had sailed from Greenock, near Glasgow, but apparently carried mainly Highlanders. In 1793, the *Argyle* deposited another 150 newcomers, again having sailed from Greenock.[35] Little more is known of these arrivals, and after 1793 the reopening of warfare between Britain and France arrested immigration to North America from the British Isles until peace was again temporarily restored in 1801. But between 1790 and 1793 nearly 900 new settlers, mainly from the western Highlands and Islands of Scotland, had arrived on the Island of St John, representing approximately 200 new families. Most were probably Gaelic-speaking Roman Catholics; Protestant Highlanders would not arrive in substantial numbers until the earl of Selkirk's ships landed on the south shore in 1803. John MacDonald wrote in 1795 that 70 families of his "countrymen" were settled on his lands, and another 150 were on adjacent estates.[36] Not all had arrived in the 1790s, of course, but many had come at that time. The brief flurry of Highland immigration between 1790 and 1793 substantially augmented the population of the Island. If Fanning's estimate of 500 families in residence in 1786 is roughly accurate – and we have no alternative figure – the addition of 200 new families of Highlanders represented an addition of 40 per cent. Moreover, the new immigration further established the Island as a prime destination for Highlanders from the western districts and islands, and many of the new arrivals in the subsequent movement after 1801 would come from this region.

Neither the Island government nor the proprietors were well prepared for the influx of new settlers in the early 1790s, and the newcomers appear to have received little assistance from either source before or after their arrival. The administration was absorbed in defending itself from new charges of malfeasance, and correspondence with the British authorities in this period makes almost no mention of the new immigration. Most of the major resident proprietors who might have been receptive to the immigrants were still in Britain, and no proprietor has ever been closely associated with this group of Highlanders. James Montgomery did respond to correspondence from his agent James Douglas in 1793 with authorization to assist the settlers with livestock, but he added that little more could be done until the question of the quitrents was settled.[37] In a letter of the same date to Governor Fanning, Montgomery approved efforts to attract the incoming Highlanders to his lands by awarding easy leases, but he emphasized that the continued rumours on the Island about large land sales of proprietorial holdings for non-payment of quitrents would undoubtedly discourage people from taking long leases, no matter how generous were the terms.[38] Montgomery subsequently made plain that he was not at all interested in assisting Highlanders to immigrate to the Island, but was prepared to allow them lands once they had arrived.[39] This position was probably typical of that of even potentially active proprietors. A vicious circle was again being created that would be virtually impossible to break.

One of the proprietors who might well have been expected to respond favourably to the new immigration was Captain John MacDonald. Although he had planned to return to the Island in 1790, he did not manage to depart in that year, and his attitude towards the new administration gradually became less enthusiastic. MacDonald had initially been much impressed with Jack Stewart, despite cautions from his sisters about the notorious violent temper, writing in March 1789 that he saw "no such thing as violence, but on the contrary, much honest good sense, Moderation and Candour."[40] At this point he confessed that "the Success I look for, will be much assisted by the Contribution of Mr. Stewart from first to last ... and I only have cause to regret ... that Mr. Stewart and I were not as well acquainted with one Another, as we are now, from the begining of the Affair." While Stewart may have been of considerable assistance in the prosecution of Walter Patterson and his cohorts, by the summer of 1790 Captain John had a far less favourable view of "that wonderful Philosopher" and of the Fanning administration in general. To his sisters he wrote, "I do not care much for the difference between the old & the new Sett, for I do not believe there is any in it. It is only deep far fetched despicable Yankey cunning instead of audacious open tyranny."[41] He was particularly upset by the alleged arrangement between Robert Gray and Stewart over the post of receiver-general of quitrents, commenting:

The truth is that Gov'r Fanning, Gray, & our hero Jack, knowing that Government never thinks of calling the Receiver Generals to Account thought they could afford to make these Sacrifices of half-pay, & hush money, to one another, by getting some hundred pounds of Quitrents every year into their hands without accounting to Government. Thus every farmer in the Island will be obliged to pay twelve, eight, or four Shillings a year of cash every year, & the Proprietors must pay the rest, which will Strip the Island once a year of every farthing of ready money in Circulation. And all this, not to benefit Government, but in order to make a parcel of idle fellows live without work, and drink wine & debauch girls.

Although the proprietors had been relatively united in their opposition to the Patterson regime, attitudes toward Fanning's government considerably complicated proprietorial politics in the summer of 1790.

Captain John MacDonald was in the chair at Munday's Coffee House in Maiden Lane on 17 June 1790 when the proprietors again assembled for the first time after their victory over Walter Patterson. As usual, not everyone attended. The meeting included a number of old hands, but Robert Gray, George Burns, Thomas Wright, and John Stewart – Island residents all – were also present.[42] While the official minutes are singularly unrevealing, Jack Stewart apparently raised the issue of the quitrents in some form that frightened the meeting. Many proprietors were already concerned by the news from the Island about the customs-house activities against Hill and Cambridge, as well as by continuing reports that "Elections and divisions run as high as ever."[43] Captain John reported to his sister:

There must be an end of this Work. Some of the proprietors are of Opinion, that it will not do for them to venture sending out Men, & there never will be peace or happiness or Safety in the Island till it is joined again to Nova Scotia. They laugh at the Idea of the Lands in the Island not being worth a penny per acre in that case. They say that there are parts of Nova Scotia as far from Halifax as the Island, that a Judge will be sufficient to administer Justice according to the Laws of Nova Scotia, which are better, than those the shabby Assemblies of St. John's are capable of making ... that there will be peace & Quietness when there is no Electioneering, and when the ambitious Demagogues, such as Stewart, Paterson and the other officers will have no Offices to grasp after nor any thing to take them off their farms ... It is only the people who are interested, & affraid of losing their offices, that will say otherwise.[44]

Most ominously of all, MacDonald added, were rumours "that Governor Fanning is going to erect a court of escheats for forfeiting Lands before we can have time to look about us."

While the proprietors in Britain had long been suspicious of the resident officials of the Island – and the Patterson performance had certainly given them cause – hostility to local administration was being entrenched. The presence in London of resident officers such as Jack Stewart clearly did not assuage suspicions, and probably raised them. A pattern of deep-seated antagonism between the absentee proprietors in Britain and the government of the Island was congealing. The events of the next few months would only help to solidify and complicate the existing sentiments.

Despite Captain John's bluster, the proprietors agreed to a modest petition to government, calling for a remission of quitrent arrearages and a reduction of payments to a level similar to that in practice in Nova Scotia. The petitioners proposed to employ the money saved on quitrents to convey "useful Subjects" to the Island from Europe and the United States.[45] They did not raise publicly the problem of the disparity between the standing definition of acceptable settlers and those who were actually arriving on the Island. Nor did they point out that the significant feature of Nova Scotia practice was that quitrents were not collected. No evidence exists to suggest that a substantial number of proprietors, especially the major British ones, would have taken advantage of any reduction in quitrent payments to become active developers. Most proprietors who had been active had seen their investments disappear into the maw of wilderness settlement and Island politics and were not feeling very bullish. In any event, twenty-five proprietors, hardly a majority, subscribed to the petition, although John Hill, John Cambridge, and William Bowley were all signatories. This petition was soon lost in the furore arising shortly after its generation, instigated by the Hill consortium.

Equally overlooked in the Hill controversy was a separate initiative from the lord chief baron of Scotland, James Montgomery, that recommended a discharge of all quitrents owing up to 1792 upon payment of a composition of one-fourth to one-fifth of the amount in arrears.[46] This proposal was made after consultation with Jack Stewart, and probably began with him.[47] Montgomery also recommended a lower quitrent schedule and the elimination of the insistence upon foreign Protestants as acceptable settlers. He pointed out that proprietors who had invested nothing and were in arrears on their quitrents were not likely to put money in the Island while their lands were subject to seizure for non-payment of quitrents. That Montgomery's proposal met with no action suggests that highly placed proprietors did not always have positive influence on the British government.

The proprietorial situation altered perceptibly for the worse in January 1791. Before a fairly full audience of proprietors on 27 January, John Hill – just arrived in England from the Island – brought an address to the proprietors and merchants in Britain complaining bitterly of the conduct of the officers of the Fanning government. Hill spoke to the complaints at some length, and proposed a committee to examine the charges.[48] He was fully supported by the friends of Walter Patterson, and the committee formed was chaired by Joseph Kirkman, a London brewer. The ultimate result was a memorial to the British authorities dated 19 July 1791, which registered a complaint against "almost all the officers of Government in that Island who by a Combination amongst themselves and their gross Misconduct of the Government have greatly retarded the Settlement obstructed and oppressed the Commerce and discouraged the Fisheries of your Majesty's said Island."[49] This "Destructive Combination," the petition alleged, was formed principally by Fanning, Chief Justice Peter Stewart, Attorney-General Joseph Aplin, and Collector of Customs William Townshend, in collaboration with the remainder of the council. Although a number of proprietors had been involved in the committee stage and found their names attached to the memorial, only six remained formally connected with it. The remainder disavowed the document.[50] Besides Kirkman, those accepting responsibility were Samuel Yockney, John Harris, Alexander Fletcher, John Hill, and John Cambridge. The first three were old friends of Patterson as well as partners of Cambridge, and Fletcher had been the ex-governor's chief political henchman on the Island. Captain John MacDonald was sympathetic, but later claimed he was too wrapped up in personal matters to play an active role.[51]

. From the outset, the memorial faced several critical obstacles in gaining credibility from either proprietors or the British government. In the first place, the memorialists got themselves trapped in the language of conspiracy, always one of the most difficult charges to document. To some extent this interpretation of the behaviour of the Island's officers was a result of the memorial's second problem, its obvious association with the discredited Patterson faction of the 1780s. Implicit recognition that Patterson had indeed orchestrated a combination led Fanning's critics to assume that an alternative organization had been created to counter it. Finally, far too much of the critique of Fanning and his officers involved petty details of local factional maoeuvring and contradictory evidence. The charges and counter-charges were – and are – impossible to sort out, for as William Townshend at one point lamented in his defence, "In this Island ... affidavits are frequently but too easily obtained.[52] Essentially, Fanning was accused of undue political manipulation, especially in obtaining an assembly favourable to him, while Stewart and Aplin were charged with denying justice in the courts and Townshend with unwarranted harassment of legitimate businessmen.

Whatever the legitimacy of the charges, Fanning and his officials were forced to take them seriously, leading to a virtual paralysis of public activity on the Island until matters were sorted out. The Island did not need another hiatus of this sort. The governor again sent

Robert Gray to England to act on his behalf, writing to Henry Dundas that "it may easily be conjectured what trouble you are likely to have from this Island, if the Memorialists should be listened to with too easy a Credulity."[53] All the officers involved generated large packets of justification. While Jack Stewart operated behind the scenes on behalf of his father, Robert Gray succeeded in gaining for Fanning the approbation of several leading proprietors, particularly James Montgomery and Lord Townshend. Although the proprietors could not control British policy, they could provide support for their clients in a political system that was based on such influence. Montgomery advised Gray not to permit a private dismission of the memorial but to seek a public acquittal. He added, "Take care that the Prosecutors dont print a Case, and You print none."[54] To members of the Privy Council, including old colleague Henry Dundas, Montgomery made clear that he found the charges unsubstantiated and politically inspired.[55] Not surprisingly, the Lords of the Committee of the Privy Council, in the spring of 1792, found the aggregate of charges devoid of proof and the separate ones fully answered by those accused. They concluded, "The Whole Accusation is Groundless," with complaints either lacking in specific documentation or answered with contradictory evidence.[56] The Fanningites immediately put the report into print as a pamphlet. Fanning and his officials were fully vindicated, and the Patterson faction was, at long last, rendered politically harmless.

The reconvened House of Assembly in November 1792 rubbed salt into the wounds of Fanning's critics. Charles Stewart Sr moved to consider a piece of "Abuse and Slander" produced by John Cambridge in the course of the late complaint, and the motion carried easily.[57] Stewart Sr then moved that the words of Cambridge were "false, malicious, factious, libellous, and highly reflecting on Members of this House," with similar results.[58] A day later, the House unanimously resolved that Cambridge should make "some concessions" for his offense. When he refused, the offending passage was ordered burnt under the public gallows. Among other business dealt with by this session was the money due the Loyalists from Walter Patterson. Edmund Fanning reported that £253 had been recovered from Patterson with the assistance of Attorney-General Aplin, and the money was ordered distributed. The governor had finally managed to obtain a copy of the 1783 draft bill, "so mutilated and changed that it became impossible to discover what its Original Contents really were," and so the house proceeded with a fresh bill to void the 1780–1 sales, which passed easily.[59] The last "business arising" from the Patterson regime on the Island was now concluded.

Six years after his first arrival on the Island, Edmund Fanning was finally in complete control of its administration. Or was he? His struggles with the Pattersonians had its price. The complaint of John Hill and his associates had been under consideration by the British authorities just as the matter of a new governor for Nova Scotia had come up in London, and Fanning found himself ignored in favour of John Wentworth as John Parr's successor.[60] In terms of Island politics, Fanning found himself far more dependent upon the ancient anti-Patterson faction than was wise for any chief executive, both because that faction's continued presence kept alive the political memories of the 1780s and because its leading members were not a particularly attractive or competent lot. The Hill complaint had made the mistake of relating the activities of Peter Stewart and William Townshend to the "combination" allegedly headed by Fanning, and the failure to prove this case meant that the British authorities overlooked several rather substantial criticisms of performance levelled against these officers that might otherwise have been taken more seriously. The behaviour of Jack Stewart and Robert Gray in London had made a number of proprietors suspicious of the Stewarts and of Fanning's intentions. Some renewed Island initiative against inactive proprietors may well have been delayed by the charges against Fanning and his officers.

Most important of all, the Hill complaint had been not only clumsy but premature. Its dismissal by the British government meant that a better-documented case could not later be mounted against the same people for the same sorts of offences. Subsequent criticisms of similar import, often by those involved in the earlier action, would be dismissed too readily by those in authority. Fanning and his administration were relatively safe from criticism, but nevertheless the governor had not been able to arrest either local factionalism or blatant instances of official rapaciousness. Moreover, he was unable to enlist the proprietors in a concerted program of Island development and settlement.

The Hill/Cambridge critique of 1791 had been fairly easily set aside. But many proprietors continued to harbour a deep-seated suspicion of the motives of Island officials and politicians, while Islanders in turn increasingly articulated their conviction that the proprietors were a negative force in Island development. The next few years would see these antagonisms further extended and refined, embedded into a permanent pattern from which there was no escape and to which there was no solution.

CHAPTER TEN

The Rise of the Escheat Movement, 1792–1798

With his administration fully vindicated by the British government in 1792, Edmund Fanning was in a position of real strength for the first time. His old enemies for the most part finally accepted the inevitable, making their peace with the governor. But the achievement of political harmony was only temporary, for most leading Islanders remained singularly unhappy with the proprietorial system, and agitation for local and imperial action against absentee landlords quickly resurfaced. Distraint had not worked, and the new demand was for the establishment of a court of escheat, similiar to that in Nova Scotia, to deal with those proprietors who were not actively developing their lands. A legislative report of 1797, drafted by Jack Stewart, documented the proprietorial failure as a preliminary to a call for escheat.

Not everyone on the Island was sympathetic to the new movement. Opposition centred around Captain John MacDonald, who saw nefarious motives behind the escheat movement and with the support of James Douglas and Joseph Aplin managed to demonstrate that the Fanning administration really had hands no cleaner than those of the Patterson regime a decade earlier. Fanning was able to suppress his critics locally, but their remarks did not go totally unheeded by either the proprietors or the British authorities in London. In 1798, the first detailed census of the Island under British rule was taken, probably to provide additional ammunition for the escheat agitation. While it had little immediate political impact, the census did provide a sort of progress report on the extent of Island settlement at the close of the eighteenth century and on the eve of the renaming of the Island after one of the sons of George III. Symbolically, census and a new name brought to an end the first tumultuous era of Island development.

Edmund Fanning's role in the political developments of the mid

1790s was a complicated, complex, and controversial one. On the one hand, he clearly recognized the power of the absentee proprietors, and made every effort to ingratiate himself with them, continually reassuring them of the benevolent intentions of his administration. On the other hand, he was also active in acquiring land on the Island and himself becoming a major resident proprietor, chiefly by purchasing the holdings of the now-bankrupt Walter Patterson at bargain prices. Moreover, Fanning had no objections to plural office holding among his friends, and allowed the expansion of a system of interlocking office holders that prevented any system of checks and balances, especially in the courts, from developing. While it was easily possible to document these facets of Fanning's administration, more problematic was his involvement in various efforts to get even with his political opponents and his connection with the growing movement of escheat. These operations were not executed directly by Fanning, but by his political associates through the mediums of the judicial system and the legislative process. His critics were fully convinced that Fanning's friends could hardly have acted without his tacit approval, but they had to admit the difficulties of finding evidence of the governor's positive engagement. The misconduct, wrote John Hill, was "of a nature not capable of that proof by evidence which would be required in a Court of Law."[1] Whether Fanning was a supremely subtle and capable political operator or the impotent captive of political factions that he did not attempt to control remains an unanswered and basically unanswerable question.

By 1793, Fanning was able to report to the British government that he was personally supervising the Island holdings of James Montgomery, Lieutenant-General Cunningham, Lieutenant-General Walsh, Marquis Townshend, Robert Shuttleworth, and Major Samuel Holland.[2] Not only did these agencies bring him control of a good deal of Island property, but they also demonstrated the confidence that a number of major proprietors had placed in Fanning, a matter of some import. To these absent landholders, Fanning kept up a reassuring correspondence. James Montgomery was informed, for example, that Fanning positively rejected any policy of selling lands for non-payment of quitrents. The quitrents, he insisted, were simply not worth differing over with "such a numerous and respectable Body of Noblemen & Gentlemen as the Proprietors are."[3] Whether this categorical denial was really significant is an interesting question. By this time Fanning had probably accepted the arguments of Jack Stewart that the way to challenge the proprietors was through the issue of development rather than through the quitrents. Fanning did not deny the possibility of escheat to Montgomery, but merely that of distraint along the Patterson lines.

Two years later, the governor reported to Marquis Townshend that the coming of war had retarded settlement, and not until peacetime could Townshend expect "an increased annual Remittance."[4] Fanning also indicated to Townshend his hope that the quitrent payments could be reduced to amounts similar to those in Nova Scotia, New Brunswick, and Cape Breton. But again, he did not discuss escheat. Between the letters to Montgomery and Townshend, Fanning had personally headed an arbitration commission that had settled the long-standing dispute between the lord chief baron and David Lawson, declaring Lawson in debt to Montgomery by a total of £9,219.12.2½.[5] In this decision Fanning had plainly taken the side of the absentee proprietor rather than that of the resident agent, but it must be remembered that Lawson had been a chief Patterson supporter in the 1780s.

While he may have been opposed to selling proprietorial land for non-payment of quitrents, Fanning had no objection to auctioning such land to satisfy private debts. Interestingly enough, the main target of such sales was ex-governor Walter Patterson. In 1794, for example, one-half of lot 19, one-half of lot 50, one-half of lot 65, and lot 67 – all held by Patterson – were publicly auctioned to satisfy the claims of James Montgomery against Patterson.[6] They were knocked down for a total of £107 – to an agent acting on behalf of Edmund Fanning. According to later assertions by James Douglas, he had ceased bidding on these properties when informed that the actual purchaser was his employer, and was amazed later to discover that the lands ended up in the hands of the governor.[7] Fanning also perpetuated an interlocking system of office holding typical of what later reformers would call a "compact," appointing his friends Robert Gray and Joseph Aplin as assistant judges of the Supreme Court, although they were already members of the council. When a chancery court was created, ostensibly to provide some mechanism for legal appeals within the Island, the court of appeals was located directly in the council, which included not only Gray and Robinson but Chief Justice Peter Stewart. Critics understandably complained that appeals went "from the Chief Justice and Assistant Judges to the Chief Justice and Assistant Judges."[8] Indeed, Robert Gray was exactly the sort of plural office holder Fanning had been twenty years earlier in North Carolina when the Regulators had singled him out for attack. Such policy was worthy of Walter Patterson himself, as were the court actions of 1793 and 1794 involving John Cambridge, William Bowley, and John Hill.

The Cambridge affair began in 1793 when those officials charged before the British Privy Council in 1791 sued John Cambridge for damages in the Island's supreme court for malicious prosecution in preferring the complaints. The use of private suits to recover damages in public actions had initially been suggested by Captain John MacDonald, to be employed against Walter Patterson's councillors, although it was never pursued in that context.[9] But the value of the technique as an instrument of retribution was well demonstrated with the Cambridge cases. Cambridge attempted unsuccessfully to get the venue changed to Nova Scotia. The first action heard was that of Joseph Aplin, who was awarded £253.5.0 in damages and expenses by a jury.[10] William Townshend then received £248 from a separate jury. In both cases, Peter Stewart presided over trials that would set precedents for his own action.

Not surprisingly, Cambridge made no further attempts to defend himself, and simply confessed judgment to Fanning of £1,371.0.0 and to Stewart of £604.4.0. Unable to pay these judgments, Cambridge with the assistance of Charles Stewart and Joseph Aplin, brought a separate series of actions against John Hill and William Bowley for their share of the money. Bowley's case was heard first, a jury finding for Cambridge for £1,268.16.6 and costs. Bowley appealed to the new-organized Chancery Court on the Island, but found his case being heard by Fanning and the Supreme Court judges in their capacity as members of the Chancery Court. The appeal was dismissed, and Bowley's property was seized and sold. John Hill had no legal assistance and did not plead – Cambridge winning his case by default and ending up with most of Hill's seized property. Although Captain John MacDonald, upon his return to the Island in 1794, attempted to reopen the Hill case with new evidence and opinions of prominent English barristers that Cambridge could not maintain his action, he was no more successful than local lawyers. MacDonald did obtain a new trial in June 1794, but the jury cast the legal objections aside and continued to support Cambridge. Both Hill and Bowley appealed their cases to the king in council, and both judgments were eventually overturned.[11] But getting new trials and property returned was another matter entirely, and legal matters dragged on until the early years of the nineteenth century.[12] Cambridge, Bowley, and Hill were all rendered temporarily impotent as active proprietors by the court battles, although both Cambridge and Hill continued to operate as businessmen on the Island for some years.[13]

John Hill always insisted that he did not dispute the right of the Island's officers to sue the complainants of 1791, but he did question the propriety of the suits being heard in the courts of the Island, particularly given the intimate connections of the plaintiffs in the judicial system.[14] Hill was understandably persuaded of the existence of another conspiracy. To James Montgomery he wrote of the "*grand*

Evil – namely the Conduct of the Parties" who had prompted Cambridge.[15] He maintained that the Island could never prosper until the "present bad men" were removed, and added darkly, none "who values his Character of Property will adventure amongst such unprincipled people, they have ruined every man who has hitherto attempted to Carry on business there." Hill pleaded desperately for assistance, for "it is very hard for me alone to Fight the Battles of all the proprietors." He complained bitterly about the legal ignorance of Chief Justice Peter Stewart, and concluded by reporting that Captain John MacDonald had said to tell Montgomery "his Connections here are to a man D-m-d Scoundrels and disgrace his Interest." Like other absentee proprietors, Montgomery was not impressed. Hill had exhausted his credibility prematurely in 1791 and 1792.

As for John MacDonald, by 1795 he was virtually the only independent proprietor in residence on the Island, totally convinced that justice would not be obtained in this world. In a lengthy letter to Colonel Joseph Frederick Wallet DesBarres, who would a decade later be appointed as Fanning's successor, MacDonald offered some heartfelt advice. DesBarres held extensive property in Nova Scotia, and had asked MacDonald to act as his agent. Captain John began his first report to DesBarres in a mood of general pessimism:

It does not signify, deny it who will, Power is every where equally oppressive all over the world. I see no Odds between that modification which appears in speculation the best, and that, which appears in speculation to be the worst. In the former, Power is not a Jott better for the being more divided – but it is in practice worse, because the most of mankind are rascals, and power is so much the more oppressive for being subdivided among a greater number of rascals, whose great support is to unite and play into one another's hands, in order to prove too strong for the oppressed Individual ... They are fools that strive to mend it through seas of blood. Power will only change hands, and be sure to get into the hands of rascals to play the like cards over again.[16]

The main burden of MacDonald's advice, that DesBarres give up public life and retire to his North American estates, obviously reflected an extension to others of what MacDonald was attempting himself to execute. It was a strategy born of a number of factors, including ill health, disillusionment with the results of his own public efforts, and particularly a cynical but all too accurate assessment of conditions in North America.

While MacDonald's analysis of the North American landlord was hardly typical of the thinking of Island proprietors, it was based on considerable experience. His insistence was that the proprietor himself must manage his holdings, based on two general arguments. In the first place, there were many complex decisions to be taken, which only the landlord could do. "It is a delicate Matter," MacDonald insisted, "for an Agent to yield up upon his own mere Judgment material points of another man's property." Moreover, he added, tenants would "at the Hands of the Owner ... allow what they would Scant at the hands of a Stranger." Second, MacDonald emphasized the difficulty of acquiring competent and dependable agents:

Tell me if you Know a Proprietor living in England, that has ever been able to hold an Estate in America. I will even venture to say that an American living always here, holding an Estate in England, would lose it at the hands of Any one Steward in five hundred. When one succeeds to or Acquires an Estate, he takes up a trade – the trade of a Land Lord, or manager, of that Estate, which if he does not attend to regularly will be sure to fail; for it is a very minute trade requiring intimate Acquaintance with the Subject, renewed occasionally as former Circumstances alter or new ones occur. He must watch the Conduct of every one connected with it. He must be employed constantly on contriving. If this is the case in respect to Estates in Settled regular Countries, how much the more so in America, where the Estates are in a Manner in the State of Creation, and where the preying upon one another is reduced to a sort of legal System, & where Circumstances vary every day? It is true a good Agent may do it all. At the same time, how many do you know capable of so acting & susceptible of the trust?

Here MacDonald put his finger on the obvious disadvantages of absenteeism, stressing that while the situation might be more severe in North America, the problem was a universal one. Proprietors such as James Montgomery or Lord Selkirk a few years later could have testified to the wisdom of Captain John's remarks.[17]

Unfortunately, few proprietors of the Island followed MacDonald's lead. There were several major obstacles to the transplanting of experienced European landlords to the Island in the formative years of development. One was the isolation from the centres of society, wealth, and power. Only a marginal figure like Captain John, whose Highland tacksman background and Catholic religion set him apart from most of his contemporaries, was prepared to take the step. A related difficulty, however, was the experience of those few like John MacDonald who attempted to manage actively their Island property. In Britain such men could be expected to dominate and lead their local governments. On the Island they often found themselves beleaguered voices crying in the wilderness. While it may be difficult to sympathize totally with Captain John's subsequent problems on the

Island in the 1790s, his situation must be fully appreciated, for it would ultimately help discourage others.

Although MacDonald had vowed in 1795 to Joseph DesBarres that "when I finish your papers, I am resolved not to read or write above a quarter of an hour any day in my life," as well as to remain out of public affairs, these sweeping commitments were gradually forgotten.[18] His suspicions of the Fanning administration, roused in England as early as 1790, were confirmed by the court cases in which John Hill had become involved. Hill's was "another unfortunate case of oppression" to be added to a mounting list. Some opposition to the government did emerge in 1795 from an unexpected quarter, when Attorney-General Joseph Aplin broke with Fanning over an act passed by the 1795 legislature making seven years possession of land from the passage of the act sufficient for title to it.[19] Aplin opposed such legislation as an effort to undermine the proprietorial system, arguing that false conveyances were entirely too easy to acquire. He also objected to the absence of a suspending clause in the act and to Fanning's acceptance of it despite personal assurances to the contrary. Along with James Douglas and John MacDonald, Aplin became persuaded that the Fanning government was working its way toward some fresh attack on the proprietors.

Further disputes occurred in 1795 over military preparations for the Island. Once again Captain John MacDonald was at the centre of the storms of controversy. In April of that year Fanning had sent MacDonald an unsolicited commission as adjutant-general of the militia, an appointment the old Scots soldier declined. The commission was probably the governor's response to MacDonald's loudly voiced criticisms of the militia system, or rather the lack of one.[20] MacDonald had complained that the local military was officered almost entirely by Fanning's political cronies, most of whom lacked military experience and resided many miles from their potential troops. The citizenry, Captain John also claimed, were for the most part unfit to fight, badly trained, and almost totally unequipped. He had suggested to Fanning "the sole proper plan of forming and distributing a militia for the state of that Island, founded in Principles which might readily occur to any imbued with a single military Idea, or not swayed by other views."[21] Fanning replied favourably in principle to MacDonald's recommendations – he was a military man himself – but in practice merely organized two independent militia companies along the same unmilitary lines. By 1796 the question of military defence became, at least in the eyes of Captain John, interconnected with the emergence of a growing popular agitation for the establishment of an escheat court.

Suspicions about the intentions of the government increased in 1796, when Robert Hodgson and his father-in-law Joseph Robinson began a new movement for escheat. Hodgson was well known on the Island as a supporter of Fanning and a chief beneficiary of his patronage, and Robinson was an old colleague of the governor.²² Hodgson travelled the Island collecting signatures on petitions to the government for escheat, and distributed a pamphlet written by Robinson on the subject. No evidence exists to demonstrate collusion between the government and Robinson over the pamphlet, which was probably motivated largely by its author's own philosophy, reinforced by his inability to purchase outright the land he was occupying as a tenant of James Montgomery. As a former resident of the American colonies, where freehold tenure was the norm, Robinson was genuinely appalled by the Island's landholding system and by the difficulties farmers, including himself, faced in bringing their lands under cultivation. The year 1796 was a particularly trying one for Island agriculture, because of the reappearance of one of those periodic infestations of field-mice. Farmers were undoubtedly feeling beleaguered and were receptive to any proposals to improve their situation.

Robinson's pamphlet was hardly as unreasonable and extreme as his opponents liked to paint it. It began by pointing out the problems faced by Island farmers. Many were natural obstacles. The growing season was short, the quality of land was not uniform, and clearing the land of trees and stumps took up to ten years. Robinson, like many Loyalists, was experiencing the cultural shock of having to begin anew as a pioneer. Moreover, as a native of the American south, where the climate was considerably milder, Robinson obviously had serious difficulties in coming to terms with the Maritime winter. In a curious aside, for example, he insisted that during the winter months the condensation of air diminished and collapsed the lungs, so that the blood accumulated on the brain to produce symptoms resembling apoplexy.²³ But he reserved his heaviest strictures for the land system and the absentee landlords, who had not settled their lands and failed to pay quitrents, but were "determined most seriously that the settlers on these lands shall pay rents to them." The result was a people living in a state of "low spirits, in much want, misery and distress: devoid of animation," who were caught in a system of slavery that could easily "become a grotesque picture of the highland Clans."

Although he sought an end to the proprietorial system, Robinson was opposed neither to quitrents nor to tenancy. What he advocated was escheat, the legal reassumption by the Crown of the lands, with the Crown then acting directly as the landlord of the small holder of

100 to 300 acres. Quitrents would continue to be paid to the government. Robinson suggested that the people petition the Crown through their assembly to enquire into the failure of the proprietors to fulfil the conditions of their grants and into the feasibility of the establishment of a court of escheat. The royal beneficence would thus produce "Harmony, happiness, and tranquillity," instead of "contention, misery, and distress," an the inhabitants would no longer seek to leave the colony for other jurisdictions where "men only look up to God and their King!" Robinson concluded, characteristically, by emphasizing the landlords made sense in Britain, where the enviroment was less oppressive, but not in the extreme wilderness conditions of the Gulf of St Lawrence.

While there was little in Robinson's pamphlet or in the circulating petition that justified the extreme reactions of Captain John MacDonald, who claimed the presence on the Island of a levelling party of dangerous tendencies similar to that in France, it is impossible to gain any real impression of the way in which the public responded to Robinson's arguments. To hear MacDonald's version, the popular deductions "equalled the chatoic dreams of all levellers in all ages."[24] Some joined the militia to get land, others refused to join if they were required to defend proprietorial property. Undoubtedly there was loose talk. But Captain John's paranoia was quite extreme. From his perspective, the agitation was the same "as might be supposed to occur in Great Britain and Ireland, if the tenantry were told from any Appearance of Authority or force that they might supercede their Rents and Landlords altogether."[25] Such a characterization of the early escheat movement was hardly fair. The major target was the existing system of large land holdings. Whether such an attack was indeed dangerous to social order was a separate question, as was the related one of whether eliminating the proprietor would really work to the benefit of the average small landholder. Indeed, the critics of the escheat movement of the late 1790s were on much stronger ground in doubting the popular advantage rather than in claiming social levelling. "Once the proprietor was drawn off the Island," argued Captain John, the escheat mongers "could pack the cards and play into one another's hands, as they might please." Given the past record of Island officialdom, converting the Island government into the landlord was not necessarily to the advantage of the settlers. In any fresh allocation of land, the official class was likely to end with the lion's share.

As the only open critic of the escheat movement on the Island, John MacDonald inevitably became increasingly loud and shrill in his opposition, undoubtedly dragging in the private behaviour of what he described as "the Circle" in the process. As an old-fashioned exponent of traditional morality, Captain John revelled in exposing the peccadillos of his fellows. One of the earlier subjects of his strictures had accused him of a pretence of "so much Sanctity of manners and Purity of religion," in which he was "but the barest of all Hypocrites."[26] In any event, over the winter of 1796/7, Captain John made some unguarded remarks about Jack Stewart at the garrison, and as he described the aftermath, while stepping into his carriage

bound up in two Heavy Watch Coats, and loaded with other defences from the Cold, so as to be able scarcely to move, having previously watched he [Stewart] insulted me in the public streets in the presence of spectators. I instantly made him turn his back and fly to a distance. When seeing that I was unable to follow or stirr from the spot, provided only with a side arm dirk fourteen inches long and without a Guard, he drew a prodigious long cut and thrust sword and coming down put me upon my defence for a considerable time which I could not have effected if his Sword Arm had not trembled.[27]

As usually was the case, spectators separated the combatants before serious damage was done. Early in 1797, MacDonald asked Attorney-General Aplin whether the pamphlet distributed by Hodgson could be publicly prosecuted. Aplin's response was that he would not prosecute it against "the strong Current of popular Prejudice" and doubted whether a jury would convict its author of seditious libel.[28] MacDonald took this cautious opinion to mean that the pamphlet was libellous. In April 1797, he therefore put pen to paper and produced a lengthy diatribe addressed to Edmund Fanning.

Admitting he realized he was regarded as "one of the greatest Malcontents on the Island," probably standing "the first on the Obnoxious List," MacDonald proceeded to explain his "despair of the possibility of my living under the actual State of this Government."[29] No reparations had been effected in the Hill affair and the party calling for escheat and land division had been disseminating levelling principles among the tenantry for over a year. Fanning had done nothing. Captain John insisted that the proper venue for discussion of escheat was the Privy Council in England, "where there is discrimination, Judgment, and Justice," rather than the Island assembly, "a Tribunal of the Mobility" where "almost every mind is more or less tainted." Insisting that no proprietor could engage in settlement while escheat was in agitation, MacDonald called for Fanning to declare his position.

The governor responded that MacDonald had merely produced

ill-founded facts from which preposterous inferences were drawn in a tone of unprovoked rancour and invective.[30] There was no levelling party on the Island such as existed in France. Fanning called for specific charges so that wrongdoers could be prosecuted. MacDonald refused to appear before the council, claiming ill health and the absence of any support.[31] Not surprisingly, the council denied any knowledge of a levelling party and branded MacDonald a trouble-maker. On 29 May 1797 MacDonald sent Fanning another letter, which the governor returned unopened. In it MacDonald claimed that he dared not make public charges, since he would face prosecution in a Supreme Court totally dominated by Fanning's principal supporters. He called for the establishment of an indepen-dent court system for the Island.[32] Upon return of his letter, Captain John resubmitted it to Fanning and asked the governor to forward it to the British authorities.

Such was the background of the reconvening of the Island assembly in July 1797, the main issue on its agenda being the petitions for an escheat court. Before the House turned to the land question, however, it spent a good deal of time debating Captain John MacDonald and his charges of the existence of a levelling party of dangerous principles. Such an accusation was an explosive one, particularly given the repression of radicalism currently under way on the part of the British government at home. The leaders of escheat probably quite rightly regarded the label as unfair, since social levelling was not high on their own list of priorities. Upon request, Fanning tabled MacDonald's correspondence. The House sent its sergeant-at-arms to Tracadie to summon Captain John to appear beore it, but MacDonald personally abused this messenger and wrote instead directly to Fanning, complaining about hostile behaviour against him and particularly protesting the appearance of a sealed letter intended for the British government among the documents sent to the assembly.[33] The matter was dropped by the assembly at this juncture, as the House turned instead to the substantive questions of land and settlement.

After only two days of considering the land question, the 1797 assembly adopted a series of detailed resolutions, which had obvious-ly been drafted in advance, probably by Jack Stewart. These resolutions distinguished four categories of lots on the Island, ranging from those totally unsettled to those settled in accordance with the provisions of the original grants. In the first category of totally unsettled went twenty-three townships totalling 458,000 acres (lots 1, 2, 3, 7, 8, 9, 10, 12, 15, 22, 29, 44, 45, 46, 51, 52, 53, 57, 58, 60, 62, 66, and 67). Twelve townships were in the virtually unsettled second

category, their 243,000 acres containing a total of only thirty-six
families (lots 4, 5, 6, 11, 23, 30, 31, 35, 61, 63, 64, and 65). In category
three were six townships with seven to nine families each (lots 13, 14,
20, 25, 27, and 42). Finally, there were twenty-six townships that the
assembly was prepared to recognize as settled according to the
provisions of the original grants (16, 17, 18, 19, 21, 24, 26, 28, 32, 33,
34, 35, 36, 37, 38, 39, 40, 41, 43, 47, 48, 49, 50, 54, 56, and 59) and a
few additional lots (7, half of 12, 30, and 57, belonging to James
Montgomery, and 5, 63, and 64 owned by Edward Lewis, John Hill,
and John Cambridge), which it accepted as held by active proprietors.
Category four was extremely generous to the proprietors, for if
emphasis were placed on a strict interpretation of the original
conditions, particularly direct assistance to settlers and to their
non-British Protestant origins, probably no lot on the Island had been
properly settled.

The emphasis of the assembly appears to have been to attempt to
identify those lands where proprietors had been grossly negligent.
Unfortunately, this approach did not really make any significant
distinctions. Most of the lands in category four did not owe their
settlement to major expenditures on the part of their proprietors, but
to their locations adjacent to Charlottetown and the Hillsborough
River, to reputations as good sites for farming, and to historic
accident, such as being among the Loyalist lots. Thus, while category
four included all the active proprietors, it also encompassed a good
many who had done nothing. Lot 66, moreover, which was royal
demesne, was totally unsettled, demonstrating that the colony itself
was not necessarily more active than the proprietors.[34]

With the land categorized, the assembly turned to escheat. It began
by insisting that the failure of the proprietors to fulfil their grants had
been ruinous to the Island and its inhabitants. Most proprietors, it
claimed, merely speculated on the industry of a few. Regrettably, the
assembly itself had not distinguished carefully between the speculators and the active investors. The Island if fully settled could hold up
to half a million inhabitants, claimed the assembly. This calculation
was based on extrapolations from West Indian sugar islands, which
critics of the assembly roundly disparaged. Progress in the neighbouring colonies, the assembly insisted, particularly in New Brunswick, came because escheat had permitted the regranting of small
tracts to actual settlers. The assembly called for land on the Island to
be actually settled or returned to the Crown, which would grant
"small tracts to actual Settlers," and voted the preparation of an
address to the British government on the subject. No mention was
made of the form of tenure for the small grants. The assembly then

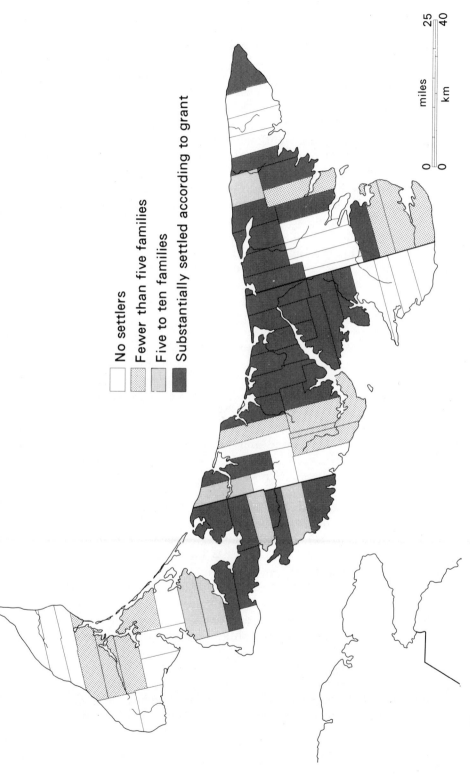

No settlers

Fewer than five families

Five to ten families

Substantially settled according to grant

miles

km

0   25
0   40

Figure 2   Island of St John: settlement of the lots in 1797 (after *Journal*, House of Assembly, 22 July 1797)

moved on to condemn Captain John MacDonald's "Scurrility, Mis-representation and Falsehood," accounting him so turbulent and factious that enforcing his attendance before the house might gratify him and raise him in importance.[35]

In a subsequent letter to the Duke of Portland, Edmund Fanning vociferously denied the circulation of seditious and inflammatory petitions, insisting moreover that the council had begun the consideration of an escheat court long before receiving any public memorials.[36] A separate letter of the same date, however, implicitly admitted that there was some substance to John MacDonald's charges. When Colonel Robinson had mustered the militia at Princetown on 22 August 1794, Fanning reported, the people refused to obey him until they were given "the same Conditions with respect to Lands as the People of Nova Scotia" and were freed from taxes.[37] Fanning himself had gone to Princetown with a company of light horse, and had arrested the leaders of the protest. He had enforced a muster there and at Grand Rustico, maintaining that the people were misled by "some secret Emissaries and unprincipled advocates of Mischief." There were "some *very few restless* Individuals," Fanning allowed, who were prepared to defy constituted authority. But Fanning made absolutely clear that his government was not tolerating such activity, and Portland accepted Fanning's explanations, writing in reply that MacDonald's charges were "totally without foundation" and his conduct "perfectly unwarrantable."[38]

Fanning's few other local critics were neutralized as well. Attorney-General Joseph Aplin found himself facing private charges of legal malpractice as well as public ones of "rash" criticism of the governor before the council. Aplin resigned bitterly from the council in January 1798, complaining of the presence of "implacable Emnities" on the Island. He added, "If the want of bread does not overrule my inclination, I shall never see the Island again ... My wish is to get rid of the Island and all its Quarrels."[39] James Douglas was forced to answer a complaint from Customs Collector William Townshend of improper practices, particularly in admitting vessels on site in remote harbours rather than at the customs house in Charlottetown. Douglas admitted the technical violation, but insisted it was normal and necessary, especially in the winter months. While he felt able to clear himself, Douglas wrote James Montgomery, he also anticipated being "attacked by the party with the Governor either underhandedly or openly till such time as I shall be wearied out and obliged to leave the Country, or ruined by them." Insisting that the attacks on both himself and Aplin were inspired by their opposition to escheat, Douglas was convinced that Fanning was behind them.[40] He observed a few months later that "No one is safe from his [Fanning's] malice, and the power he has to gratify it, having all the different departments of Justice and the Government at his discretion," and added, "nothing can protect a man in a Country where the different departments of Government play into one another's hands."[41] Like other critics of escheat and Fanning, Douglas would become an advocate of annexation to Nova Scotia as the solution to the Island's problems.

Whether he was a "tame dupe" or a "wielder of misapplied power" – the alternatives were those of Joseph Aplin – Edmund Fanning in 1798 had on his hands the most powerful and persuasive attack yet mounted against the proprietors. Although we have no details regarding the thinking that led to Fanning's order of 1798 to take a careful census of the inhabitants of the Island, the timing suggests it was probably intended in part to provide documentation for the assembly report of 1797 assessing the state of settlement. Unfortunately, the census of 1798 survives only as reprinted by historian Duncan Campbell later in the nineteenth century. Campbell reproduced the nominal information, but it is impossible to tell whether additional data, such as amounts of land cleared or livestock held, was originally included.[42] While early census taking in Canada was notoriously unreliable, and this one was probably limited in ambition, it does provide us with some opportunity to assess the progress of settlement on the Island beyond the assertions of the assembly.

By and large, the census does confirm the 1797 report of the assembly, particularly regarding the unsettled townships of category one and the virtually unsettled ones of category two. The census indicates that the occasional lot in categories two and three held a few more inhabitants than the assembly had claimed, while several lots in category four (lots 40, 41, 54, and 59) contained substantially fewer families than their inclusion there would justify. The chief factor uniting these latter townships appears to have been the agency of Edmund Fanning. According to the census, there were 744 heads of families and a total of 4,372 inhabitants, for an overall family size of just under six persons per family; the census takers did not distinguish servants from other family members, however. Of the 744 heads of families, 39 resided in Princetown and 78 in Charlottetown, which meant that 117 families, or just over 14 per cent, lived in places even resembling village conditions. These 117 families contained 667 inhabitants, giving a village family size of 5.6, slightly less than for the Island as a whole. The census also documented the gender imbalance typical of newly settled regions in Canada. There were 78 females and 104 males above 60 years of age, 867 females and 1,014 males

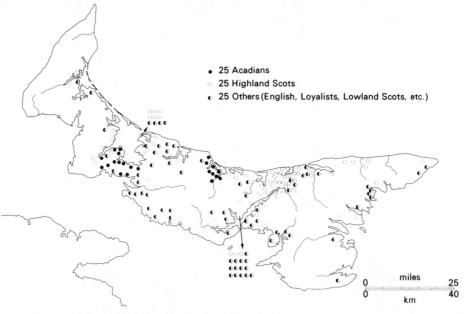

Figure 3   Island of St John: distribution of population, 1798

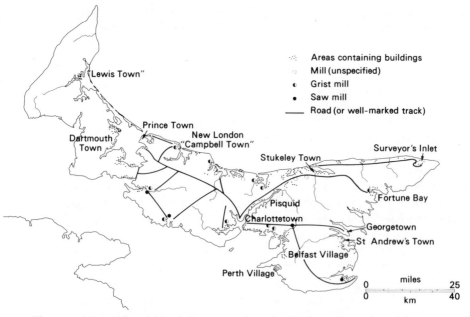

Figure 4   Prince Edward Island: houses, roads, and mills about 1800 (adapted from Stewart [1806] and other sources)

between 16 and 60, and 1,092 females and 1,217 males under the age of 16. Shortfalls of females occurred in every category, even among children, suggesting that the Island was not yet experiencing much natural increase (where males and females would be randomly more equal in number) and that immigration continued to concentrate in families where young males predominated.

According to Andrew Hill Clark, who attempted to assign ethnic origins for this census on the basis of surname, the 1798 population contained 669 Acadians, 1,814 Highland Scots, 310 Lowland Scots, and 1,579 others, chiefly of initial English extraction.[43] As Clark also observed, the Acadians were concentrated in three major areas: the Bay of Fortune district to the east (lot 43); the Rustico Bay district on the north-central shore (lot 24); and the south shore of Malpeque Bay (lots 13, 14, 16, and 17). The Highlanders were concentrated in Princetown and adjacent lot 18, as well as on lots 34 to 39 along the Hillsborough River. English names were chiefly to be found in and around Charlottetown.[44]

The 1798 census also makes it possible to offer some ultimate assessment of the impact of the Loyalists on the Island. Of 464 individuals identified as either refugees or disbanded soldiers, 128 (or 25.2 per cent) persisted to the 1798 census. Fifty-three of 180 refugees (29 per cent) and 69 of 284 disbanded soldiers (24 per cent) were among those enumerated. Among the persisting soldiers, 15 were from the St John's Volunteers, 18 from the King's Rangers, and 9 from the Nova Scotia Volunteers, for a total of 42 (or 60+ per cent) of the 69 persisters in this category. On the whole, therefore, while refugees were marginally more likely than disbanded soldiers to remain on the Island, if the large number of soldiers who had previous connections there during or before their military service are excluded, refugees comprised the bulk of the persisters. Perhaps the most significant fact about the disbanded soldiers who persisted, apart from their previous relationship with the Island, was their marital status. Of the forty-three disbanded soldiers for whom marital status at the time of settlement is known, twenty-two (or 51 per cent) were still in residence on the Island in 1798. Undoubtedly a relationship existed between previous connections and marital status. Insufficient information makes it impossible to attempt any generalization about the marital status of the refugees. But it appears likely that single soldiers and refugees did not persist.

Another striking feature of the Loyalists who remained on the Island in 1798 is the fact that very few were still located on the lands they had been originally allotted in the 1780s. Only a handful of Loyalists had taken advantage of the legislation of 1790 to obtain title to the lands they had originally been granted, but one of the conditions of that law was that they must still be resident on them. Thus the mobility of the Loyalists rather than government neglect appears to account for their failure to request titles.[45] The extent of Loyalist mobility probably also explains why so many contemporary observers insisted that few Loyalists remained. It is obviously quite impossible to assess motivation from the limited data available, but it would appear likely that many of the Loyalists, who tended to gravitate toward the more highly developed parts of the Island in and around Charlottetown, were attracted by a more sophisticated economy and the opportunities for markets.

What the census of 1798 disclosed was a relatively small colony that was growing, albeit sporadically, in terms of population and extent of settlement. Outside of Charlottetown and Princetown, there were few agglomerations of population. Most of the settlers were widely scattered across the Island, although there were large areas (particularly in western Prince County, western Queen's County, and the southernmost portions of Queen's and King's Counties) where virtually no one resided. An examination of Samuel Holland's original surveys would have indicated a strong correlation between those townships that Holland had initially found most attractive, because of soil fertility and location, and those that were indeed most heavily settled. In part this correlation was self-fulfilling, since active investors were influenced by Holland's assessments, but largely it followed from the cumulative decisions of pioneers, both individually and in groups, as to the best places to locate. Proximity to water, availability of a market, ease of clearing, and congeniality of neighbours were all factors in such calculations. Although the efforts of a few active proprietors such as James Montgomery and John MacDonald had created beachheads of settlement that attracted others, most pioneers acted in accordance with obvious criteria that had been apparent to Holland. Government policy, most evident in the allocation of Loyalist lands, had not been particularly effective in directing settlement, a fact that did not in some ways bode well for the scheme of escheat currently under discussion on the Island. One of the most obvious characteristics of Island settlement was the tendency of ethnic groups to gather together, a feature particularly marked among the Highland Catholic and Acadian population. But government had no policy for Acadians and none for immigrants of any description.

What the census of 1798 did not illuminate was the economic situation of the colony, or its prospects. In this respect, it was little different from the legislative report of 1797. Nevertheless, the economy of the Island remained, as it had been from the outset, agrarian and unspecialized. Virtually every family, from that of the governor down, produced most of its own food. While the term subsistence suggests a degree of self-sufficiency that would be misleading, most Islanders marketed a surplus rather than produced chiefly for the market. Cash was in extremely short supply, and most transactions were conducted on barter principles or on credit. Public office holding was virtually the only way to assure a regular income, thus explaining the incredible attraction of office, however minor, to the inhabitants, as well as the tendency among those not among the privileged few funded from the civil list to accumulate as many petty functions as possible. While the office-holding class was relatively open – many critics of the government complained constantly of the menial origins of those who had risen to prominence – it nevertheless constituted a relatively tiny elite centred in Charlottetown. For the vast majority of the population, either in the capital or in the back country, regular incomes were inconceivable, and money was obtained wherever possible through a variety of activities. Island farmers grew foodstuffs for themselves, and little beyond livestock for the market. They engaged in fishing, in timbering, in boat building, in a variety of artisan activities, and in unskilled labouring jobs whenever the opportunity presented itself.

The diary of Benjamin Chappell offers one of our few opportunities to glimpse the unspecialized nature of employment for those who were not part of the ruling elite. A skilled mechanic and woodworker, Chappell was not himself necessarily typical of early Islanders, but even he was forced to turn his hand to many occupations, public and private. He worked sporadically in the forests, especially in his earlier years on the Island, but in 1778 he removed to Charlottetown, settling on town lot 20, where he completed his house in 1780.[46] Economic opportunities were obviously expanded in the capital, and Chappell worked as a house carpenter for a succession or governors and other leading citizens, built boats, and even tried such unusual projects as making a saddle for Parson Desbrisay. In 1780, he agreed with Governor Patterson to maintain the town pump for £6 per annum, and he served the parish for years as churchwarden and overseer. Between his outside employments, Chappell laboured in his workshop, producing almost anything the market required, but basically specializing in spinning wheels and hand barrows. Not until after 1800 would Charlottetown society demand more sophisticated products such as house furniture, coach carriages, and sleighs, and throughout his working life the mainstay of Chappell's shop was the humble spinning wheel. The production of over 600 spinning wheels by Chappell tells us much about the importance of domestic industry on the Island in the early period.

The very isolation and economic self-sufficiency of the Island help account for Benjamin Chappell's success as a local artisan. Island women used the wheels to manufacture homespun, and importing them was not sufficiently attractive to make them an article of commerce. Whether Chappell would ultimately have benefited or suffered from a thriving trade with the outside world is an interesting question. But it was one which at the end of the eighteenth century he did not have to face. Although most of the available evidence on Island commerce at this time comes from critics of the Fanning administration, their assessment was never contradicted by anyone in authority. Controversy revolved around who was responsible for the moribund state of Island commercial development, not over its extent.

Merchant John Hill, writing in 1801 with information supplied him by John MacDonald and James Douglas, offered the only detailed contemporary analysis of Island commerce. Hill's assessment must be tempered both by the realization that he hated the Island's government and that he was describing a wartime period during which European investment in British North America had virtually ceased. Nevertheless, there exists no evidence to contradict his assertion that at the close of the eighteenth century there was not one active merchant to be found on the entire Island. Most retailing, Hill maintained, was done by petty hucksters from Halifax at a 200 per cent mark-up, and less than £500 in specie was in circulation, inevitably gravitating into the hands of the petty traders. Only one of many sawmills constructed over the preceding years was in operation, and boards and planks from the Island were estimated by James Douglas in the late 1790s at little more than 100,000 feet per year, with an annual value of just over £100. Only seven of nine gristmills were in operation. Customs revenue in 1792 had been £1.18.6 in exports, £132.15 in imports, and although a 1795 duty on spirits had raised total customs receipts, the real figures remained lower than in 1792, with no vessels being cleared in or out of the customs house in the final years of the decade. Hill defied Fanning to document commercial activity, but the governor never responded. No proprietor received much revenue, and the few rentals paid came in the form of produce for which there was little available market.[47] However much those favouring escheat may have talked about the oppression of tenants by their landlords, as in most pioneering situations, the tenants probably derived more economic benefit from the proprietors than the proprietors did from their inhabitants.[48]

John Hill, of course, had his own explanation for the unimproved state of the Island and the condition of its commerce, dismissing any arguments that the Island lacked economic potential. The problem was that the behaviour of the Island's leaders had "rendered fruitless every attempt" at investment, "as well as discouraged and prevented the making of more attempts."[49] Without an active commercial class to supply settlers and trade surplus, Hill maintained, no Islander would raise more produce than he could consume himself. The political situation on the Island did not encourage investment, however. Hill proclaimed, "No Man in his senses will trust his property in a place that either does not afford the institutions necessary for protection, or where those institutions are used as the means of destruction." Like other opponents of Fanning's government, Hill called for re-annexation to Nova Scotia.

Although John Hill's perspective on the affairs of the Island was that of a commercial proprietor rather than of a landholder like Captain John MacDonald, the two men were in broad agreement in terms of their overall assessment of the future of investment there. In a lengthy untitled manuscript written around the turn of the century, MacDonald outlined his case.[50] He admitted the value of escheat if too much land in a colony had been granted to non-improvers, but objected to escheat being constantly held over the heads of the proprietors, particularly when so many of the conditions of the original grants were "useless, intricate, nonsensical, even hurtful or impracticable." On the Island, moreover, the same people would be "Prosecutors, Judges, and Inquest or Jury," and all were hostile to the proprietors. The official class, which took the lead in such matters, could not "be trusted in point of Intention, probity, and truth," and it had secret designs once a quitrent court was established. The result, argued Captain John, was that "no man of produce will expend in the Settlement or Improvement of his lands until the matter shall be deliberately and justly settled upon a different scale."

Hill and MacDonald were in agreement that the proprietorial system had not succeeded and the proprietorial property was valueless. Neither man, of course, was prepared to follow the argument to its logical conclusion. Why defend such a hopeless system, particularly in the face of concerted local hostility? However beseiged the proprietors might feel, they were never really prepared to examine alternatives, beyond demanding reform of the anachronisms of the system in their favour. By the end of the eighteenth century, the lines of conflict had been plainly drawn between Islanders and proprietors. Islanders were scoundrels, proprietors were parasites. The particular issues of the land question would alter over the ensuing generations, but the substance remained unchanged.

Epilogue

By the close of the eighteenth century, the direction of development, the problems faced by the Island, and the debate over those problems, were all firmly in place. The Island's early experience had been one in which the expectations of those responsible for planning its development had been thoroughly frustrated, as the proprietorial system, the autonomous government, and settlement – all of which were supposed to work together harmoniously – had instead produced hostility and confusion. By 1798 the proprietorial system was obviously in disarray and under attack, especially on the Island itself. The explanation of what had gone wrong, however, was hardly an easy one to make, and conflicting views on the subject were held by those who had been most actively involved.

The simplest explanation was one favoured by spokesmen for the Island, which insisted that the proprietors had never intended to live up to the terms of their original grants and in their failure had so greatly retarded the development of the Island that they deserved to be cast aside. This position had long been inherent in the actions of the Island government, was implicit in the 1797 assembly report, and became enshrined in print in John Stewart's history of the Island first published in 1806.[1] It has been the prevailing interpretation ever since.[2] The contrary view was one put forward by some of the most active and articulate proprietors. It insisted that the proprietors had never been given a fair chance to develop their holdings, and blamed this failure on the actions of the Island's ruling class. While this explanation was never clearly expressed in print in the early years, it did have considerable influence through private statements on a British government that by the end of the eighteenth century, was being asked to deal with the shambles of the original visions for the colony.

Although the proprietorial interpretation should not be accepted uncritically, it does deserve a more serious hearing than it has hitherto received, particularly since its credibility does help explain the reluctance of the British authorities to accept enthusiastically the demands of the Island for the wholesale abandonment of the proprietorial system. Moreover, a realistic analysis of the early dynamics of the Island helps put into perspective a good many of the Island's historic grievances and problems. As the foregoing pages have attempted to demonstrate, no simple explanation will suffice to explain the early development of Prince Edward Island. Instead, a series of interconnected and constantly escalating factors – some attributable to human instrument but many beyond the control of those involved – contributed to producing an ultimate chaos that would have required the wisdom of Solomon, and his despotic power, to resolve.

While it is tempting to begin by condemning the British authorities for their initial establishment of an anachronistic landholding system for the Island in the 1760s, that system was neither anachronistic nor totally without merit at the time. The French had employed very similar land-granting devices in their attempt to establish a colony, and the allocation of large land grants to proprietors with concomitant obligations for settlement and revenue through quitrents was a time-honoured British device as well, often used throughout North America and especially common in the Maritime region in the mid eighteenth century. What was distinctive about the extension of the system to the Island of St John was, ironically enough, an element of serious advance planning and the deliberate effort to use the quitrent revenue as the financial basis of an independent colonial administration. The initial British mistake was not so much the allocation of Island land to absentee proprietors who were expected to develop a wilderness with their own resources, but wedding that system of land-granting to the premature establishment of a colonial government. Indeed, the case could well be made that the critical decision of the British authorities was not the lottery of 1767, but the acceptance of an autonomous government for the Island in 1769. The consequent politicization of the land system on the Island made it quite impossible to deal with it as would be done in Nova Scotia, New Brunswick, and Cape Breton, by a sweeping wholesale escheat of vast undeveloped tracts of land.

Further complicating the possibility of any general escheat were other factors. Some proprietors had invested in the early settlement of the Island and many had paid something toward the quitrents, making it more difficult for authority on or off the Island simply to reassume for the Crown the land allocated by lottery in 1767 on the grounds of general and total non-performance of obligations. The earliest policy regarding proprietorial failure was not one of escheat, but of distraint, involving the transfer of land from one proprietor with British connections to another with Island connections, rather than in straightforward reassumption. This policy in turn resulted directly from the pressing financial needs of the Island's officers, but was in practice carried out under extremely dubious circumstances following the incredible confusion of the American rebellion, resulting in further complications that were almost impossible to disentangle.

The period of the American rebellion further enhanced a trend already in evidence before 1775, which saw a growing distinction between residents of the Island and forces without – notably the bulk of the proprietors and the British government. A sense of Island distinctiveness was increased by the establishment of a legislative assembly in 1773. Like the earlier creation of an independent government, the formation of an assembly was premature, caused chiefly by the financial needs of the Island's office holders to put pressure on the proprietors regarding the payment of quitrents. Quite apart from the inflated sense of importance the assembly gave to Island political leaders, its presence also made it far more difficult for the British authorities ultimately to reorganize jurisdictions in the region. In 1820, Cape Breton Island – no more isolated or underdeveloped than Prince Edward Island – was re- annexed to Nova Scotia, and one of the major reasons this political realignment was possible related to its lack of a popular House. As the problems of merging assemblies in the Canadas would later demonstrate, their presence made jurisdictional readjustment exceedingly difficult. When the Maritime region was reorganized following the American war and the coming of the Loyalists, an Island of St John without its own assembly, still operating with governor and council, might well have found itself part of Nova Scotia or merged with Cape Breton.

Finally, muddying an already complex situation were the policies of Governor Walter Patterson in the 1780s. Auctioning the distrained lots of some of the proprietors in 1781 was a terrible blunder on Patterson's part, especially given the failure to observe legal niceties and the presence of obvious self-interest. But Patterson was not content to stop here. Settling the incoming Loyalists upon the auctioned lots, in the full knowledge that the land titles were in dispute, made matters worse, and the transparent attempts of Patterson to defy the British authorities with the collaboration of his local legislature merely completed the process. In the end, Patterson succeeded in cementing a number of unfortunate hostilities and antagonisms. The absent proprietors were encouraged to think of the Island government as more than merely an adversary, but as a collection of rapacious scoundrels willing to go to any lengths to feather their own nests at the expense of the land system. The British authorities were led to the general perception that the Island was a defiant and essentially nasty little colony from which no statesmanlike policies could be anticipated and in which none could be executed. The perpetuation of the politicization of the land question made a solution to the problems even more difficult. Instead of approaching the failures of the proprietorial system from the standpoint of the need for better policies, Patterson merely established the principle that Island political leaders could manipulate the existing system – and Island politics – for their own advantage.

While there can be no question of the negative influence of Walter Patterson, an assessment of the first decade of the administration of Edmund Fanning is considerably more difficult. Certainly Fanning had a difficult time in his early years, and he did more or less succeed in settling the colony down after the Patterson fiasco. But on the whole, while the constraints upon him are understandable, Fanning's policies were singularly unconstructive. Whatever his own thinking about local politics, Fanning did not succeed in escaping from local rapaciousness and self-interest, and in some instances he clearly exacerbated the frustrations for outsiders dealing with Island officials. The establishment of a Chancery Court was a good idea, for example, but allowing it to be composed as it was of the same people whose judicial decisions were to be appealed was hardly very satisfactory. While the creation of an escheat court would be in principle a legitimate step forward, the way in which the escheat movement was orchestrated was reminiscent of Patterson, albeit more subtle. In the end, the Fanning regime would settle for a bargain with the proprietors, in which quitrent arrearages would be wiped clean in return for payment of a proportion of the amount owing. The arrangement ignored the development failures of the proprietors.

Whatever Fanning stood for, it was not the legitimate interests of the average inhabitant of Prince Edward Island. In his efforts to tread a tightrope between the conflicting forces of Island office holders and absentee proprietors, Fanning succeeded by failing to offer far-sighted administration. He made no effort to legitimize the proposal that the Island government take over for the proprietors by indicating any serious interest in directing and supervising the process of immigration and settlement. A thousand Highland Scots had arrived on the Island in the years immediately preceding the resumption of war between France and Britain in 1793, but they had not found a government prepared to assist and direct them. Criticisms of Fanning's administration could not be countered by evidence of positive action. Fanning survived, but the price the Island paid was a high one.

In his initial report on public affairs upon assuming the governorship in 1805, J.F.W. DesBarres had observed that matters "seem more and more to have been in a strange and incompatible state from the beginning, and the different points of which in the progress of above thirty years induced such further confusion and intricacy, pervading the whole, as to render them extremely difficult to be unravelled."[3] DesBarres was supposed to bring about reform, but like a series of Island governors in the nineteenth century, he would be totally frustrated in the attempt. In one fundamental sense the critics were correct. Overcoming the complexities created over the first thirty years of Island history under the British would require not merely reform of the land system, but a complete remodelling of the political system of the Island. Land and politics were inseparably intertwined on Prince Edward Island, and the price of political autonomy would for many years continue to be the failure to bring about the elimination of the proprietors.

Notes

BL   British Library, London
BT   Board of Trade, London
CO   Colonial Office Series, Public Record Office, London
DCB   *Dictionary of Canadian Biography*, Toronto
NLS   National Library of Scotland, Edinburgh
PAC   Public Archives of Canada, Ottawa
PANS   Provincial Archives of Nova Scotia, Halifax
PAPEI   Provincial Archives of Prince Edward Island
PRO   Public Record Office
PRO BT   Public Record Office, Board of Trade
PRO PC   Public Record Office, Privy Council
SCA   Scottish Catholic Archives, Edinburgh
SPPAC   Selkirk Papers, PAC
SRO   Scottish Record Office, Edinburgh
SRO GD   Scottish Record Office, Gifts and Deposits
UBC   University of British Columbia Library, Vancouver

PROLOGUE

1 H.P. Biggar, ed., *The Voyages of Jacques Cartier* (Ottawa 1924), 43; W.F. Ganong, ed., *Description and Natural History of the Coasts of North America by Nicholas Denys* (Toronto 1908), 208–9.

2 A.H. Clark, *Three Centuries and the Island: A Historical Geography of Settlement and Agriculture in Prince Edward Island, Canada* (Toronto 1959).

3 D.C. Harvey, *The French Regime in Prince Edward Island* (New Haven 1926), 40–1.

4 John Reid, *Acadia, Maine, and New Scotland: Marginal Colonies in the Seventeenth Century* (Toronto 1981).

5 Harvey, *French Regime*, 40–55; "Gotteville de Belile," *DCB* 2 (Toronto 1969): 254–5.
6 Clark, *Three Centuries*, 28; Harvey, *French Regime*, 63–4.
7 Harvey, *French Regime*, 64–72; Clark, *Three Centuries*, 29–30.
8 Harvey, *French Regime*, 73–93; the quote is on 92. See also "Roma," *DCB* 3 (Toronto 1974): 566–7.
9 "David Higgins," *DCB* 4 (1979): 352–3.
10 Harvey, *French Regime*, 109–18.
11 Ibid., 121–45.
12 Harvey, *French Regime*, 121–74; Clark, *Three Centuries*, 32–3. For a discussion of British policy, see Naomi E.S. Griffiths, ed., *The Acadian Deportation: Deliberate Perfidy or Cruel Necessity?* (Toronto 1969).
13 Clark, *Three Centuries*, 32–40; Harvey, *French Regime*, 163–87.
14 Harvey, *French Regime*, 144.
15 Ibid., 175–87.
16 *Report of the Canadian Archives* (Ottawa, 1905), 2: 77–165.
17 Ibid.
18 See, for example, James T. Lemon, *The Best Poor Man's Country: A Geographical Study of Early Southwestern Pennsylvania* (Baltimore 1972); A.H. Clark, *Acadia: The Geography of Early Nova Scotia to 1760* (Madison 1968), 233–44.
19 Harvey, *French Regime*, 201–11.
20 Rousseau de Villejouin to ---, 8 September 1758, quoted in Harvey, *French Regime*, 190–4.
21 Boscawen to Pitt, 13 September 1758, CO 412/3.
22 Harvey, *French Regime*, 193.
23 J. Henri Blanchard, *The Acadians of Prince Edward Island 1720–1964* (Ottawa 1964); A.B. Warburton, *A History of Prince Edward Island* (Saint John, NB, 1923), 99–100.

CHAPTER ONE

1 For some notion of the vehemency still possible against the proprietors, see Milton Acorn, *The Island Means Minago* (Toronto 1975) and Errol Sharpe, *A People's History of Prince Edward Island* (Toronto 1976).
2 Most of the standard accounts view events from an Island perspective. See, for example, Duncan Campbell, *History of Prince Edward Island* (Charlottetown 1875), 10–17, which contains the fullest account of the Egmont schemes, as well as A.H. Clark, *Three Centuries and the Island: A Historical Geography of Settlement and Agriculture in Prince Edward Island, Canada* (Toronto 1959), 42–50, and F.W.P. Bolger, ed., *Canada's Smallest Province: A History of P.E.I.* (Charlottetown 1973), 33–42. In *The*

Atlantic Provinces: The Emergence of Colonial Society 1712–1857 (Toronto 1965), 64–6, W.S. MacNutt makes some attempt at a broader perspective.

3 Adam Shortt and Arthur G. Doughty, eds, *Documents relating to the Constitutional History of Canada, 1759–1791* (Ottawa 1907), 1: 85–6.

4 Thomas Pichon, *Lettres et memoires pour servir a l'historie ... du Cap Breton et Isle Saint Jean* (Paris 1760). In English, *Genuine Letters ...*

5 *Genuine Letters*, 65–6.

6 "Remarks relative to the Sketch of the Island of St. John's in North America, where I was employ'd by order of the General to run over that Island," Hardwicke Papers, BL Add. MSS 35914, 95–9ff.

7 *Journal of the Commissioners for Trade and Plantations, January 1759 to December 1763* (London 1935), 369.

8 Ibid., 406.

9 Most of the critical documents are reprinted in Shortt and Doughty, *Documents* 1: 93–122.

10 C.V. Alvord, *The Mississippi Valley in British Politics* (New York 1959), 1: 157–210; R.A. Humphreys, "Lord Shelburne and the Proclamation of 1763," *English Historical Review* 49 (1934): 241–64; Jack M. Sosin, *Whitehall and the Wilderness: The Middle West in British Colonial Policy 1760–1775* (Lincoln, NE, 1961), 52–78; John Shy, *Toward Lexington: the Role of the British Army in the Coming of the American Revolution* (Princeton 1965), 140–231; Franklin B. Wickwire, *British Subministers and Colonial America 1763–1783* (Princeton 1966), 88–96.

11 Shortt and Doughty, *Documents* 1: 121.

12 *London Gazette*, number 10368 (22–26 November 1763).

13 *Journals of Commissioners ... January 1764 to December 1767* (London 1936), 6–7.

14 *To the King's Most Excellent Majesty, the Memorial of John Earl of Egmont* (n.p., n.d., but January 1764), 1.

15 For John Perceval, second earl of Egmont (1711–1770), see *Dictionary of National Biography* 15 (Oxford 1921), 815–18.

16 John Stewart, *An Account of Prince Edward Island, in the Gulph of St. Lawrence, North America* (London 1806), 155.

17 Petition of Sir Charles Saunders et al., 15 November 1765, BL Add. MSS 35914, 48–9ff.

18 First Memorial of John Earl of Egmont, BL Add. MSS 35914, 68–9ff.

19 Particularly the suggestions of William Knox, who ironically became the London agent of Prince Edward Island in 1801. See Leland J. Bellot, *William Knox: The Life & Thought of an Eighteenth-Century Imperialist* (Austin, TX, and London 1977), 46–55.

20 *The Memorial of John Earl of Egmont*, 1n.

21 *Acts of the Privy Council of England, Colonial Series*, vol. 6 (London 1912), no. 401 (10 April 1728).

22 Ibid., no. 584 (5 January 1764).
23 *The Memorial of John Earl of Egmont*, 21–2n.
24 Shy, *Towards Lexington*, 140–231.
25 *The Memorial of John Earl of Egmont*, 25.
26 Leading members of the board at this time were the earl of Hillsborough (the American secretary of state), Soame Jenyns, Bamber Gascoyne, and Lord Orwell.
27 "The Report of the Board of Trade upon the Earl of Egmont's First Memorial, 13 February 1763," BL Add. MSS 35914, 70–1ff; Victor Hugo Paltsits, ed., *Narrative of American Voyages and Travels of Captain William Owen, R.N. ... 1766–1771* (New York 1942), 19.
28 BL Add. MSS 35914, 72–3ff.
29 Third Memorial of John Earl of Egmont, BL Add. MSS 35914, 73–4ff.
30 "Report of the Board of Trade in Consequence of the Earl of Egmont's Third Memorial, 23 March 1764," BL Add. MSS 35914, 75–6ff.
31 "Observations on the Report of the Board of Trade in Consequence of the Earl of Egmont's Third Memorial, transmitted by the said Earl to the Committee of Council," BL Add. MSS 35914, 77–82ff.
32 *Journal of the Commissioners 1764–1767*, 53.
33 Petition of Admiral Charles Knowles et al., 14 May 1764, BL Add. MSS 35914, 84f.
34 Quoted in Campbell, *History of PEI*, 15–16. For the Rockingham government, see Paul Langford, *The First Rockingham Administration 1765–1766* (Oxford 1973).
35 Petition of Sir Charles Saunders et al., BL Add. MSS 35914, 47f.
36 Ibid., 47–52ff.
37 BL Add. MSS 35914, 89f.
38 Edmont to Charles Yorke, 26 April 1766, BL Add. MSS 35914, 86f.
39 *Journal of the Commissioners 1764–1767* (8 May 1766), 277–8.
40 Charles Yorke and W. DeGray to the Right Honourable the Lords of the Committee for Plantation Affairs, 1 August 1766, BL Add. MSS 35914, 87–93ff.
41 Ibid., 93f.
42 *Journal of the Commissioners 1764–1767*, 393–4.
43 Saunders and Keppell remained at the Admiralty, Saunders as first lord, until November 1766. Their continuation in office probably accounts for the delay until 1767 of the implementation of the Board of Trade's scheme.
44 *Journal of the Commissioners 1764–1767*, 394. Documents on proceedings from this point are most accessible in PAC *Sessional Paper Number 18* (Ottawa 1906), 3–22.
45 Edmont to Lords of Trade and Plantations, 6 June 1767, CO 217/22/57.
46 PAC *Sessional Paper no. 18*, 7.

47 Ibid., 7–9.
48 Ibid., 10–11.
49 See, for example, Beverly W. Bond, *The Quit-Rent System in the American Colonies* (New Haven 1919); Sung Bok Kim, *Landlord and Tenant in Colonial New York: Manorial Society 1664–1775* (Chapel Hill, NC, 1978).
50 Margaret Ells, "Clearing the Decks for the Loyalists," *Canadian Historical Association Annual Report*, 1933, 43–58.

CHAPTER TWO

1 Minutes of Meeting of His Majesty's Commissioners for Trade & Plantations, 8 July 1767, PAC *Annual Report*, 1906, 6–9.
2 Ibid., 6.
3 Cited in John Brebner, *The Neutral Yankees of Nova Scotia: A Marginal Colony during the Revolutionary Years* (Toronto 1969), 85.
4 Hillsborough to Francklin, 26 February 1768, PANS A81, 135. The letter is partially reprinted in A.B. Warburton, *A History of Prince Edward Island* (Saint John 1923), 132–3.
5 PANS 167, 66ff.
6 Brebner, 85–6; Warburton, 133–41.
7 PRO CO 226/1/1–6. For an example of criticism, see F.W.P. Bolger, ed., *Canada's Smallest Province* (Charlottetown 1973), 42–3. Significantly, Bolger does not mention Nova Scotia.
8 PRO CO 226/1/1–6.
9 Ibid.
10 Ibid.
11 For Patterson, see DCB 4 (Toronto 1979), 605–11.
12 For Desbrisay, see DCB 5, 249–50.
13 These instructions have been reprinted in Warburton, 450–64, and in Frank MacKinnon, *The Government of Prince Edward Island* (Toronto 1951), 327–43.
14 For Higgins, see DCB 4: 352–3.
15 Hillsborough to D. Higgins, 7 July 1769, CO 226/4/1–2.
16 John Moreaú to M. Francklin, 10 November 1769, CO 226/4/5–6; State of the Receipts and Issues of Dry Stores belonging to the Government of Charlotte Town, CO 226/4/9–10.
17 David Higgins to John Pownall, 4 December 1769, CO 226/4/29–32; for the buildings, see Warburton, *A History*, 144–5.
18 W. Patterson to Hillsborough, 23 May 1770, CO 226/4/37–8.
19 Proprietors' Petition to Lords of Treasury, June 1770, CO 226/4/47–8.
20 Hester Patterson to William Pitt, no date, CO 226/16/54–5.
21 Patterson to Hillsborough, 24 October 1770, CO 226/1/23–7; Patterson to Hillsborough, 25 October 1770, CO 226/1/31–3.

22 CO 226/4/123–5.

23 CO 226/4/126ff.

24 Patterson to Hillsborough, 1 June 1771, CO 226/1/51.

25 Ibid.

26 Patterson to Hillsborough, 25 October 1770, CO 226/1/13–14; Patterson to Hillsborough, 25 October 1770, CO 226/1/39–40.

27 Hillsborough to Patterson, 2 January 1771, CO 226/4/73–5.

28 Beverly Bond, *The Quit-Rent System in the American Colonies* (New Haven 1919).

29 James Montgomery to John MacKenzie, 14 April 1770, NLS MS 1399/70–1.

30 Bond, *Quit-Rent System.*

31 John Duport to Hillsborough, 23 April 1771, CO 226/4/84; Hillsborough to Duport, 3 July 1771, CO 226/4/87.

32 CO 226/1/59–60; CO 226/4/257.

33 Patterson to Hillsborough, 24 July 1771, CO 226/1/69–71.

34 CO 226/4/161–5.

35 Patterson to Hillsborough, 3 September 1771, CO 226/1/91–2.

36 Duport to Hillsborough, 3 September 1771, CO 226/1/73–7.

37 Patterson to Hillsborough, 18 October 1771, CO 226/4/189–91.

38 Hillsborough to Patterson, 27 March 1771, CO 226/5/9.

39 CO 226/1/80–6.

40 John Robinson to John Pownall, 4 March 1772, CO 226/1/79.

41 Hillsborough to Patterson, 7 August 1772, CO 226/5/17.

42 Leonard Labaree, *Royal Government in America: A Study of the British Colonial System before 1783* (New Haven 1930), 172–217.

43 Dartmouth to Patterson, 4 November 1772, CO 26/5/46–7.

44 CO 226/5/98–100.

45 Patterson to Dartmouth, 17 February 1773, CO 226/5/87–9.

46 Patterson to Dartmouth, 20 May 1773, CO 226/5/103–10.

47 This comment has become part of the folklore of the Island, but it does not appear in any of the contemporary evidence.

48 The personnel of the first assembly is listed in Bolger, ed., *Canada's Smallest Province*, 49.

49 George Tead to John Pownall, 26 September 1772, CO 226/1/99–100; George Tead to Lords of Trade, 1 October 1772, CO 226/1/103–4.

50 Patterson to Dartmouth, 15 July 1773, CO 226/5/119–21.

51 Dartmouth to Patterson, 1 December 1773, CO 226/5/151–7.

52 Report of Richard Jackson, 23 March 1774, CO 226/1/175–81.

53 Patterson to Dartmouth, 7 June 1773, CO 226/5/115.

54 Patterson to Dartmouth, 15 July 1773, CO 226/5/119–21.

55 Patterson to Dartmouth, 2 September 1773, CO 226/5/139–40.

56 Dartmouth to Rev'd Mr. Caulfield, 26 November 1773, CO 226/5/143–4.

57 Dartmouth to Patterson, 7 January 1775, CO 226/6/55–7.
58 See *DCB* 6, forthcoming, for a biographical sketch.
59 Patterson to Dartmouth, 20 August 1774, CO 226/6/59.
60 Patterson to Dartmouth, 1 May 1774, CO 226/6/13–28.
61 Patterson to Dartmouth 2 September 1774, CO 226/6/32.
62 *Journal of the House of Assembly, St. John's Island, 1774,* 1–2; CO 226/6/95–9.
63 Charlottetown Land Register, PAPEI.
64 Dartmouth to Patterson, 7 January 1775, CO 226/6/55–7.

CHAPTER THREE

1 For the terms of the grants, see "Land Grants in Prince Edward Island 1767" in *Report of the Canadian Archives,* 1906, 7–9.
2 The first concerted attempted in print to explain the failure of the proprietors comes in John Stewart's *An Account of Prince Edward Island, in the Gulph of St. Lawrence, North America* (London 1806), essentially hostile to the proprietors. Such hostility is a continual theme in Island historiography. See my paper, "'The Only Island There is': The Writing of Island History," in V. Smitheram et al., eds, *The Garden Transformed: Prince Edward Island 1945–1982* (Charlottetown 1982). Recent accounts may be found in Frank MacKinnon, *The Government of Prince Edward Island* (Toronto 1951); Andrew Hill Clark, *Three Centuries and the Island: A Historical Geography and Settlement and Agriculture in Prince Edward Island, Canada* (Toronto 1959), F.W.P. Bolger, ed., *Canada's Smallest Province: A History of P.E.I.* (Charlottetown 1973).
3 For a further discussion, see my book, *The People's Clearance 1770–1815* (Edinburgh and Winnipeg 1982).
4 Clarence W. Alvord, *The Mississippi Valley in British Politics: A Study of the Trade, Land Speculation, and Experiments in Imperialism Culminating in the American Revolution* (New York 1959), 2: 141ff.
5 See my paper, "Things in the Womb of Time": Ideas of American Independence, 1633 to 1763," *William and Mary Quarterly,* 3rd ser., 31 (1974): 533–64.
6 Winthrop P. Bell, *The Foreign Protestants and the Settlement of Nova Scotia* (Toronto 1961).
7 See my paper, "Highland Emigration to the Island of St. John and the Scottish Catholic Church, 1769–1774," *Dalhousie Review* 58 (1978): 511–27.
8 For Robert Clark, see *DCB* 4 (Toronto 1979), 152–3.
9 George D. Langdon, Jr, *Pilgrim Colony: A History of New Plymouth 1620–1691* (New Haven and London 1966).
10 K.R. Williams, "Social Conditions in Nova Scotia 1749–1783," unpub-

lished MA thesis, McGill University, 1936. See also my book, *Henry Alline 1748–1784* (Toronto 1971), 6–28, and Gordon Stewart and George Rawlyk, *A People Highly Favoured of God: The Nova Scotia Yankees and the American Revolution* (Toronto 1972), 3–44.

11 See the introduction to this work.

12 In fairness to Holland, he did note "a great part of the lands formerly cleared are so much over-grown with brush and small wood that it will be extremely difficult to form a true estimate of the cleared lands, or to make it fit for the plough again" (Alexander Warburton, *A History of Prince Edward Island* ... [Saint John, NB, 1923], 124).

13 "An Account of the Settlement of Prince County as giving [*sic*] by the first immigrants," PAPEI 2702.

14 D.C. Harvey, "Early Settlement and Social Conditions in Prince Edward Island," *Dalhousie Review* 11 (1931/2): 450.

15 "An Account," PAPEI 2702.

16 Harvey, "Early Settlement," 450.

17 See my paper, "Sir James Montgomery and Prince Edward Island, 1767–1803," *Acadiensis* 7 (1978): 76–102.

18 James Montgomery to John Mackenzie, 14 April 1770, NLS MS 1399/70–1.

19 DCB 4: 352–3.

20 Job Prince to James Montgomery, 30 December 1788, SRO GD 293/2/78/30.

21 "Leases granted by D. Higgins, May 1775," SRO GD 293/2/79/52.

22 James Montgomery, "Scroll Memorial 1791," SRO GD 293/2/79/1.

23 Carl Bridenbaugh, ed., "Patrick M'Robert's Tour through Part of the North Provinces of America," *Pennsylvania History* (1935): 162.

24 "Contract of Agreement for the Lord Advocate of Scotland and David Lawson, 1769," SRO GD 293/2/79/38; James Montgomery to David Lawson, 20 June 1769, SRO GD 293/2/78/9.

25 James Montgomery to John Mackenzie, 14 April 1770, NLS 1399/70–1.

26 James Montgomery to John MacKenzie, 24 April 1770, NLS 1399/72–3.

27 "A General Abstract of the Debit of the Lord Chief Baron Montgomery Account against David Lawson [1793]," SRO GD 293/2/79/25.

28 Reverend George Patterson, *Memoir of the Rev. James MacGregor D.D.* (Philadelphia 1859), 212.

29 Harvey, "Early Settlement," 449.

30 David Lawson, "A Copy of the Misfortunes I met with since my landing the 8th of June 1770," SRO GD 293/2/79/5.

31 A graphic description of runaway fires is in Walter Johnstone, *A Series of Letters, Descriptive of Prince Edward Island*, reprinted in D.C. Harvey, ed., *Journeys to the Island of St. John* (Toronto 1955), 104–7.

32 See David Weale, ed., "Diary of William Drummond," *The Island Magazine*, no. 2 (1977): 28–31.

33 David Lawson, "Copy"; "A list of Cattle in Stanhope Farm 1774," SRO GD 293/2/79/27.
34 The best description of the Stanhope Farm buildings is in James Douglas to James Montgomery, 20 August 1802, SRO GD 293/2/20/8.
35 Montgomery, "Scroll Memorial 1791."
36 Bridgenbaugh, ed., "M'Robert's Tour," 163.
37 James Montgomery to Edmund Fanning, 30 April 1798, UBC.
38 Ibid.
39 George Hay to John Geddes, 11 November 1770, Blairs Letters, SCA.
40 See my paper, "Highland Emigration to the Island of St. John and the Scottish Catholic Church, 1769–1774," *Dalhousie Review* 58 (1978): 511–27.
41 John MacDonald Glenaladale to George Hay, 8 November 1771, SCA.
42 George Hay to Peter Grant, 25 November 1771, SCA.
43 John Macdonald Glenaladale to George Hay, n.d., but March 1772, SCA.
44 George Hay to John Geddes, 20 April 1772, SCA.
45 "John Macdonald of Glen'll to Donald MacDonald Dr. 1772", SCA.
46 George Patterson, *History of Pictou, Nova Scotia* (Montreal, 1877); Alexander MacKenzie, "First Highland Emigration to Nova Scotia: Arrival of the Ship 'Hector,'" *Celtic Magazine* 8 (1883): 140–4.
47 John MacDonald Glenaladale to George Hay, 19 January 1773, SCA.
48 A.H. Clark, *Three Centuries and the Island*, passim.
49 Father James MacDonald to John Grant, 9 June 1773, SCA. The Vatican refused to put the St John's mission directly under its authority and continued the Island under the jurisdiction of the bishop of Quebec.
50 Ibid.
51 See, for example, John Fraser to James Stewart, 8 November, 1806, SPPAC, 14918–14920.
52 John MacDonald Glenaladale to George Hay 16 April 1773, SCA.
53 John MacDonald Glenaladale to George Hay, 16 October 1773, SCA.
54 Bishop John MacDonald to George Hay, 25 October 1774, SCA.
55 Ada MacLeod, "The Glenaladale Pioneers," *Dalhousie Review* 11 (1931/ 32): 311–24; Rev. Allan F. MacDonald, "Captain John MacDonald, 'Glenaladale,'" *Canadian Catholic Historical Association Report*, 1964, 21–37.
56 Alexander MacDonald to George Hay, 25 September 1774, SCA.
57 Thomas DesBrisay to John Pownall, 22 November 1773, CO 226/ 5/147–9.
58 Walter Patterson to Dartmouth, 20 August 1774, CO 226/6/57.
59 SPPAC 59: 10–15.
60 Ibid.
61 Harvey, "Early Settlement," 451(n).
62 See my book, *The People's Clearance: Highland Emigration to British North America 1770–1815* (Edinburgh and Winnipeg 1982), 232–3, 235–7.

63 Quoted in Harvey, "Early Settlement," 452.
64 Ibid.
65 Ibid. See also Benjamin Chappell's diary, PAPEI.
66 Quoted in Harvey, "Early Settlement," 452.
67 Ibid.
68 Testimony of Edward Allen before House of Assembly, 11 April 1786, *Journals of House ... 1786.*
69 For Chappell, see my forthcoming sketch in DCB 6. See also Ada Mac-Leod, "The Oldest Diary on Prince Edward Island," *Dalhousie Review* 9 (1929/30): 461–74.
70 Thomas Curtis, "Voyage to the Island of St. John's" in Harvey, ed., *Journeys to the Island of St. John* 10.
71 Quoted in MacLeod, "The Oldest Diary," 462.
72 Chappell diary, PAPEI.

CHAPTER FOUR

1 Peter Stewart to James Montgomery, 20 July 1775, SRO GD 293/2/78/66.
2 D.C. Harvey, "Early Settlement and Social Conditions in Prince Edward Island," *Dalhousie Review* 11 (1931/2): 455–6.
3 George Patterson, *A History of the County of Pictou* (Montreal 1877), 94; John Budd to earl of Dartmouth, 8 December 1775, CO 226/6/251–5.
4 See my account of Higgins in DCB 4 (Toronto 1979), 353–4.
5 D.C. Harvey, ed., "Thos. Curtis Voyage to the Island of St. John's 1775," in *Journeys to the Island of St. John or Prince Edward Island 1775–1832* (Toronto 1955), 23ff.
6 Phillips Callbeck to Lord Dartmouth, 5 January 1776. CO 226/6/153–4. See also Helen J. Champion. "The Disorganization of the Government of Prince Edward Island during the American Revolutionary War," *Canadian Historical Review* 20 (1939): 37–9, and Wilfred Brenton Kerr, *The Maritime Provinces of British North America and the American Revolution* (Sackville, NB, 1941), 105ff.
7 Harvey, "Curtis Voyage," 39.
8 Ibid., 10.
9 Ibid., 39.
10 Ibid., 45.
11 Ibid., 56–9.
12 16 George III, c. iv.
13 Petition of Proprietors of St John's Island to King in Council, CO 226/1/207–14; for disclaimers, see for example Lord George Germain to Walter Patterson, 10 April 1777, CO 226/2/53–4.
14 Callbeck to Dartmouth, 5 January 1776, CO 226/6/153–4.

15 CO 226/1/207–14.
16 CO 226/1/215–26.
17 CO 226/1/205–6.
18 CO 226/1/245–7.
19 CO 226/1/251.
20 Germain to Callbeck, 1 April 1776, CO 226/6/181–7.
21 Howe to Callbeck, 6 February 1776, CO 226/6/193–5.
22 Callbeck to Germain, 20 May 1776, CO 226/6/241–3.
23 Howe to Callbeck, 4 June 1776, CO 226/6/267–8.
24 Memorial of Council and House of Assembly to Lord Howe, 12 August 1776, CO 226/6/331–7.
25 See, for example, council minutes of 21 February 1777, CO 226/6/331–7.
26 Germain to Callbeck, 18 August 1777, CO 226/6/365–6.
27 Callbeck to Germain, 1 July 1777, CO 226/6/13–18.
28 William Nisbett to Germain, 22 January 1780, CO 226/7/13–15.
29 Lieutenant-Governor Thomas Desbrisay to Germain, 7 December 1779, CO 226/7/87–90.
30 Callbeck to Dartmough, 15 January 1776, CO 226/6/165–71.
31 Callbeck to Germain, 25 June 1776, CO 226/6/263–6.
32 Callbeck to Dartmouth, 15 January 1776.
33 Callbeck to Germain, 1 July 1777, CO 226/6/369–72; "A list of provisions ... to supply 110 men under Callbeck's command," CO 226/7/32; Thomas Desbrisay to Germain, 1 May 1780, CO 226/7/91–3; "Calculation of cost St. John's Volunteers annually if completed to 100 men," CO 226/7/195–6.
34 William Nisbett to Thomas de Gray, 15 December 1779, CO 226/7/119.
35 Ibid.
36 William Nisbett to Germain, 22 January 1780, CO 226/7/13–15. Nisbett was Walter Patterson's brother-in-law, and was highly critical of Callbeck's operations in the period before the governor's return to the Island.
37 Benjamin Chappell diary, passim.
38 Peter Stewart to James Montgomery, 27 April 1783, SRO GD 293/2/79/46.
39 Germain to Callbeck, 18 August 1777, CO 226/6/365–6.
40 William Nisbett to Lord George Germain, 22 January 1780, CO 226/7/13–15; "A Calculation of the Annual Expence to Government of the Six Companies stationed at the Island of St. John," CO 226/7/199–202.
41 Germain to Callbeck, 4 November 1778, CO 226/7/63–5.
42 Germain to Callbeck, 6 May 1779, CO 226/7/67–8.
43 Germain to Callbeck, 19 May 1780, CO 226/7/127–8.
44 Germain to Patterson, 28 February 1781, CO 226/7/239–45.
45 H. Clinton to Major Hierlihy, 12 September 1778, CO 226/7/211.

46 Executive Council Minutes, 4 November 179, CO 229/1/164.

47 Executive Council Minutes, 6 and 10 January 1780, CO 229/1/165–6.

48 Executive Council Minutes, 21 July 1780, CO 229/1/169–70.

49 Germain to Patterson, 10 April 1777, CO 226/2/53–4; Germain to Patterson, 7 May 1778, CO 226/7/37; Memorial of Walter Patterson to Board of Trade, 23 July 1779, CO 226/2/9–20.

50 Lieutenant Walter Young to Charles Middleton, 13 May and 29 June 1779, in Sir John Knox Laughton, ed., *Letters and Papers of Charles, Lord Barham* 1 (London, Navy Record Society, vol. 32, 1907), 50–2.

51 See *DCB* 5: 249–50, and Desbrisay's Memorial of 30 December 1777, CO 26/6/385–7.

52 Desbrisay to Germain, 7 December 1779, CO 226/7/87–90; Desbrisay to Germain, 1 May 1780, CO 226/7/91–3; Desbrisay to Germain, 15 August 1780, CO 226/7/159–62.

53 Patterson to Germain, 20 September 1780, CO 226/7/159–62.

54 Memorial of Timothy Hierlihy, 27 August 1779, CO 226/7/83–6. See also C.J. MacGillivray, *Timothy Hierlihy and His Times* (Antigonish, NS, 1935).

55 Hierlihy to Germain, 27 August 1779, CO 226/7/79–80.

56 See *DCB* 5: 776–9.

57 Stewart to Germain, 10 July 1779, CO 226/7/75–8.

58 Thomas de Gray to Stewart, 4 November 1779, CO 226/7/101.

59 Stewart to James Montgomery, 3 June 1775, SRO GD 293;2/78/65; Stewart to Montgomery, 1 November 1779, SRO GD 293/2/78/59.

60 Patterson to Germain, 6 July 1780, CO 226/7/141–4.

61 Stewart to James Montgomery, 1 November 1779, SRO GD 293/2/78/59.

62 Helen MacDonald to John MacDonald, 2 September 1779, PAPEI 2664.

63 *DCB* 5, 513–14.

64 Callbeck to Germain, 18 May 1776, CO 226/6/237–9.

65 Executive Council Minutes, 16 March and 16 May 1778, CO 226/7/60–2.

66 19 George III, c. I is titled, "An Act for Continuing Sundry *Laws* that are near expiring."

67 20 George III, c. II and c. III.

68 20 George III, c. IV.

69 Desbrisay to Germain, 1 May 1780, CO 226/7/95–8.

70 20 George III, c. II.

71 20 George III, c. IV.

72 20 George III, c. VI.

CHAPTER FIVE

1 Thomas Desbrisay to Lord George Germain, 27 October 1781, CO 226/7/271–8; same to same, 18 November 1780, CO 226/7/283.

2 Walter Patterson to Germain, 21 September 1780, CO 226/7/163–4.

3 Desbrisay to Germain, 23 November 1780, CO 226/7/219–23.

4 Memorial of Thomas DesBrisay to Lord George Germain and Articles of Complaint against Walter Patterson, 23 November 1780, CO 226/7/227–8; Desbrisay to Germain, 27 October 1781, CO 226/7/271–8.

5 Timothy Hierlihy to Germain, 25 November 1780, CO 226/7/247–9.

6 Executive Council Minutes, 11 November 1780, CO 226/7/247–9.

7 Ibid., 26 November 1780, CO 229/1/185.

8 Patterson to Germain, 15 November 1783, CO 226/8/63–7.

9 Executive Council Minutes, 19 February 1781, CO 229/1/190.

10 "Evidence taken before the House of Assembly ... Relative to the Sale of Lands &c on the Island in the Years 1780 and 1781," *Journals of the House of Assembly, 1786*, CO 226/10/253–94.

11 Testimony of Lt John Stewart, 10 April, 11 April 1786, ibid.

12 Testimony of David Lawson of Stanhope, 13 April 1786, ibid.

13 Copy of Memorial from Chief Justice Peter Stewart, 30 May 1789, PAPEI 2652/4.

14 John MacDonald to his sisters [Halifax, 26 June 1781], PAPEI 2664.

15 Affidavit of James Curtis, 15 December 1784, BT 6/102.

16 Testimony of Samuel Braddock of Nans-ville, 11 April 1786, *Journals of the House ...*

17 Testimony of Lt John Stewart, 11 April 1786, ibid.

18 Curtis affidavit, 15 December 1784.

19 Ibid.

20 Ibid.; extracts of letters from Walter Patterson to John Stuart, CO 226/9/55–62.

21 Ibid.; Patterson to Lord Sydney, 10 April 1784, CO 226/8/72–80.

22 Peter Stewart to Sydney, 2 June 1784, CO 226/9/71.

23 Testimony of Lt John Stewart, 11 April 1786, *Journals of the House ...*; "Account of Sales of sundry Townships and half Townships sold by Public Auction at the suit of His Majesty for non payment of Quit Rents due to the 1st of May 1781," SPPAC 56: 15049–50.

24 Patterson to Sydney, 10 April 1784, CO 226/8/72–80.

25 Ibid.

26 Extracts of letters, Patterson to Stuart, CO 226/9/55–62.

27 John MacDonald to Nelly MacDonald, London, 19 July 1783, PAPEI 2664.

28 Patterson to Germain, 25 January 1783, CO 226/8/1–3.

29 Executive Council Minutes, 1 December 1781, 6 December 1781, CO 226/8/4–5.

30 "An Act to Enable Proprietors to divide their Lands held in Common," 20 George III, c. II.

31 Executive Council Minutes, 2 February 1782, CO 226/8/6–7.

32 Executive Council Minutes, 4 May, 3 June, 1 and 28 August 1783, CO 226/8/16–31.
33 DCB 4, 353.
34 Peter Stewart to Lord Sydney, 2 June 1784, CO 226/9/71–3.
35 Examination of Annabella Stewart, Executive Council Minutes, 30 November 1784, CO 226/8/318–20.
36 Patterson to Lord Sydney, 12 December 1784, CO 226/8/169–70.
37 Executive Council Minutes, 2 January 1783, CO 226/8/72.
38 Executive Council Minutes, 8 January, 17, 18, and 21 March, 4 April, CO 226/8/74–89.
39 Ibid.
40 Ibid.
41 Patterson to Committee of Council for Trade & Planations, 16 July 1783, CO 226/8/105–12.
42 [John MacDonald], *Narrative of Transactions Relative to St. John Island ... from the Year 1769; and Observations on the Purchases of Lands, belonging to the Proprietors, made by the Officers of that Government in 1781* (n.p., n.d.), 11.
43 Ibid.
44 Lord North Patterson, 12 May 1783, CO 226/3/61.
45 "Act for Repealing an Act ... and for the enforcing in future a due and regular payment of the Quit Rents," CO 226/3/62–71.
46 John MacDonald to Nelly MacDonald, 19 July 1783, PAPEI 2664.
47 Patterson to North, 15 November 1783, CO 226/8/63–7.
48 Extracts of letters, Patterson to Stuart, CO 226/9/55–62.

CHAPTER SIX

1 The only scholarly monograph on the Loyalists and Prince Edward Island remains Wilbur H. Siebert and Florence E. Gilliam, "The Loyalists in Prince Edward Island," *Transactions Royal Society of Canada*, 3rd ser., 4 (1910), section 2: 109–17. But see also Robert Allan Rankin's undocumented "An Island Refuge: The American Rebellion and Loyalist Settlement on the Island of Saint John 1783–1795," in Orlo Jones and Doris Haslam, eds, *An Island Refuge: Loyalists and Disbanded Troops on the Island of Saint John* ([Charlottetown] 1983), 1–14, and Donald Wetmore's semi-fictional "William Schurman of Bedeque Prince Edward Island" in Phyllis R. Blakeley and John N. Grant, eds, *Eleven Exiles* (Toronto and Charlottetown 1982), 169–94.
2 Captain John MacDonald to his sisters, 27 June 1785, PAPEI 2664.
3 Esther Clark Wright, *The Loyalists of New Brunswick* (Fredericton 1955), 27–45.
4 CO 226/9/3–6.

5 Rankin, "An Island Refuge," 10.
6 Wright, *The Loyalists*, 31–2.
7 Ibid., 41–2.
8 Ibid.
9 CO 226/8/45–7.
10 CO 226/8/160–1. Colony agent John Stuart insisted in transmitting the petition that it should be seen as distinct from the quitrent business. Stuart to Colonel North, 19 June 1783, CO 226/9/13–14.
11 "Scroll Memorial for Lord Chief Baron of Scotland, about the Quitrent &c of the Island of St. John, 1791," SRO GD 293/2/79/1.
12 Margaret Ells, "Clearing the Decks for the Loyalists," *Canadian Historical Association Annual Report*, 1933, 43–55.
13 Council minutes, 30 September 1783, CO 226/8/248.
14 Ibid.
15 Quiet Rent Account Book, ca 1817, PRO T1/4144.
16 Council Minutes, 30 September 1783, CO 226/8/248.
17 Council Minutes, 13 October 1783, CO 226/8/247–8.
18 Council Minutes 14 October 1783, CO 226/8/61–2.
19 Patterson to North, 14 October 1783, CO 226/8/61–2.
20 See Bumsted, "Loyalists and Nationalists: An Essay on the Problem of Definition," *Canadian Review of Studies in Nationalism* 6 (1979): 218–32, and Jo-Ann Fellows, "Would the Real Loyalists of the American Revolution Please Stand Up?" *The Humanities Association Review* 27 (1976): 83–8. Consult also Bumsted, *Understanding the Loyalists* (Sackville 1986).
21 Council Minutes, 6 November 1783, CO 226/8/263–4.
22 Ibid.
23 Council Minutes, 28 October 1783, CO 226/8/258–9.
24 Council Minutes, 28 October 1783.
25 Patterson to Sydney, 10 October 1784, CO 226/8/108–9.
26 Philip R.N. Katcher, *Encyclopedia of British, Provincial, and German Units 1775–1783* (London 1973).
27 Council Minutes, 28 October 1783.
28 See Jones and Haslam, eds, *An Island Refuge*, 348–50.
29 Council Minutes, 19 November 1783, CO 226/8/137.
30 Katcher, *Encyclopedia*.
31 Council Minutes, 1 November 1783, CO 226/8/211–12.
32 Council Minutes, 12 February 1784, CO 226/8/137.
33 Quitrent records.
34 A.H. Clark, *Three Centuries and the Island: A Historical Geography of Settlement and Agriculture in Prince Edward Island, Canada* (Toronto 1959), 57–8, does not make this point sufficiently clear.
35 Patterson to North, 15 April 1784, CO 226/8/81–9. For Stewart, consult F.L. Pigot, *John Stewart of Mount Stewart* (Summerside, PEI, 1973).

36 Examination of Cornelius, Council Minutes, 29 November 1784, CO 226/8/313–17.
37 Examination of David Lawson, Council Minutes, 27 November 1784, CO 226/8/304–9.
38 For the British background, see Caroline Robbins, *The Eighteenth-Century Commonwealthman: Studies in the Transmission, Development and Circumstance of English Liberal Thought from the Restoration of Charles II until the War with the Thirteen Colonies* (Cambridge, MA, 1959). For the American side, consult Bernard Bailyn, *The Ideological Origins of the American Revolution* (Cambridge, MA, 1967).
39 For accounts of the critical 1784 assembly, see F.W.P. Bolger, ed., *Canada's Smallest Province: A. History of P.E.I.* (Charlottetown 1973), 58–9, and Frank MacKinnon, *The Government of Prince Edward Island* (Toronto 1951), 23–4.
40 Council Minutes, CO 226/8/301ff. For earlier American parallels, see C.S. Sydnor, *American Revolutionaries in the Making* (New York 1965).
41 Council Minutes, CO 226/8/301ff.
42 Examination of D. McEwan, 6 December 1784, Council Minutes, CO 226/8/351–3.
43 Patterson to North, 15 April 1784.
44 *Journals of the House of Assembly, 1786.*
45 CO 226/3/165–6.
46 CO 226/8/268.
47 CO 226/8/269–73.
48 Copy of Memorial from Chief Justice Stewart St. John's Island to the Imperial Privy Council relative to the Governor's Conduct, 30 May 1789, PAPEI 2652/4.
49 Council Minutes, 20 March 1784, CO 226/8/269–73.
50 Examination of John Stewart, 4 December 1784, Council Minutes, CO 226/8/337–43.
51 Peter Stewart to Sydney, 2 June 1784, CO 226/8/251.
52 Patterson to North, 15 April 1784; Patterson to John Parr, 23 May 1784, CO 226/8/125–6.
53 DCB 6.
54 Charles Stewart to Colonel Winslow, 5 June 1784, PANS RG 1 376.
55 Ibid.
56 Stewart to ---, 25 June 1784, ibid.
57 Patterson to Sydney, 10 August 1784, CO 226/8/96–100.
58 Patterson to Sydney, 10 August 1784.
59 Patterson to Parr, 24 September 1784, CO 226/8/121–2.
60 Patterson to Sydney, 12 July 1784, CO 226/8/94–5.
61 Stewart to ---, 25 June 1784.
62 Jones and Haslam, eds, *An Island Refuge*, 366–8.

63 CO 226/9/211–14.
64 Jones and Haslam, eds, *An Island Refuge*, 15–337.
65 Wright, *The Loyalists*, 249.
66 J. Potter, "The Growth of Population in America, 1700–1860," in D.V. Glass and D.E.C. Eversley, eds, *Population in History: Essays in Historical Demography* (Chicago 1965), 631–68; Philip Greven, "Historical Demography and Colonial America," *William and Mary Quarterly*, 3rd ser., 24 (1967): 438–54.
67 CO 226/8.
68 30 George III, c. 5, "An Act to empower the Lieutenant Governor to give grants of lands ... to such Loyalists and Disbanded Troops, as are in the occupation therof by virtue of Locations formerly made by the Governor and Council ..."
69 See, for example, William H. Nelson, *The American Tory* (Oxford 1961), 85–115.
70 John MacDonald to his sisters, 27 June 1785, PAPEI 2664.
71 Minutes of the Committee of Council for the Consideration of Trade and Foreign Plantations, 27 August 1784, PRO BT 5/2/21.
72 Ibid.
73 Patterson to North, 10 April 1784, CO 226/8/72–80; John MacDonald to Nelly MacDonald, 17 September 1784, PAPEI 2664.
74 Fawkener to Sydney, 3 September 1784, PRO BT 6/102.

CHAPTER SEVEN

1 Patterson to Lord North, 10 April 1784, CO 226/8/72–80.
2 Patterson to Lord Sydney, 20 November 1784, CO 226/8/112–20.
3 Patterson to Lord Sydney, 1 December 1784, BT 6/102.
4 Patterson to Sydney, 2 December 1784, CO 226/8/162–8. Although technically both Patterson and his successor were hereafter lieutenant-governors, I have continued to refer to them in the text as governor.
5 Peter Stewart to Sydney, 10 December 1784, CO 226/9/102–6.
6 Examination of Annabella Stewart, Council Minutes, 30 November 1784, CO 226/8/318–20.
7 Affidavit of Charles Stewart, 10 December 1784, CO 26/9/107–8; Peter Stewart to Sydney, 10 December 1784.
8 Patterson to Sydney, 12 December 1784, CO 226/9/169–70.
9 CO 226/9/164–7.
10 Phillips Callbeck to Patterson, 10 December 1784, BT 6/102.
11 Peter Stewart to Patterson, 1 December 1784, BT 6/102.
12 Certification of Peter Stewart and John Budd, 13 December 1784, BT 6/102.
13 Affidavit of James Curtis, 15 December 1784, BT 6/102.

14 Affidavit of William Nisbett, 14 December 1784, BT 6/102.
15 Affidavit of Thomas Wright, 15 December 1784, BT 6/102.
16 Affidavit of James Campbell, 15 November 1784; affidavit of John Russell Spence and Alexander Acheson, 15 December 1784, BT 6/102.
17 Affidavit of Thomas Wright, 16 December 1784, BT 6/102.
18 Affidavit of Walter Berry, 15 December 1784, BT 6/102.
19 Assembly to Sydney, 4 December 1784, CO 226/9/84–94.
20 A Summary of Facts regarding Governor Patterson's Conduct toward the Assembly, CO 226/9/94–5.
21 Affidavits of Thomas Wright and James Curtis, 14 October 1784, CO 226/9/184–91.
22 Examination of William Craig, Council Minutes, 6 December 1784, CO 226/8/244–53; Council Minutes, 16 December 1784, CO 226/8/201–2.
23 Council Minutes, 25 February and 16 March 1785, CO 226/8/208–9.
24 Patterson to Sydney, 20 April 1785, CO 226/8/171.
25 Copy of a letter from Saint John candidates to Mr Roberts, 20 May 1785, CO 226/9/198–201.
26 Helen Taft Manning, *British Colonial Government after the American Revolution 1782–1820* (New Haven 1933), 100–26, especially 111.
27 Protest of candidates against the sheriff at the general election in March 1785, CO 226/9/202ff.
28 Ibid.
29 Ibid.
30 *Remarks on the Conduct of the Governor and Council of the Island of St. John's, in Passing an Act of Assembly in April 1786, to Confirm the Sales of the Lands in 1781 ... (n.p., n.d.), 53.*
31 Ibid., 29.
32 Copy of the Poll taken at the General Election at Charlotte Town in the Island of Saint John on the 15th 16th and 17th March 1785, CO 226/9/211–14.
33 Council Minutes, 22 March 1785, CO 226/8/219.
34 Council Minutes, 24 and 26 March 1785, CO 226/8/220–2.
35 *Journals of House of Assembly, 1785*, CO 229/1/131–2.
36 Council Minutes, 1 April 1785, CO 226/8/225.
37 25 George III, c. 1–14, CO 228/2. The Quaker bill is c. 11, the fee bill is c. 9, the recording of deeds bill is c. 12.
38 25 George III, c. 2, CO 228/2.
39 PRO PC 2/134/155.
40 John MacDonald to his sisters, 29 June 1785, PAPEI 2664.
41 Ibid.
42 Memorial of proprietors to Lord Sydney, 4 May 1785, CO 226/9/162–3.
43 PRO PC 2/130/211–12.
44 Abel Jenkins to William Birch, 4 May 1785, PAPEI.

45 William Birch to Abel Jenkins, 6 May 1785, PAPEI.

46 John MacDonald to his sisters, 27 June 1785, PAPEI 2664.

47 Council Minutes, 19 July 1785, CO 226/10/161; Council Minutes, 12 May, 17 June, 12 July, 2 and 6 September, 8 October, 2 November 1785, CO 226/10/156–66.

48 Council Minutes, 7 February 1786, CO 226/10/169–74.

49 Ibid.

50 Minutes of Lords of Committee of Council, 7 July 1785, BL add. MSS, 38394/5b.

51 Conduct of Lt. Gov. Patterson, 26 October 1785, CO 226/10/310–12.

52 Considerations for removing the respective Officers and Council of St. John's Island humbly Submitted to the Right Honourable Lord Sydney by Capt. MacDonald, 5 November 1785, CO 226/10/313–18.

53 Sydney to Board of Trade, 13 January 1786, BL Add. MSS 38389/17b–19b.

54 Minutes of the Committee of Trade, 14 January 1786, BL Add. MSS 38389/14.

55 Patterson to Sydney, 10 January 1786, CO 226/10/11–13.

56 Patterson to Sydney, 24 January 1786, CO 226/10/16–17. This problem may help explain why so few Island Loyalists submitted claims to the Claims Commission.

57 Council Minutes, 17 March 1786, CO 226/10/185.

58 *Journals of Assembly*, 19 March 1786, CO 226/10/218; Council Minutes, 21 March 1786, CO 226/10/187.

59 *Journals of Assembly*, CO 226/10/220.

60 Advertisement, 31 March 1786, CO 226/10/133.

61 Petition of John Cambridge to House of Assembly, 1 April 1786, CO 226/10/135–6.

62 Ibid.

63 Petition of John Cambridge, 7 April 1786, CO 226/10/137–43.

64 *Journals of Assembly*, 7 April 1786, CO 226/10/238.

65 "Evidence Taken before the House of Assembly ... Relative to the Sales of Lands &c on this Island in the Years 1780 and 1781," *Assembly Journals*, 1786, CO 226/10/263–94. This evidence has been discussed in detail in chapter five above.

66 Examination of Ronald MacDonald, 11 April 1786, *Assembly Journals*.

67 CO 226/10/249–53.

68 *Assembly Journals*, 20 April 1786, CO 226/10/263.

69 Council Minutes, 22 April 1786, CO 226/10/200.

70 Patterson to Sydney, 1 May 1786, CO 226/10/94–126.

71 John MacDonald to Evan Nepean, 21 July 1786, CO 226/10/329–30.

72 John Patterson to Evan Nepean, 29 June 1786, CO 226/10/327–8.

73 Sydney to Patterson, 30 June 1786, CO 226/10/1.

CHAPTER EIGHT

1 *DCB* 5, (1983), 308–12; see also W.S. MacNutt, "Fanning's Regime in P.E.I.," *Acadiensis* 1 (1972): 37–53.

2 A.P. Hudson, "Songs of the North Carolina Regulators," *William and Mary Quarterly*, 3rd ser., 4 (1947): 477.

3 Lorenzo Sabine, *Biographical Sketches of Loyalists of the American Revolution* 1 (Port Washington, NY, 1864), 415–19.

4 Carl Bridenbaugh, *Myths and Realities: Societies of the Colonial South* (Baton Rouge 1952), 16–7; H.T. Lefler and A.R. Newsom, *North Carolina: The History of a Southern State*, 3rd ed. (Chapel Hill 1977), 180–90.

5 Edmund Fanning to Evan Nepean, 16 November 1786, CO 226/10/39–40.

6 Fanning to Lord Sydney, 8 November 1786, CO 226/10/21–2.

7 Patterson to Sydney, 5 November 1786, CO 225/10/18–20.

8 Patterson to Fanning, 7 November 1786, CO 226/10/23–4.

9 Patterson to Nepean, 30 July 1789, CO 226/11/280–6.

10 Patterson to Sydney, 7 November 1786, CO 226/10/144–6.

11 Extract of Report to the Surveyor General of the Customs, CO 226/12/26–9.

12 *Cursory Remarks upon a Memorial Proposed to be Addressed to Parliament for a Suspension of the Navigation Laws* (n.p., n.d., but London 1789), 14.

13 Address of inhabitants to Fanning, 7 November 1786, CO 226/10/29–30.

14 Council Minutes, 8 November 1786, CO 226/10/205.

15 *Journals of House of Assembly*, November 1786, CO 226/10/295–303.

16 See chapter 7 above.

17 *Journals of the House* ...

18 Council Minutes, 18 November 1786, CO 226/10/211.

19 Ibid.

20 Fanning to Sydney, 17 November 1786, CO 226/10/41–2.

21 Fanning to Sydney, 8 March 1787, CO 226/10/72–6.

22 CO 228/2/18 (November 1786).

23 Patterson to Sydney, 19 November 1786, CO 226/10/149–52.

24 Address of inhabitants to Fanning, 1 December 1786, CO 226/10/57–9; same to same, 5 March 1787, CO 226/10/77–83.

25 Patterson to Sydney, 6 December 1786, CO 226/10/153–4.

26 Fanning to Nepean, 23 December 1786, CO 226/10/62–3.

27 Fanning to Sydney, 4 February 1787, CO 226/10/54–5.

28 Thomas Desbrisay to Fanning, 27 February 1787, CO 226/10/60.

29 Desbrisay to Fanning, 27 February 1787, CO 226/10/62–3.

30 Memorial of John Budd, 5 February 1787, CO 226/10/339–40.

31 Address of inhabitants to Fanning, 5 March 1787.

32 Fanning to Sydney, 10 May 1787, CO 226/10/84–6.

33 Proclamation of Walter Patterson, 12 April 1787, CO 226/10/90–1.
34 Council Minutes, 12 April 1787, CO 226/11/15.
35 Fanning to Sydney, 10 May 1787.
36 Fanning to Nepean, 11 May 1787, CO 226/10/92–3.
37 Fanning to Sydney, 10 June 1787, CO 226/11/5.
38 Dorchester to Fanning, 14 June 1787, CO 226/11/58–9.
39 Council Minutes, 6 June, 17 and 18 July 1787, CO 226/11/89–100.
40 Council Minutes, 17 June 1787.
41 Ibid.
42 Ibid.
43 Ibid.
44 Council Minutes, 18 July 1787.
45 *Report of the Right Honourable the Lords of Committee ... on Certain Complaints against Lieutenant Governor Fanning* (n.p., n.d., but London 1792), 15.
46 Council Minutes, 20 August 1787, CO 226/11/104–13.
47 Ibid.
48 Council Minutes, 17 September 1787, CO 226/11/116–21.
49 Council Minutes, 20 August 1787, CO 227//11/104–13.
50 Council Minutes, 17 September 1787.
51 Fanning to Sydney, 3 October 1787, CO 226/11/133–7.
52 Nepean to Fanning, 22 September 1787, CO 226/11/304.
53 Fanning to Sydney, 4 October 1787, CO 226/11/146–9.
54 Sydney to Patterson, 5 April 1787, CO 226/10/230–1; Fanning to Nepean, 4 October 1787, CO 226/11/150–61.
55 It appears, for example, in neither Baglole's sketch of Patterson in the *DCB* nor in Bolger's account of the Patterson regime in *Canada's Smallest Province: A History of P.E.I.* (Charlottetown 1973).
56 James Montgomery to Walter Patterson, 28 February 1787, SRO GD 293/2/78/6.
57 Edward Allen to Captain Mainwaring, 28 October 1787, CO 226/11/170–1.
58 Fanning to Nepean, 1 November 1787, CO 226/11/168.
59 Terms of leasing lands on lot 47, 11 October 1787, CO 226/11/172–3.
60 Copy John Patterson Arrangement with Gov'r Fanning, 10 October 1797 [*sic*], Fanning Papers, PAC; Fanning to Sydney, 1 November 1787, CO 226/12/1–2.
61 Council Minutes, 29 October 1787, CO 226/12/113.
62 Council Minutes, 26 November 1787, CO 226/12/112.
63 Fanning to Sydney, 15 April 1788, CO 226/12/30–3.
64 *Journals of House of Assembly, 1788*, CO 226/12/52–87.
65 Ibid., CO 226/12/80.
66 Fanning to Nepean, 30 April 1788, CO 226/12/95.
67 *The Royal American Gazette*, 6 March 1788, CO 226/12/34–5.

68 Fanning to Sydney, 15 April 1788, CO 226/12/30–3.
69 Sydney to Fanning, April 1788, CO 226/12/22–3; W. Townshend to Sydney, 14 August 1788, PAPEI 2825/74a; Petition of John Dowling, 23 June 1788, PAPEI 2702; Council Minutes, 2 July 1788, CO 226/12/137.
70 Bumsted, "Sir James Montgomery and Prince Edward Island, 1767–1803," *Acadiensis* 7 (1978): 88–9.
72 Ibid.
73 "Lord Chief Baron's directions for Stating Accounts," SRO GD 293/2/79/31.
74 David Lawson to William Montgomery, n.d. but 1788, SRO GD 293/2/79/16.
75 Bumsted, "Sir James Montgomery," 91.
76 SRO GD 292/2/17/4.
77 Power of Attorney to Governor Fanning, James Douglas, and David Irving, SRO GD 293/2/80/22.
78 For Douglas, see *DCB* 5: 262–4.
79 *Cursory Remarks upon a Memorial*, 7–9.
80 Ibid., 22.
81 Patterson to Nepean, 12 March 1789, CO 226/12/259.
82 *Petition of the Proprietors of Lands in the Island of St. John* ... (n.p. n.d., but London 1789).
83 Ibid.
84 John MacDonald to his sisters, 9 March 1789, PAPEI 2664.
85 Ibid.
86 Handwritten notation at end of PAC copy of *The Criminating Complaint of the Proprietors of the Island of Saint John* (London 1789).

CHAPTER NINE

1 John MacDonald to his sisters, 12 September 1789, PAPEI 2664.
2 Ibid.
3 Ibid.
4 Walter Patterson to Evan Nepean, 18 July 1789, CO 226/12/278–9; Patterson to Nepean, 30 July 1789, CO 226/12/280–6.
5 Walter Patterson to Evan Nepean, 31 July 1789, CO 226/12/287.
6 *The Criminating Complaint of the Proprietors of the Island of St. John* ... (London 1789).
7 John MacDonald to his sisters, 12 September 1789.
8 *DCB* 4: 610.
9 *Some Facts Stated, Relative to the Conduct of Walter Patterson, Esq; Late Governor and Lieutenant-Governor of the Island St. John. Of Edmund Fanning, Esq; the Present Lieutenant-Governor; and of Peter Stewart, Esq; Chief Justice of the said Island; Occasioned by some Notes, Contained in a Pamphlet,*

Entitled THE CRIMINATING COMPLAINT, *&c, &c.* (n.p., n.d., but London 1789).

10 Ibid., 1–11, 37.

11 Ibid., 15–17.

12 Minutes of appeal in Hayden in demise of Clark v. Patterson, CO 226/13/76–91.

13 Copy, circular letter to proprietors, 30 September 1789, SPPAC 59: 180–4.

14 John MacDonald to his sisters, 12 September 1789.

15 Ibid.

16 Ibid.

17 PEI Customs Letter Book 1789–1809, PAC.

18 "Supplemental Affidavits and remarks thereon, together with a Brief Review of the evidence adduced in support of the Charges. By Lt. Governor Fanning," Fanning Papers, PAC.

19 William Patterson to Thomas Hooper, 25 February 1790, Fanning Papers, PAC.

20 John Hill, "A Detail of Various Transactions at Prince Edward Island," CO 226/17/213ff.

21 *Journal of House of Asembly, 1790,* CO 226/13/126–326.

22 30 George III, c. 5. It was confirmed by the king in council on 31 July 1793.

23 *Journal of the House … 1790.*

24 30 George III, c. 7.

25 "Supplemental Affidavits by Fanning," Fanning Papers.

26 Hill, "A Detail."

27 "A Return of the Tennants of the Right Honourable James Montgomery Lord Chief Baron of the Court of Exchequer in Scotland, on lot no. 30, 34, &c. in the Island of Saint John, with the rents now payable, received this year, now due, and the Times of their Encrease," 15 November 1790, SRO GD 293/2/17/2.

28 "Supplemental Affidavits by Fanning."

29 John MacDonald to his sisters, 29 June 1785, PAPEI 2664.

30 Augustin MacDonald to his sister, 29 June 1786, PAPEI 2664; same to same, 4 July 1791, PAPEI 2664.

31 These lists are reprinted in full in Bumsted, *The People's Clearance: Highland Emigration to British North America 1770–1815* (Edinburgh and Winnipeg 1982), 238–41. Originals are in SCA, Oban Papers.

32 Bumsted, "Scottish Emigration to the Maritimes 1770–1815: A New Look at an Old Theme," *Acadiensis* 10 (1981): 71.

33 James Montgomery to James Douglas, 16 April 1793, SRO GD 293/2/21/8.

34 Michael F. Hennessy, ed., *The Catholic Church in Prince Edward Island*

1720–1979 (Charlottetown 1979), 22–57; Edward MacDonald, "The Good Shepherd: Angus Bernard MacEachern, First Bishop of Charlottetown," *The Island Magazine*, no. 16 (1984): 3–8.

35 "St. John's Island: List of Shipping Inward," PAPEI; Orlo Jones and Douglas Fraser, "Those Elusive Immigrants," *The Island Magazine*, no. 16 (1984): 37.

36 John MacDonald to J.F.W. DesBarres, 8 November 1795, DesBarres Papers, PAC.

37 James Montgomery to James Douglas, 16 April 1793.

38 James Montgomery to Edmund Fanning, 16 April 1793, SRO GD 293/2/21/16.

39 James Montgomery to James Douglas, 25 March 1794, SRO GD 293/2/21/7.

40 John MacDonald to Helen MacDonald, 29 March 1789, PAPEI 2664.

41 Ibid., 7 July 1790, PAPEI 2664.

42 "Minutes of the Proceedings of the Proprietors of St. John's Island 17 June 1790–27 January 1791," PAPEI 2702.

43 John MacDonald to Helen MacDonald, 7 July 1790.

44 Ibid.

45 "Minutes of Proceedings," 2 September 1790.

46 Memorial of James Montgomery, 1791, SRO GD 293/2/79/18.

47 James Montgomery to Edmund Fanning, 16 April 1793.

48 "Minutes of Proceedings," 27 January 1791.

49 "Copy of Memorial & Charges exhibited against Governor Fanning and his answers thereto," Fanning Papers, PAC.

50 *Report of the Right Honourable the Lords of the Committee ... on Certain Complaints against Lieutenant Governor Fanning* (n.p., n.d., but London 1792), 1.

51 John MacDonald to Helen MacDonald, 4 July 1792, PAPEI 2664.

52 William Townshend to the Right Honourable the Lords of the Committee, 1791, Fanning Papers, PAC.

53 Fanning to Henry Dundas, 1 January 1792, CO 226/14/9–10.

54 James Montgomery to Robert Gray, 8 March 1792, Fanning Papers, PAC.

55 James Montgomery to Henry Dundas, 26 March 1792, Macmillan collection, UBC.

56 *Report of the Right Honourable the Lords of the Committee*, 3–4.

57 *Journal of the House of Assembly, 1792*, CO 226/14/101–37.

58 Ibid.

59 Edmund Fanning to Henry Dundas, 24 November 1792, CO 226/14/94–100.

60 For the Nova Scotia appointment, see Brian C. Cuthbertson, *The Loyalist Governor: Biography of Sir John Wentworth* (Halifax 1983), 51–3.

CHAPTER TEN

1 John Hill, "A Detail of Various Transactions at Prince Edward Island," CO 226/18.
2 Edmund Fanning to Henry Dundas, 20 September 1793, CO 226/14/181–90.
3 Fanning to James Montgomery, 20 November 1792, SRO GD 293/2/79/23.
4 Fanning to Marquis Townshend, 20 August 1794, PAPEI 2702.
5 Bumsted, "Sir James Montgomery and Prince Edward Island, 1767–1803," *Acadiensis* 7 (1978): 94–6.
6 Copy of Sheriff's Sale, 28 May 1791, PAPEI 2702.
7 James Douglas to James Montgomery, 15 September 1800, SRO GD 293/2/19/9–10.
8 Hill, "A Detail."
9 See chapter 9 above.
10 These events are outlined at length in Hill's "A Detail" and in a Report of Committee of Council for hearing appeals from the Plantations on Petition of William Bowley to Privy Council, heard 6 March 1799, in PAPEI Chancery Court loose papers.
11 PAPEI Chancery Court loose papers.
12 Ibid.
13 John Cambridge letter book, PAPEI.
14 John Hill, "A Detail."
15 John Hill to James Montgomery, 20 May 1795, SRO GD 293/2/78/25–7.
16 John MacDonald to J.F.W. DesBarres, 8 November 1795, DesBarres Papers, PAC.
17 See Bumsted, "James Montgomery" and also "Lord Selkirk of Prince Edward Island," *The Island Magazine*, no. 5 (1978): 3–8.
18 MacDonald to DesBarres, 8 November 1795.
19 Hill, "A Detail," 224.
20 Ibid.
21 MacDonald to Fanning, 19 July 1797, CO 226/15/230–40.
22 For biographical sketches, see DCB 5.
23 [Joseph Robinson], *To the Farmers in the Island of St. John, in the Gulf of St. Lawrence* (n.p., n.d, but 1796), PAPEI 2702.
24 John MacDonald, untitled manuscript on the land question on PEI, SPPAC, 2546–85.
25 Ibid.
26 Copy letter Major McDonald to Captain John McDonald, 26 April 1787, SCA, Oban Papers.
27 MacDonald to Fanning, 19 July 1797.
28 Joseph Aplin to John MacDonald, 25 March 1797, CO 226/15/178.

29 Captain MacDonald to Fanning, 15 April 1797, CO 226/15/209–17.
30 Fanning to MacDonald, 28 April 1797, CO 226/15/217–19.
31 MacDonald to Fanning, 29 April 1797, CO 226/15/219–22.
32 MacDonald to Fanning, 29 May 1797, CO 226/15/240–8.
33 MacDonald to Fanning, 19 July 1797.
34 *Journals of House of Assembly*, July 1797, CO 226/15/171–2.
35 Ibid., CO 226/15/172–5.
36 Fanning to Portland, 30 September 1979, CO 225/15/176–7.
37 Fanning to Portland, 30 September 1979, CO 225/15/264–66.
38 Portland to Fanning, 8 February 1798, CO 226/15/278–9.
39 Council Minutes, 3 January 1798, CO 226/15/285–95.
40 James Douglas to James Montgomery, 26 November 1797, SRO GD 293/2/19/9.
41 James Douglas to James Montgomery, 26 April 1798, SRO GD 293/2/19/6.
42 Duncan Campbell, *History of Prince Edward Island* (Charlottetown 1875), 207–24.
43 A. H. Clark, *Three Centuries and the Island: A Historical Geography of Settlement and Agriculture in Prince Edward Island, Canada* (Toronto 1959), 60–1.
44 Ibid.
45 This explanation is quite different from that favoured by Loyalist descendants in *Journal of the House of Assembly of Prince Edward Island, Anno Tertio Regis Gulielmi IV* (Charlottetown 1833), and repeated in Siebert and Gilliam, *Transactions Royal Society of Canada*, 3rd ser, 4 (1910), section 2: 109–17.
46 Diary of Benjamin Chappell, PAPEI.
47 John Hill, "A Detail."
48 See, for example, Richard Colebrook Harris, *The Seigneurial System in Early Canada: A Geographical Study* (Madison 1966).
49 Hill, "A Detail."
50 SPPAC, 2546–85.

EPILOGUE

1 John Stewart, *An Account of Prince Edward Island, in the Gulph of St. Lawrence, North America* (London 1806).
2 See Bumsted, "'The Only Island There Is': The Writing of Prince Edward Island History," in Verner Smitheram et al., eds, *The Garden Transformed: Prince Edward Island, 1945–1980* (Charlottetown 1982), 11–24.
3 J.F.W. DesBarres to Edward Cooke, 4 December 1805, CO 226/20/103–4.

A Note on Sources

As the notes to this work suggest, the basic documentary source for the history of Prince Edward Island in the eighteenth century is the collection of Colonial Office Papers at the Public Record Office in Kew, London. There are three series – CO 226 (letters and dispatches), CO 227 (assembly and council minutes), and CO 228 (legislative enactments). The Public Record Office also contains material in other series of inestimable value to the Island historian, particularly in the Treasury Papers and the Board of Trade records. At the same time, it should be equally apparent that the early history of the Island cannot be written solely from the perspective of the Public Record Office. The British Library, for example, holds in its Additional Manuscripts the Hardwicke Papers, invaluable for the dealings of the 1760s and occasionally for later British policy. The Scottish Record Office in Edinburgh has the Montogmery Papers, and additional Montgomery material is available in the Scottish National Library, also in Edinburgh. The Scottish Catholic Archives in Edinburgh, especially in its Blairs letters, remains a hitherto largely neglected source for early Highland Catholic immigration to the Island, especially that involving the MacDonald family. On the Canadian side of the Atlantic, the Public Archives of Prince Edward Island has a constantly expanding collection of manuscript sources, of which the most valuable for this study were the MacDonald Papers, the Smith-Alley Collection, the John Cambridge Letter Book, and the diary of Benjamin Chappell. The Public Archives of Nova Scotia (PANS) in Halifax holds copies of its own Colonial Office series dealing with the early development of the Island, as well as Charles Stewart's Loyalist muster rolls and other scattered material. The Public Archives of Canada (PAC) in Ottawa contains the Fanning Papers, the DesBarres Papers, and the Selkirk Papers, as well as other documents such as the Customs House Letter Books. The PAC, the National

Library of Canada in Ottawa, the Toronto Public Library, and the PANS hold rare and in some cases unique copies of printed pamphlets relevant to the early Island. Contemporary printed materal is far more extensive than any bibliography has hitherto suggested, and it desperately needs collecting and reprinting. Scattered but important Island material comes constantly to light in unexpected places: the MacMillan collection at the University of British Columbia in Vancouver, for instance, contains a number of letters of Edmund Fanning and James Montgomery for the 1790s. There are undoubtedly other similar holdings that I have not consulted.

Very little reprinted source material on the early history of the Island is available, although *Public Archives Sessional Paper Number 18* (Ottawa 1906, 3–22) does reprint the documentation on the land grants of 1767, and several general series of British colonial papers contain material useful for policy decisions. One major reprinted document is Thomas Curtis' "Voyage to the Island of St. John's," in D.C. Harvey, ed., *Journeys to the Island of St. John* (Toronto 1955), 3–69. David Weale has edited the 1770 "Diary of William Drummond" in *The Island Magazine*, no. 2 (1977): 28–31. John Stewart's *An Account of Prince Edward Island, in the Gulph of St. Lawrence, North America* (London 1806) is the pioneer historical account by a participant in many of the events described, and it deserves to be treated at least in part as a primary source.

While no one could claim that the early history of the Island has attracted a great deal of scholarly attention, there does exist a useful secondary literature. Much of the good recent work has been published in the pages of *The Island Magazine* and *The Dictionary of Canadian Biography* (*DCB*). Particularly important is the re-evaluation of Walter Patterson by Harry Baglole in volume 4 of the *DCB*, which anticipates many of the points made in more detail in this study. On the early Acadian presence, the reader should consult D.C. Harvey, *The French Regime in Prince Edward Island* (New Haven 1926), and J.H. Blanchard, *The Acadians of Prince Edward Island 1720–1964* (Ottawa 1964). A number of general histories of the Island are also available, including Duncan Campbell, *History of Prince Edward Island* (Charlottetown 1875); A.B. Warburton, *A History of Prince Edward Island* (Saint John 1923); F.W.P. Bolger, ed., *Canada's Smallest Province: A History of P.E.I.* (Charlottetown 1973); and Errol Sharpe, *A People's History of Prince Edward Island* (Toronto 1976). Although not a standard historical survey, A.H. Clark's *Three Centuries and the Island: A Historical Geography of Settlement and Agriculture in Prince Edward Island, Canada* (Toronto 1959) remains important and useful, although Clark's reliance on printed sources is limiting. W.S. MacNutt's *The Atlantic Provinces: The Emergence of Colonial Society 1712–1857*

(Toronto 1965) puts the early history of the Island in the context of the region's development.

The standard work on the government of the Island continues to be Frank MacKinnon, *The Government of Prince Edward Island* (Toronto 1951), heavily dependent upon published sources. Some context on the early government and administration of the Island may be found in Beverly Bond, *The Quit-Rent System in the American Colonies* (New Haven 1919); Sung Bok Kim, *Landlord and Tennant in Colonial New York: Manorial Society 1664–1775* (Chapel Hill 1978); Leland J. Bellot, *William Knox: The Life & Thought of an Eighteenth-Century Imperialist* (Austin and London 1977); Leonard W. Labaree, *Royal Government in America: A Study of the British Colonial System before 1783* (New Haven 1930); Margaret Ells, "Clearing the Decks for the Loyalists," *Canadian Historical Association Annual Report*, 1933, 43–58. Works on early settlement include my own *The People's Clearance: Highland Emigration to British North America 1770–1815* (Edinburgh and Winnipeg 1982); D.C. Harvey, "Early Settlement and Social Conditions in Prince Edward Island," *Dalhousie Review* 11 (1931/2); D.C. Harvey, ed., *Journeys to the Island of St. John* (Toronto 1955); Ada MacLeod, "The Glenaladale Pioneers," *Dalhousie Review* 11 (1931/2); Rev. Allan F. MacDonald, "Captain John MacDonald, 'Glenaladale,'" *Canadian Catholic Historical Association Report*, 1964. On the period of the revolutionary war, see Helen J. Champion, "The Disorganization of the Government of Prince Edward Island during the American Revolutionary War," *Canadian Historical Review* 20 (1939); Wilfred Brenton Kerr, *The Maritime Provinces of British North America and the American Revolution* (Sackville 1941); and C. J. MacGillivray, *Timothy Hierlihy and his Times* (Antigonish 1935). For the Loyalists, consult Wilbur H. Siebert and Florence Gilliam, "The Loyalists in Prince Edward Island," *Transactions Royal Society of Canada*, 3rd ser., 4 (1910), section 2: 109–17; Orlo Jones and Doris Haslam, eds, *An Island Refuge: Loyalists and Disbanded Troops on the Island of Saint John* ([Charlottetown] 1983); Phyllis Blakeley and John N. Grant, eds, *Eleven Exiles* (Toronto and Charlottetown 1982); E.C. Wright, *The Loyalists of New Brunswick* (Moncton 1955); and my *Understanding the Loyalists* (Sackville 1986). For the post-revolutionary period, see Helen Taft Manning, *British Colonial Government after the American Revolution 1782–1820* (New Haven 1933); F.L. Pigot, *John Stewart of Mount Stewart* (Summerside 1973); W.S. MacNutt, "Fanning's Regime in Prince Edward Island," *Acadiensis* 1 (1972); Michael F. Hennesy, ed., *The Catholic Church in Prince Edward Island 1720–1979* (Charlottetown 1979); and Edward MacDonald, "The Good Shepherd: Angus Bernard MacEachern, First Bishop of Charlottetown," *The Island Magazine*, no. 16 (1984).

Index